TITANIC VOICES

MEMORIES FROM THE FATEFUL VOYAGE

Written, compiled and edited by
DONALD HYSLOP, ALASTAIR FORSYTH AND SHEILA JEMIMA

Photography by
JOHN LAWRENCE

ST. MARTIN'S GRIFFIN ❧ NEW YORK

ISBN 0-312-21792-7 paperback

Library of Congress Cataloging-in-Publication Data

Titanic voices: memories from the fateful voyage / written, compiled
and edited by Donald Hyslop, Alastair Forsyth, and Sheila Jemima:
photography by John Lawrence.
   p.   cm.
  Includes bibliographical references.
  ISBN 0-312-17428-4 (cloth)
  ISBN 0-312-21792-7 (paperback)
  1. Titanic (Steamship) 2. Shipwrecks—North Atlantic Ocean. I. Hyslop,
Donald. II. Forsyth, Alastair. III. Jemima, Sheila.
G530.T6T586 1997
363. 12'3'091631—dc21   97-2253
                                               CIP

First published in 1994 by Southampton City Council

First published in hardcover in the United States of America in 1997

First St. Martin's Griffin edition: May, 1999

10 9 8 7 6 5 4 3 2 1

CONTENTS

Editors' Introduction

It is now over eighty years since the *Titanic* disaster sent shock waves throughout the world. The disaster struck at the heart of both the United States and British establishments. Among the passengers were some of the United States' most powerful businessmen and other elements of high society. Although not as well represented among the passengers, the sinking rocked a British establishment complacent in the belief that nature herself could be tamed.

This association with the powerful and famous, combined with the ship's indestructable tag and the huge loss of life, has seen the *Titanic* continue to fascinate and intrigue people all over the world long after other disasters have been forgotten by all except those directly involved with them. Most schoolchildren in Great Britain or the United States asked to name one ship would recite *Titanic*, while television and radio scriptwriters can always raise a laugh with reference to or mere mention of the word. Catch a taxi in Southampton and you are likely to hear a call on the radio to pick up at *Titanic*, a rank beside one of the many memorials in the city.

In both the United States and Great Britain there are *Titanic* Societies dedicated to remembering and conducting research about the ship and the disaster. It is interesting to note that one, The *Titanic* Historical Society in the United States which produces a journal, *The* Titanic *Commutator*, has a membership which would put some small political parties to shame. Throughout the world from Sweden to New Zealand many groups and individuals spend much of their spare time in researching the disaster. Many of these people have carried out painstakingly detailed studies into different aspects of the disaster.

So many books have been written about the *Titanic* disaster from every conceivable angle, be it the telegrams sent to and from the ship through to a graphologist's analysis of the handwriting of people involved with the ship. Many of these texts are listed at the back of this book but the acknowledged general texts are *The Maiden Voyage* by Geoffrey Marcus, Walter Lord's lyrical *A Night to Remember*, Eaton and Haas's fact-packed *Triumph and Tragedy* and the lavish *Illustrated History* by Marschall and Lynch.

Perhaps this all begs the question: why another book on the *Titanic*? Indeed, that is a question the editors of this book have asked themselves on more than one occasion as they have struggled to complete the task. The main reason for this book is that we wanted to look at the disaster from the perspective of the people and the town of Southampton, from where the vast majority of the crew were drawn. The *Titanic* disaster was to

Southampton what the Pan Am bombing was to Lockerbie, the Valley Parade fire to Bradford and the earthquakes to the Los Angeles area. The vast majority of the crew of 898 were domiciled in the town and only 212 returned to tell the tale. Even by the standards of a seaport used to the ravages of the sea this was a high toll and one compounded by the slaughter of the Great War just two years later. In some areas of the town many were left fatherless, as Edward Simmons remembered: '*nothing unusual about not having a father, most men around usually had something wrong with them*'. Even today, over eighty years later, many local people you meet in Southampton have a direct family connection with the disaster.

Inevitably over the years the local museum service in Southampton has come to acquire, be loaned, or gifted many items relating to the ship and particularly the crew. These range from Captain Smith's dress sword through to the personal papers of the crew members and memoriam cards printed at the time. Even today, despite a lucrative market (especially in the United States) for *Titanic* ephemera, new items of interest are still being gifted and loaned to this public body. Much of the collection is on display in the city's Maritime Museum. These objects and ephemera are supplemented by a large photographic and newspaper archive.

More recently, through our pioneering Oral History Unit, we have been able to tape-record the memories of the few survivors in Britain who are still alive, and also the sons and daughters of crew members who still live locally. In many of the other life story interviews carried out with local people, an early memory of many older Sotonians is of being taken to see the *Titanic* in Southampton Docks, or remembering the chaos that ensued in the town as the news of the sinking broke and people waited nailbitingly for days for news of loved ones.

In this book we have tried to share as much of these collections as we can with you and illustrate how much the *Titanic* and Southampton were inextricably linked from even before she was built, through to the present day.

Much of the book is made up of the first-hand accounts of survivors, relatives of crew members or people who were living in or visiting Southampton at that time. The first-hand accounts are oral histories, extracts from both the United States and British Inquiries, and newspaper interviews mostly given immediately after the disaster but in some cases from later editions of the *Southampton Echo*. When we have reproduced articles and photographs from contemporary newspaper accounts we have attempted to identify the newspaper source. However, this has not been possible in every case as many of the articles have come to us cut out and stuck in scrap albums compiled by people at the time. Where the source is uncertain they have simply been credited as City Heritage Collections, where they are held.

There is no doubt that there are factual mistakes in some of these narratives, firstly many elements of the press of 1912 were little different from today, and would not let the facts interfere with a good story; secondly, when people cast their minds back to an event the things they are less likely to remember accurately are dates and technical details. We have other ways of finding out the facts, figures and details of the *Titanic* and its untimely end and as mentioned before these are thoroughly covered in other general texts. We have therefore edited these first-hand accounts as little as possible in order to retain their immediacy.

By focusing on first-hand accounts and oral histories, warts and all, we can explore an area that even the most learned *Titanic* expert cannot fully reveal, which is to bring those dramatic days vividly to life as the people who were actually there recount their experiences and feelings of those times. There can be no doubting the power and immediacy of these narratives: the dramatic events have rarely faded from the minds of those who were there. Sixty, seventy or eighty years after the disaster these people have remembered events as if it had happened yesterday.

The photographic sources in this book are many and varied. The bulk of the photographs are from the City Heritage Collections which include the William Burrough Hill Collection (post-disaster), the Stones Album (contemporary newspapers), the Bealing Collection and the Associated British Port Collection (docks). Other sources include the *Southern Daily Echo*, Hampshire Libraries, Southampton Records Office, Father Browne Collection and many private collections often held by descendants of crew members. The colour photographs are of objects and documents held by City Heritage, members of the British *Titanic* Society and private collections. A full listing of sources and where to write for prints (if possible) is listed at the back of the book.

A full list of credits and acknowledgements also appears at the end of the book but we would particularly like to thank Pauline Moore for her hard work in laying out the book, our colleagues Rachel Wragg and Alastair Arnott who care for our wonderful collection, Peter Ashton and staff, ever helpful at the *Southampton Daily Echo*, Brian Ticehurst of the British *Titanic* Society for his help and advice, and Simon Hardy, the Heritage Services Manager, for his continued support through the long haul to bring this book to fruition. Last but not least all the *Titanic* survivors and other interviewees without whose help this book would never have happened.

Titanic leaving Southampton on her maiden voyage.

Private collection

Historical Introduction

For nearly two thousand years Southampton has served the British Isles as a port. Situated almost in the centre of the south coast, nature has provided her with a well protected harbour in Southampton Water and the Isle of Wight shielding her from the open sea. This, coupled with the famous double tide, which gives seventeen hours of rising and high water in every twenty-four, helped elevate Southampton to the 'Gateway to the World' when the ship was all powerful and the aeroplane no more than an oddity for the reckless and foolhardy.

But long before the days of the liners, Southampton and its rivers Itchen and Test were attracting people. Flint hand axes made by prehistoric peoples 40,000 years ago have been recovered from the rivers, a Mesolithic forest lies beneath part of the land reclaimed for the new docks and an Iron Age earthwork known as Aldermoor camp survives as one of Southampton's oldest historic monuments.

The Romans established a settlement at Bitterne Manor on the east of the Itchen whose purpose is something of an enigma, but archaeological finds of lead and glass suggest the settlement was involved in trade. Parts of a bath house can still be seen today and every so often local gardeners discover unexpected treasures among their potatoes.

From around AD 700 the Saxon town of Hamwic developed on the west of the Itchen, spreading to cover 40 hectares and becoming one of the largest towns in eighth-century England. Archaeological excavations in Hamwic have shown that trade was passing through the port to and from the continent. Hamwic declined in the ninth century partly due to the activity of the Vikings who were wreaking havoc around the North Sea.

While Hamwic declined, however, sometime in the tenth century a new settlement developed in the area of what was to become medieval Southampton and which today is still the site of the city centre. The accession of Henry II and the founding of the Angevin empire resulted in an expansion of the wine trade which was the basis for Southampton's prosperity in the thirteenth century. The castle became important in the shipping of royal cargoes, and town merchants built grand houses with vaulted stone cellars which survive today as testament to their wealth and influence. During the twelfth and thirteenth centuries the merchants enjoyed great wealth and the benefits of their trade with France, Spain and beyond. In the fourteenth century this trade became threatened by wars with France. Southampton merchants had been encouraged for some time to enclose the town but had left the seaward side undefended, which allowed cargoes

to be unloaded straight into their warehouses. On the morning of October 4th 1338, a French and Genoese force landed in Southampton, ransacking it and razing large parts to the ground. In the years that followed, the fortification of the town was completed and much of those walls remain today.

Henry V embarked from the town with an army destined for the battle of Agincourt in 1415, one of many armies which have left Southampton Water for foreign battlefields.

During the fifteenth century Southampton boomed again, mainly due to trade with Italian merchants who formed a significant community in the town. Following the decline of the Italian trade, a new generation of merchants with roots in London dominated Southampton. One of these, John Dawtrey, built a timber-framed building which today forms the basis of Tudor House Museum.

Gradually, however, Southampton shipping declined to the point that the town even had difficulty in supplying one vessel to the force that confronted the Spanish Armada in 1588. Although the town's population was growing considerably during this period it was not a reflection of a wealthy and successful place. Elizabethan Southampton was often described as 'decayed'.

Southampton, however, was able to re-establish itself with a new economy as a market centre serving the region. Huguenot refugees from religious persecution settled in Southampton during the sixteenth century; among them were artisans who made serge cloth which became a major industry of the time.

During this time, as the New World began to be exploited, Southampton was the point of departure for one of the most famous sea journeys ever made. On August 15th 1620 the *Mayflower* and the *Speedwell* left the port with a group of Puritan exiles bound for Virginia, America. The *Speedwell* however was 'open and leakie as a sieve' and had to be abandoned after calling in at Plymouth. The Pilgrims then continued their journey in the *Mayflower*. Over the ensuing centuries Plymouth and Southampton have contested their claims as the port of departure.

The English Civil War, which broke out in 1642 saw Southampton, like many commercial towns, on the side of the Parliamentarians. Cromwell's forces were garrisoned in all the forts around the Solent and Southampton Water.

The seventeenth century saw the town decline once more. Like the rest of Europe she fell victim to recurrent epidemics of bubonic plague. Many ships and their cargoes were lost in the frequent wars, and the industry of woollen cloth weaving disappeared. By 1700 the population had fallen about one quarter and in 1723 Daniel Defoe visited the town and lamented the decay of a once great port.

Once again it was water that was central to the town's resurgence in the eighteenth century, but not this time through ships and trade. Southampton became an unlikely venue for the fashionable who came to enjoy the spa waters and indulge in medicinal sea bathing. Patronage by royalty stimulated the town's development, which started to spread to the north and saw the Itchen bridged at Northam. During this period also, growing trade brought an extension of the docks with new quays being built on the Itchen and Test. However, it was the introduction of steam navigation that was to be the key to Southampton's growth.

Victorian Southampton was a child of the steam era. The availability of steamships made the port much more attractive than many West Country ports. The key to the future success of Southampton was in its links with London. A railway link was completed in May 1840 and two years later the Southampton dock company opened its first dock. Some had intended Southampton to be the Liverpool of the south, but it was passengers and mail rather than bulk cargoes which became her principal trade. The first shipping companies to make the port its home were the Peninsular and Oriental Company, which secured a government contract to provide a mail service to Alexandria and India and the Royal Mail Steam Packet Company, which obtained its contract in the same year for the mail service to and from the West Indies.

Between 1841 and the turn of the century, Southampton's population increased from 27,000 to 105,000. In the late 1800s the town rapidly spread over the elegant country estates that encircled it. Overcrowding in the old medieval town caused health problems and widespread concern. In 1849 a cholera epidemic killed around 240 people. In contrast to the slums this was also the period when the many parks in the town centre, a relic of the medieval common lands for which Southampton is noted, became legally enshrined as public parks.

Much of the industry of Victorian Southampton was concentrated along the banks of the Itchen. The Northam iron works of Summers and Day launched the first iron ship to be built on the Itchen in 1842. In 1876 a yard opened in Woolston building large iron sailing ships. After a succession of owners the yard was taken over by John I Thornycroft in 1904 when naval contracts were secured. The yard is still operational today as Vosper Thornycroft.

As the nineteenth century progressed the demand for ships and men and women to crew them increased. As Southampton and its people responded to the challenge they were entering some of the most challenging and turbulent times of its long history.

THE SPHERE

AN ILLUSTRATED NEWSPAPER FOR THE HOME With which is incorporated "BLACK & WHITE"

Volume XLIX. No. 640. {REGISTERED AT THE GENERAL POST OFFICE AS A NEWSPAPER} London, April 27, 1912. [WITH SUPPLEMENT] Price Sixpence.

DRAWN BY F. MATANIA

THE MODERN
MESSENGER OF DEATH:

A typical bearer of the fateful
tidings concerning the "Titanic"

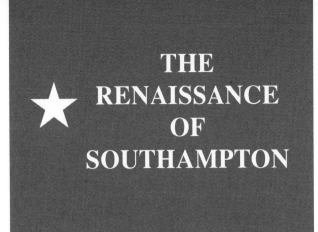

THE RENAISSANCE OF SOUTHAMPTON

"American Line to White Star"

The *Olympic* (left) and *Titanic* in the Thompson Graving Dock, Belfast.

Harland and Wolff

RMS *Titanic*, the largest liner in the world, arrived in Southampton from her builders, Harland & Wolff, Belfast, for the first time just after midnight on the morning of 4th April 1912, to prepare for her maiden voyage on the 10th. In that one intervening week she was truly a ship of Southampton, as she lay in the new White Star Dock. In Sotonian memory, and attitude today, she remains so, but as the history books all over the world recount, the *Titanic* never returned to Southampton. Supposedly unsinkable, she struck an iceberg off Newfoundland on 14th April, and sank two and a half hours later the next day, with the loss of 1503 lives. 705 survived in the few lifeboats provided on the ship and were rescued by the Cunard liner *Carpathia*.

The effects and lessons of the devastating sinking of the new ship with so many passengers and crew have made the *Titanic* immortal and are still felt in Southampton today. 686 of the crew, many of them resident in the town, were lost, 212 survived. In the days immediately following the sinking the spotlight was on Southampton as the community waited in shock for further news, then in most cases gradually received the worst, and sought to come to terms with it. This is a Southampton story, but had the *Titanic* been a smaller ship making her debut a few years before, then in some ways Southampton might not have been the setting and victim of such a tragedy.

The *Titanic* was the latest flagship of the White Star Line founded in Liverpool in 1869 by Thomas H.

Ismay, who soon established an impressive reputation for the ever improving size, speed, comfort and safety of his transatlantic liners on the Liverpool–New York run, and a worthy rival to the longer established Cunard, Guion and Inman Line. One of Southampton's famous commodores, Sir Bertram Hayes, a Captain of the *Titanic*'s sister ship *Olympic*, recalling T.H. Ismay, said

'I consider that he was the most far seeing man of steamers, and I am not sure that the travelling public have ever realised the debt they owe to his foresight. He was the pioneer in introducing most of the comforts, not to say luxuries, which they now take as a matter of course.'

In 1893, six years before his death, Thomas Ismay saw a new rival, the American Line, purchase the new flagships of the older rival Inman Line – the *City of Paris* and the *City of New York*, both briefly holders of the Blue Riband, like White Star's *Teutonic* and *Majestic*. Much more startling was the American Line's decision to immediately transfer the vessels from Liverpool to Southampton.

What was the attraction of Southampton over Liverpool? Southampton was previously best known for

its use by those British and European shipping lines that served the far corners of the Empires, particularly the Union Line to South Africa, the P & O to the Mediterranean, North Africa and India, and the Royal Mail Steam Packet Company to the West Indies and South America. These latter two companies had joined with the London and South Western Railway as shareholders in the Southampton Dock Company to build and develop Southampton Docks, while the first railway line directly from London to Southampton was opened during 1840. LSWR used Southampton as a base for its steamers to France and the Channel Islands. Only the German transatlantic lines, Norddeutscher Lloyd and Hamburg America Line regularly used Southampton as an intermediary port from the late 1850's, either using the docks or more often tendering in Southampton water.

Southampton had several advantages over Liverpool however, as a transatlantic terminal port. One was its relative depth, another its famous double high

tides, which saved long and costly waits for ships outside the harbour. From 1892 both the docks and railways were under the control of the London South Western Railway, so that as one of their 1911 guides put it

'The traveller is in the care of one company's staff, obviating confusion and trouble.'

Southampton was much nearer to London than

Empress Dock c1900.

Southampton City Heritage Collections

The Docks, Southampton c1893.

Southampton City Heritage Collections

Liverpool, and also near enough to France, to allow a call at Cherbourg for the capital, Paris, popular with wealthy American tourists and business travellers, as well as to collect European emigrants. At the same time Southampton was still convenient for Queenstown, the traditional outward call to pick up Irish emigrants at the height of the emigration era.

A new deep water dock, the Empress Dock, had been built in Southampton in 1890 with a £250,000 loan from the LSWR, and opened by Queen Victoria. Finally, Southampton's fifth new dry-dock was being built; 745 feet in length, it was the largest in the world. It was completed in 1895 as the Prince of Wales Graving Dock, opened by its namesake. Equally important, a new coal barge dock on the river Itchen would be completed in 1898-9.

The American Line's successful move to the Southern port was enthusiastically received. Twenty years later the Southampton Pictorial recalled 1893 as *'The renaissance of Southampton and the coming of the American Line'*. Southampton was established as a major terminal for the growing transatlantic trade, as liners of the Cunard, White Star, American Line, NDL and Hamburg America Lines increased in size and speed, and the competition intensified. Once again, more dry dock accommodation was needed in Southampton if there was any hope to attract them to or keep them in the port. In January 1900, LSWR awarded a contract to J. Aird for a sixth graving dock. The western edge of the docks now saw extensive excavations (266,200 cubic yards) to create the dock, 875 feet long, 90 feet wide, 33 feet deep; the dock formally opened as Trafalgar Dock for the centenary of the battle – 1905.

At the same time Southampton's biggest hotel, the

Advert for South Western Hotel, Canute Road.

Southampton City Heritage Collections

South Western, opened in 1867 to architect John Norton's design as the Imperial Hotel, re-named in 1870, and purchased by LSWR in 1882, was modernised and altered by Maples, the famous London decorating firm. New iron trellis panelling above the handrails to a Grill room, and new coppered door furniture were provided. Ornamental panels were re-painted in blue and gold and the kitchens and offices renewed. New electric lifts were provided to all floors. It all cost £28,000. In March 1904 the famous *'time ball'* was moved here from God's House Tower. Shipping office commissionaires used to stand at their doors in Canute Road and when the ball dropped, shout the time through the buildings. The hotel adjoining the old town station and near the dock gates was ideally placed to accommodate the town's most exclusive and demanding clients, and was also the scene of many a function, or dinner organised by the LSWR or one of the shipping lines. By 1912 it had its own garage.

South Western Hotel under scaffolding during repair and alterations in 1900.

Bert Moody Collection

"Porters in red livery and a motor bus meet all express trains at Southampton West station. Incoming liners are wired from Hurst Castle for the convenience of guests awaiting arrival of old friends. One of the best family and commercial hotels in the Country" the LSWR could rightly declare. Many of its staff worked there for decades, including Frank Regler who became Maître d', Fred Veale who eventually became Head Porter, and Edward McClure who became Head Waiter.

Extra provision began to be made in the town to accommodate emigrants or organise their movements, as the figures rose. At the same time a vicious price war between the steamer companies was gradually bringing down the price of a one-way steerage ticket to £8, and later on even less.

Late in 1900, the American Line was involved in a dramatic business development which would have far reaching effects in Southampton, including the *Titanic*. The line's owners, the International Navigation Company of Philadelphia, who also owned the Red Star Line, supported ambitions of the American financier, steel magnate and railway baron, J. Pierpoint Morgan, to create a huge American owned shipping syndicate that

would dominate the Atlantic, and connect it with the US railroad and lake steamer system. Gradually all the American shipping lines were acquired and incorporated including two of the most important clients of the Belfast shipbuilders, Harland and Wolff. Harland's also built the White Star liners, many of the steamers of Southampton's RMSP Co., and the newly merged Union Castle Line. Harland and Wolff's chairman, W.J. Pirrie, sensing both danger and business potential, swiftly made contact with Morgan, and became his European negotiator. By July 1901 he was promoting Morgan's American Syndicate Scheme with Albert Ballin, Chairman of the Hamburg America line, and J. Bruce Ismay, the new chairman of White Star Line, despite their reservations. Ismay's first reaction was to declare *'the whole thing for a swindle and a humbug'*. But Pirrie, already trapped with his shipyard so dependant on the new syndicate's building custom, was desperate to win the support of White Star, Hamburg America and the Norddeutscher Lloyd for the scheme. Harland and Wolff duly entered the scheme, contracting to supply their ships, and Pirrie hammered out a deal in November 1901 with White Star, Hamburg America (HAPAG) and NDL, assuring them that the syndicate

L.S.W.R. boat train awaits disembarking passengers from a White Star liner at Southampton c1907.

Southampton City Heritage Collections

Steam Navvy used to excavate land for the White Star Dock. May 1908.

Southampton City Heritage/A.B.P. Collections

White Star Dock nears completion c1910–11. Union Castle liner *Carisbrook Castle* is already moored at berth 46.

Southampton City Heritage/A.B.P. Collections

was *'something magnificent and ingenious'*. The financial reward was one the White Star shareholders could not refuse, whatever the personal feelings of the Ismay family. White Star was bought for £10,000,000.

On Morgan's behalf Harland and Wolff also bought a 51% share in the Holland America Line. (One of its directors Herr von Reuchlin would be a passenger victim on the *Titanic*). The new syndicate was to be known as the International Mercantile Marine, and under a provisional agreement

'all orders for new vessels and for heavy repairs…. done at a shipyard of the United Kingdom to be given to Harland and Wolff'.

The combine would have dearly liked Cunard to join, but all approaches were abortive. The merger became public in April 1902, and among its thirteen directors (eight of them Americans) two were J. Bruce Ismay and W.J. Pirrie. In effect the vessels of the White Star Line were now virtually American ships, although they remained under the British flag, and Admiralty and Government requirements in time of war were unaffected. After an awkward start to the combine, the highly able J. Bruce Ismay was asked to become President and Managing Director of the IMM and its subsidiaries.

Ismay's ships had always been favoured by Morgan. Sir Bertram Hayes recalled

'He was always, it seems to me, associated with the White Star Line. I remember him crossing with us when I was Fourth Officer on the Teutonic and at intervals in various other ships until his death …. In his later years Mr Morgan had the rooms he liked reserved for several dates, in various ships till he could settle when he wished to cross'.

One of the medical officers on the *Olympic*, J.C.H. Beaumont, remembered

'Most of us were a little frightened of him,

class only of passengers is taken by these vessels, which sail every four weeks, and with Colonials in particular they are warm favourites, owing to their exceptionally fine accommodation.

The other great British Colony in Southern Seas, New Zealand, is also served by the White Star Line in conjunction with the Shaw, Savill and Albion Co., Ltd. In this instance the steamers leave London every four weeks, calling at Plymouth, Tenerife, Cape Town and Hobart en route, whilst on the return voyage—which is made *via* Cape Horn—Monte Video or Rio de Janeiro, Tenerife, and Plymouth are touched at before arriving at London. The New Zealand steamers are the largest despatched from the United Kingdom to the Colony, and carry first, second, and third class passengers.

The White Star Line's operations consist of the following services:—

Southampton-Cherbourg-Queenstown-New York.
Via Queenstown (Westbound) and Plymouth (Eastbound).
Liverpool-Queenstown-New York.
Liverpool-Queenstown-Boston.
Liverpool-Quebec-Montreal.
Liverpool-South Africa-Australia.
Liverpool-Australia (direct), Cargo only.
Liverpool-New Zealand „ „ „
London-South Africa-New Zealand.
New York-Azores-Mediterranean.
Boston-Azores-Mediterranean.

WHITE STAR TRAINING SHIP "MERSEY."

THE years 1907-1909 were of such supreme importance in the annals of the White Star Line that a brief account of the various alterations then made in its services will doubtless prove of interest to the travelling public.

Up to some 10 to 15 years ago, London was the main objective of the American tourist, and the New York-Liverpool service of the White Star Line then admirably served every need of the traveller. But time effects many changes, and of recent years the trend of American travel has been directed to an almost equal extent towards Paris, with the result that such passengers as desired to visit the Continent of Europe in the first instance, demurred to the necessity of crossing the Channel after landing in England. It was to meet the requirements of these that, after mature consideration, the Managers of the White Star Line decided to remove its Royal and United States Mail service from Liverpool to Southampton, calling at Cherbourg and Queenstown Westbound, and Plymouth and Cherbourg Eastbound, and thus affording its patrons the opportunity of embarking and disembarking either at a French or English Channel port. The new service was most happily inaugurated by the new "ADRIATIC," 25,000 tons (the largest of all British twin-screw steamers, and one replete with many innovations), which sailed from Southampton June 5th, 1907, and the support since given to this and the

R.M.S. "ADRIATIC."
FIRST CLASS READING ROOM.

White Star Line fold-out brochure c1912.

Southampton City Heritage Collections

unnecessarily, for although apparently austere he had a very kind heart. I always think of him at Church Service on board, attended regularly, joining us lustily in his favourite hymns, with a deep basso voice'.

From the start the White Star Line was the combine's showpiece, particularly the luxurious *Oceanic* (built 1899) and the "Big Four" liners (*Celtic, Cedric, Baltic* and *Adriatic*) built between 1901-7 at Harland's. For a short time they were the largest liners in the world, though not the fastest. Comfort was White Star's priority now. During 1906, observing the success of the American Line and the development of Southampton Docks and the LSWR, Ismay, Pirrie and Morgan decided to move White Star's *"express"* service from Liverpool to Southampton, an even bigger blow to Liverpool than the sale and move of the Inman liners. The new Trafalgar dry dock was an especial lure, apart from the lucrative continental traffic unobtainable in Liverpool.

One resident, G.E. Hopcroft, remembered

'We of Southampton, impressed by the marvel of the Oceanic, were accustomed to speak of the White Star Line with bated breath. In those far off days we could hardly dare to hope that the Line's mail steamers would make their home with us.

......It was the coming of the White Star Line which put a hustle into our local authorities.'

Southampton's only previous sight of White Star liners had been the old *Britannic* trooping from the port during the Boer War, the *Teutonic* off Spithead in the 1889 and 1897 Royal Naval Reviews, and the *Germanic* in 1898 and 1905 under temporary charter to the American Line. The *Celtic* soon made two trial trips for the American Line before returning to Liverpool. In 1906 the White Star Line appointed George William Bowyer, popularly known as *'Uncle George'*, of the famous Southampton piloting family, as their representative to attend the Harbour Board's meetings to press for extra dredging in readiness for the big ships. The brand new *Adriatic* (to be joined by the older *Oceanic, Teutonic* and *Majestic*) was chosen to officially inaugurate and maintain the new Southampton service from 5th June 1907. White Star opened offices with the American Line in Canute Road. (The offices stood between what was then Dock House, the North German Lloyd offices and Maritime Chambers. Hamburg America Line had offices opposite North German Lloyd and their agents.) White Star/American Line's were managed by Philip E. Curry with staff of under managers, secretaries, booking

CONCERNING THE CELTIC.

The monster Celtic, sister ship to the Cedric, presented a most imposing side when mooring at the Ocean Quay, her draught aft showing 26 feet, and about 24 feet at the stem, the bow at the load line being marked 37 feet. Her dimensions are somewhat under those of the Adriatic, which are 725 x 75½ feet, and a depth of 50 feet, with 12 bulkheads, and 9 decks; but the Celtic exceeds 700 feet on the load line, with a beam of 75 feet, and a depth giving extreme stability, so that movement is scarcely perceptible to travellers in ordinary health. Deep bilge keels are fitted for over 300 feet, and on some famous Liverpool liners are made 30 inches wide with bulb edges, so that rolling is practically unknown. The floors of modern liners are nearly flat, as in battle ships, the old pattern of keel being superseded by a deep box plate keel, combining with the cellular double bottom to give enormous strength, with safety in the event of stranding. The bottom also serves for water ballast, some steamers using the space for hundreds of tons of liquid fuel, to burn it alone, or in combination with coal. About two years ago a large Atlantic liner had her hull strengthened, in the Empress Dry Dock, by having rivetted amidships long sections of plating, the work being done by pneumatic hammers, seen here for the first time. The plan enables huge hulls to resist flexure and longitudinal distortions when subjected to severe strains in heavy cross seas. This method of giving rigidity is fully carried out in the Celtic, the wide steel strap or belt – about 12 feet deep – covering the whole middle body, and giving a look of maximum strength. The vessel had also longitudinal bulkheads, extending above the water line from the bottom, the interior being thus a series of self contained cofferdams, protecting the structure against casualties of the sea. The four-cranked engines are only designed for a moderate speed, but are fine examples of Belfast skill, as are all departments of the noble craft, which may be regarded as a chef d'ouvre of the famous firm.

Newspaper cutting of White Star liner *Celtic* in Southampton Docks, 1907.

Southampton City Heritage Collections

Olympic were at pains to point out

'The management of such large steamers as the Olympic calls for perfect organisation, and though the White Star Line's biggest serving ship has her base at Southampton, the "Home" of the line is at Liverpool'.

Equally a passenger on the *Titanic*, Mr Saalfeld, could write

'The name of my friend the White Star manager in London works wonders'.

Thus were Southampton's fortunes controlled regarding the White Star Line. But all the local and day to day problems or decisions were administered from Canute Road, so handily placed for the Docks, the hotels, the railway. The offices were at the heart of the place. But from the back windows in the top floor, Curry and the staff could barely view the dock scene, the berths and the IMM Co Steamers obscured by the warehouses surrounding the Inner or the Close Dock. But the masts and the funnels and the smoke of the new giants could be glimpsed rising above the buildings.

In point of fact, who ever or wherever the controlling hands were, the White Star Line was good news for Southampton. Unemployment in Southampton was very noticeable in the early 1900's, despite the rise in Atlantic traffic. It was at its worst in the winter of 1903-4.

'In almost every street numbers of working men were aimlessly about idle. Men went out in the early morning to look for work, pulling their belts tighter to make up for their lack of breakfast, while their children went to school cold and with their hunger only partly satisfied and their weary eyed wives perhaps pawned something more in order to find some sort of apology for a dinner in the family. Large numbers of men wandered about near the docks and haunted Canute Road like ghosts, those nearest the dock gates hoping to be among the fortunate ones when workers were called for; all with a hungry look in their eyes that turned to one of hopeless misery if the work was supplied without them, and they were condemned to go home as they came out, with empty pockets as well as stomachs. Many were forced to give up the struggle and throw themselves on the

clerks, messenger boys, telephonists, cleaners and others. George Bowyer, in his memoirs, would heap praise on Curry as

'a man deserving of the highest respect, always out to help anyone and everybody within the limits of his powers. A more popular official Southampton will never see'.

Bryan Hunt remembers

'He lived a few yards from my house and he and his wife taught me to play bridge in the late 1920's. I wish that I was older then, as he had memories, documents etc of great interest.'

In 1909 Captain Ben Steele was also appointed as White Star's Marine Superintendent. Between 1907 and 1912 their first Victualling Superintendent was J. Bartholomew, with White Star since 1873 and formerly chief steward on the *Oceanic*. After the *Titanic* disaster he was promoted to Victualling Supervisor in Liverpool. For many years Edward Clibborn was White Star's Passenger Manager in Southampton, and was also well known for his work for the Society of Friends and many charitable and philanthropic institutions.

The White Star/American Line office was the local *'nerve centre'*, the relay link with London, Liverpool and New York where the major decisions were made. As late as 1919 official White Star Line brochures for the

cold mercy of the parish so that the workhouse in St Mary's Street became crowded. Even in 1907 when the distress had much diminished there were still many hundreds out of work and not till 1913 could employment be called plentiful'.

(A. Temple Patterson; drawing on the Southampton Times 21st Nov 1903, 9th Jan 1907, 30th Nov 1907, 4th Jan 1913.)

The situation was well known at the time. One of the *Titanic's* passengers in 2nd class, Mrs D Hewlett later wrote of her companions in lifeboat No 13 as

'about 50 people, mostly men of the unemployed class, stokers, stewards and cooks, not one real seaman among them'.

(Letter written from RMS Laconia 12th May 1912: Onslow's Sale 14th April 1992)

Southampton men who were unemployed were glad of any job in many cases, taking it as it arose, bluffing their way into it if need be.

Naturally, when the *Adriatic* arrived in Southampton for the first time from New York on 30th May 1907, the town was in great excitement. The main street was illuminated, town bells were rung and the Echo's correspondent noted *'the vast importance of the move South of the White Star cannot yet be estimated at its true proportions'*. The Harbour board had met on 28th May,

solemnly noting *'The Advent of the White Star Line'*. The Chairman referred to the approaching arrival of the *Adriatic*, the first of this line of steamers and it was resolved upon the proposition of Alderman E Gayton, seconded by Councillor A J Cheverton that authority be given to the General Purposes Committee to expend a sum *'not exceeding twenty pounds in order that the Board may take its share in the reception of this line.'*

By 30th May the Board had agreed to illuminate the Royal Pier for a week, engage the South Hampshire Temperance Band to play on the pier on the night of 31st May, and that *'Messrs Cox and McPherson be engaged to supply and let off some rockets, maroons and Balloons'*. The proposed engagement of local volunteer bands to play on the ship's departure on 5th June was vetoed by Councillors Beavis and Oakley.

At last the *Adriatic* arrived on 30th May, and the Mayor and Corporation set out on the chartered paddle steamer *Princess Helena* to meet her in Southampton Water where they boarded her. A commemorative luncheon was held on board on 1st June, with White Star's London Director and General Manager, Harold Sanderson hosting Mayor Andrews, LSWR's Sir Charles Scotter, and Harland and Wolff's W J Pirrie, and responding to the toast *'Success to the White Star Line'*.

George Bowyer recalled the early days of White Star in Southampton.

The new Harland & Wolff works Southampton c1908. The American Line steamer *St Paul* rests in Trafalgar dry dock.

Private Collection

'In April 1907 I piloted the White Star liner Celtic in and out twice. She took the sailings of one of the American line ships which was laid up for a time, and in the outward voyage she had the largest number of passengers on board that ever left Southampton in one ship, namely 1596. Calling at Cherbourg on the same day she took in a further 582 making a total of 2178, and including the crew there were over 2,500 souls on board. The second trip she made was in May and on the 30th of this month the Adriatic arrived under the command of the late Captain E.J. Smith. A great number of people had gathered in the quay to welcome her to the port for this was really the commencement of the coming of the White Star Line to Southampton. On the 3rd of June she was opened to the public, and 8888 people visited the ship; proceeds went to the local hospitals. On 5th June she sailed for the first time, and the Isle of Wight steamer Prince of Wales full of people followed us down as far as Osborne when they wished Adriatic Bon Voyage and returned to Southampton'.

The ship had made her mark on the town in a big way. She 'towered head and shoulders above every other ship in the docks' as G.E. Hopcroft recalled.

May 30 1907. *The attendance is slightly lowered on account of the expected advent of the 'Adriatic' in the docks this afternoon – the parents have taken the children.*
(Northam Girls' School Logs)

But the White Star Line's arrival immediately called for extra facilities in Southampton. A number of improvements to quays and buildings were made quickly to meet their requirements. LSWR had at once laid on new rolling stock for the White Star boat train from Waterloo, but the real developments were in the docks. Instead of building its own works in Southampton, like the RMSP Co for instance, White Star asked Harland and Wolff to develop repair and maintenance facilities for them in their new port. From now on, although a handful of the Belfast staff would continue to cross down to Southampton for every maiden voyage, or any crisis or urgent repair, White Star and Harland and Wolff could now count on a local workforce in Southampton. On test voyages though, the senior Belfast designers would often question and listen to the ships' crews, who usually saw things first. (*Titanic* steward H S Etches on Thomas Andrews, one of her designers *'I mentioned several things to*

SS Suevic in Trafalgar dock.

Southampton City Heritage Collections

White Star Line *Suevic.* Refloated from the rocks at the Lizard is berthed at Southampton, April 4th 1908. Her new bow was to follow.

Southampton City Heritage Collections

him and he was with the workmen having them attended to'.
(US Enquiry) In March 1907 Harland and Wolff leased a two acre site at the head of the Trafalgar Dry Dock, which they at once leased to J Thornycroft & Co for a year, while they prepared to build. Robert Crighton, the Superintendent Engineer of IMM Co's Red Star Line became the manager of the new plant constructed over the next twelve months by Waring White Building Company. Gradually there arose a platers shed, boiler shop, fitting and turning shop, smithy, brass foundry, coppersmiths, plumbers, tinsmiths, joiners, cabinet makers, pattern makers, french polishers, painters, riggers and electricians shops, a general store and offices for the manager and his assistants, clerks and draughtsman. The

floor above the platers' shed was leased by Harland and
Wolff to White Star for use as a laundry. The entire plant
cost £40,000 to build.

    As it happened, Harland's and Thornycroft were
promptly presented with a repair job for White Star
which was quite outstanding and attracted world
publicity, putting a spotlight on the Southampton and
Belfast link created by the IMM takeover and White
Star's move to Southampton. Their liner *Suevic* had
stranded on the rocks at the Lizard in March 1907. The
bow was a total loss, but the remaining three quarters of
the hull was separated from it by the Liverpool Salvage
Company and towed to Southampton. George Bowyer,
who guided her in, thought

    *'She made a curious sight coming up the water, and I
had to be most careful in putting her alongside not to let her
touch hard in case of her bulkhead giving out.... We berthed
safely and everyone was thankful when she was moored
alongside.... Then the Belfast shipyard went ahead and built a
new bow, which at that time was thought wonderful. The joke
was going about that the Suevic was the longest liner in the
world, her stern being in Southampton and her bow in Belfast.'*

    When in September 1907 the new bow was
skillfully towed to Southampton, Bowyer guided both

> *Suevic* under repair by Thornycroft Shipyard in Trafalgar
> dry dock, 1907.
>
> Southampton City Heritage Collections

sections into the Trafalgar Dock – a number of joyriders,
among them the Manager of the South Western Hotel,
Mr Banks, went round in the bow *'for the novelty of saying
they had made a short voyage in half a ship.'* The two
sections were successfully joined. One of the chargehands
during this work, Henry Creese, would later serve on
Titanic as deck engineer. The feat was celebrated as *'a
magnificent story of man's genius pitted against the great forces
of the ocean'*, and the *Suevic* resumed her career. Edward
Simmons whose father was a steward who went down on

> *RMS Olympic.* The main staircase.
>
> Southampton City Heritage Collections

21

RMS Olympic at Harland and Wolff's in Belfast just prior to her maiden voyage, 1911.

Private Collection

Louis XV style First Class Lounge, *Olympic* c1920–30's.

Southampton City Heritage Collections

the *Titanic* recalls:

" 'My mother told me that when she was very young she and my aunt walked into the docks one day when there was a big engineering job going on and everyone in the town was talking about it, it was a ship called the Suevic which had been broken in half and they towed the two halves up to the docks, put them in dry dock and welded the two halves together – my mother was about 16 years old at the time, they went in the docks – no restrictions then apparently – and my elder cousin just a baby in a pram – they were looking over the edge of the dock, and one of the dock workers came along and said 'do you want to go down and have a look girls?' So they went down the bottom of the dock to see what was going on while he looked after the baby.*"

On 1st January 1908 Harland and Wolff formally took over the works from Thornycroft and the IMM/Harland & Wolff Belfast foothold in Southampton was established.

If these developments were dramatic in themselves, they paled in the light of others planned elsewhere for Southampton. The success of the White Star 'Big Four' liners, the advent in 1907 on the Liverpool–New York run of Cunard's 31,900 ton Blue Riband winners *Lusitania* and *Mauretania*, the largest liners in the world, 80 feet longer than *Adriatic*, and the continuing fame and development of the German steamers, particularly Hamburg America's *Amerika* (1905) and *Kaiserin Auguste Victoria* (1908), encouraged IMM to go further still with the White Star Line. The idea was probably chiefly W.J. Pirrie's. From 1906–8 Harland and Wolff were already building two new slipways at Belfast with giant overhanging gantrys. Over dinner at his house in London, Pirrie and J. Bruce Ismay decided to build three superliners of 45,000 tons, 880 feet long, easily eclipsing the *Lusitania* pair in size and luxury, but running at a much more economical and comfortable service speed of 22½ knots, fast enough to permit a weekly service from Southampton to New York. The first two steamers, *Olympic* and *Titanic* would cost £3,000,000. They would cater chiefly to the American millionaires and business travellers in first class, middle class emigrants, missionaries, teachers, business travellers, farmers in second class, and the *"better class of emigrant"* in third class. A very small area was initially planned for the traditional steerage 'open berth' dormitory accommodation on the first of the pair, but this would be replaced by separate cabins on the second steamer.

In design and looks, both external and internal, the new ships were closely evolved from the *Oceanic* and the 'Big Four' – tried and tested with the White Star/Harland Wolff 'house style' – but on an unparalleled scale. For the first time there would be four funnels (one a dummy) on a White Star liner.

Vast coal bunkers would store the fuel for the boilers of the triple expansion engines which turned the three enormous propellers of each vessel. A special system of water tight compartments, with closable bulkheads was designed, capable it was thought of handling any likely emergency. The latest type of lifeboat davits was provided, designed by Welin. *Titanic* boatswain's mate Albert Haines said of the new davits, *'In the Olympic I worked with them. They worked very free.'* (**American Enquiry**)

Also provided – a barbers shop, a dark room for photographers, a clothes pressing room, a lending library, and a telephone system. Many wonderful new facilities previously tested on *Adriatic* would be provided on a larger scale, chiefly for the benefit of the first class passengers – a swimming pool, a panelled gymnasium, moorish tiled Turkish baths and cooling room, an *à la carte* restaurant in addition to the 1st class dining saloon, a reception room outside the 1st class dining saloon and trellised verandah cafés copied from the new Hamburg America liners.

Although the ships were so large, none of the public rooms was more than a deck high – most liners of this period carried their dining saloons into an upper storey, and their lounges into a domed skylight – only the main first class grand staircase foyer would be allowed to soar two decks upwards into a domed skylight. The predominant feature of the public rooms was width, the detailed carvings, mouldings and mother of pearl inlay of their woodwork and plaster work, the silks, damasks, lace and velvets of their hangings, and the numerous carpets – some plain, some flowered or foliate, and others richly oriental, all in a splendid Anglo-French-American amalgam.

Although the *Olympic* and her sisters were so large, so much more ground space was allotted to public rooms and improved staterooms that they carried fewer passengers than might have been expected, no more than the *Celtic*, half their size – *Olympic* was originally laid out for 689-735 first class passengers, 674 second class passengers and 862 third class passengers with an extra 164 third class under the old "open berth" system (soon dispensed with). Third class was divided into 66 two berth cabins, 112 four berth, 37 six berth, 5 eight berth and 2 ten berth cabins.

Although Harland & Wolff had such major maintenance works in Southampton, some of them for the interior fittings of the liners, sometimes damaged in storms, or worn out by frequent use, and carpenters and cabinet makers in Southampton might find work here, Southampton did not design the interiors of the ships which the passengers used and so many of the crew worked. This was all designed in London, Liverpool and Belfast by Aldam Heaton and Co, who had worked on earlier White Star liners and the homes of the Ismay family. Heaton himself was now dead, and Edward Croft-Smith was the senior designer/partner. With the

The Café Parisien, *Titanic*.

Private Collection

rush on in Belfast to complete the *Olympic* trio, Heaton's was 'taken over' by the IMM Co's Ocean Transport Company, effectively Harland & Wolff, so that the Belfast shipbuilders had their own 'in-house' decorators, whose style, a mixture of 'period' and late

Honour and Glory Crowning Time, carved by Charles Wilson for the *Olympic* and possibly also for the *Titanic*.

Private Collection

23

Wood carver Charles Wilson (far left) and others in a studio, location and date unknown.

Private Collection

Victorian/Edwardian contemporary was very recognisable, as it evolved through each White Star ship. What they did not design or supply themselves they ordered from other sub-contractors and suppliers in Britain and Europe. The staterooms charmed passengers like Lady Duff Gordon:

'My pretty little cabin with its electric heater and pink curtains delighted me .... its beautiful lace quilt, and pink cushions, and photographs all round ... it all looked so homely'.

Normally it was the stewards and stewardesses' chief duty, when not waiting on passengers, to clean the staterooms and public rooms. At refits, particularly later in the 1920's, White Star liners like the *Olympic* might be repainted and redecorated in Southampton, when new docks had been built, but in earlier years major work was still done at Belfast, as was her post World War I refit under Heaton's supervision.

Cabinet maker Samuel Leith would make tables and cupboards at Harland and Wolff in Belfast for the *Titanic's* cabins. Men like Leonard Waldron and Charles Wilson worked on wood carvings for *Olympic* and *Titanic*. Wilson had earlier trained in London with Aumomier's, but eventually joined Heaton's. Other freelance carvers, such as Mr Moss (Rose and Crown Passage, Cheltenham) turned wood columns. (He later worked for H.H. Martyn's, whose founder cancelled his

trip on the *Titanic*, remained in London, and neglected to tell his family in Cheltenham, who were immensely relieved to see him return home.)

Wood carving was more elaborate in the First Class Lounge, Dining Saloons and Reception Room. It was simpler and more repetitive in Second Class, but dignified. In Third Class it was mostly plain, or painted in white enamel. One hundred and eighty six men worked on the carved panelling on the *Olympic*, and the same would have been required for *Titanic*.

Charles Wilson, who carved the central portion of the Honour and Glory Crowning Time panel on the *Olympic*, and a similar or identical panel on *Titanic* remembered that when the *Titanic* finally set sail from Belfast there had not been time to set a clock into the similar ornate carved panel over her First Class Staircase, and a mirror had to be substituted until the clock arrived.

One of the wood carvers and interior designers had studied at Southampton School of Art.

'It was gratifying to notice that a former free student, Cyril Robinson, and for some time in the employ of a leading London firm, had lately executed a considerable part of the carved interior of the SS Olympic and Titanic.'
(Report of Prize Giving, Hants Advertiser, Jan 3, 1912.)

Imperator. Hamburg American Line, 1913.

Michael Cross Collection

Postcard view of White Star Dock from South Western Hotel in 1913. *Olympic* is at berth 43, with American Line steamers at 46 and 47. RMSP steamer is at berth 45.

Southampton City Heritage Collections

Another ex-student had designed the Louis XIV parlour suite on *Olympic* and perhaps also worked on *Titanic*.

It was the 'last minute' work of fitting out, painting, carpet fitting, screw turning, curtain hanging that saw a mixture of men from Harland and Wolff, White Star crew and others, all scurrying around in Southampton under the watchful eye and equally active working hand of Thomas Andrews.

Word of these new ships began to filter through to Southampton. George Bowyer recalled

'A rumour was going about that the White Star Line were going to build two large steamers of double the tonnage of the Adriatic. Of course we all took it with, as the saying goes, a grain of salt; for up to this time, upon a ship arriving at a thousand tons larger you would look upon her with astonishment, the jump from 25,000 to 50,000 tons appeared to be almost impossible.'

Yet White Star was not the only company preparing to build new giants. In June 1910 Hamburg America Line laid down the first of its own mammoth trio, the 52,117 gt *Imperator*, whose size, luxury and emigrant capacity would soon eclipse the White Star trio. She would be launched down the Hamburg slipways five

weeks after the *Titanic* disaster. Built at Vulcan's yards (the other two at Blohm and Voss), *Imperator* would carry not only 942 third class passengers, but an additional amazing 1772 steerage passengers, many still though in improved open berth dormitories.

The scale and elegance of her 1st Class public rooms, designed by Ritz hotel architect Charles Mewès, would make those of the *Olympic* and *Titanic* look almost intimate, although carrying approximately the same number of 1st and 2nd class passengers. The *Imperator* would start the trend for *less* funnels (only three). Hers would be unmistakable for their height, when she tendered off Southampton for the first time in 1913. The policy was similar to White Star in luxury and moderate speed, but grander and slightly faster. The development of these giants was logical, inevitable, but they were leaping ahead at astonishing speed.

Over in St Nazaire the French Line were planning to lay down their luxurious 23,666 tons *France*, a fast vessel and their only 'four funneller'. She was not expected to affect Southampton as at this stage French Line called at Plymouth, and did not call in Southampton until the 1930s. But curiously enough the *France*, whose maiden voyage began a week after the loss of the *Titanic*, made a surprise appearance in Southampton's Prince of Wales Dry Dock in January 1913.

Inauguration of the Trafalgar dry dock.

Southampton City Heritage/A.B.P. Collections

Cunard was soon preparing to build an *Olympic/Imperator* type giant, the *Aquitania*, for the Liverpool run, completed in 1914. Eventually she would be well known in Southampton.

It was against this climate that railroad chairman and *Titanic* passenger victim, Charles M. Hays, made his remark recorded by Archibald Gracie, a fellow passenger.

"The White Star, the Cunard and the Hamburg American lines are now developing their attention to a struggle for supremacy in obtaining the most luxurious appointments in their ships, but the time will soon come when the greatest and most appalling of all disasters at sea will be the result."

If it is ironical that one of the biggest financial beneficiaries and promoters of advanced transport, linked with the IMM, should have perceived the danger, the evidence suggests that many of the dockworkers and seafarers of Southampton did not. How many of them, so eager for any chance of work, can have seen a blot on the glittering prospects of new ships and work? Southampton morale was generally high at the prospect of these ships, although their size could be intimidating. Captain Smith

himself, a seasoned sea-dog if ever there was one, was apparently supremely confident in the developing giants of the new age. On the maiden arrival of the *Adriatic* in New York he had actually said

'I cannot imagine any condition which would cause a ship to founder. I cannot conceive of any disaster happening to this vessel. Modern shipbuilding has gone beyond that…'

At the same time that these giants were being conceived outside Southampton, the LSWR, spurred on by the arrival of the White Star Line, the prospect of the growing Atlantic trade, and the increasing size of the vessels, prepared to build yet another wet dock between the Empress Dock and Trafalgar Dry Dock. Between 1907 and 1911 White Star liners would only berth at Berths 38 to 41 on the Ocean or Test Quay. The new dock would cover 16 acres, LSWR awarding the building contract to Topham Jones and Railton in October 1907, at an estimated cost of £492,231. 3,840 feet of quay were to be constructed, with a depth of 40 feet at low water. Four large cargo and passenger sheds with waiting rooms and lavatories were to be erected on what became 43, 44, 46 and 47 berths. The entire project was to be completed in 40 months and was supervised by the newly appointed New Works Engineer, Mr F.E. Wentworth-Shields who soon became Docks Engineer.

Once work began there were 850 to 1,200 men

on site, with 85 machines, including locomotives and steam navvies to excavate 873,00 cu.yds of material and load it into hoppers, build a chalk bank across the site at the southern end, in effect a temporary dam, and build berths 48-9 by submarine construction, lowering 8-ton concrete blocks into position with the help of divers. At 41 berth a wall was built in a dry trench and sunk into the heart of the bank. A large temporary stage was erected over the River Test, to carry two railway tracks, so that trucks loaded with excavated material could easily run on to the waiting hoppers who would dump it off the Isle of Wight. The rest of the material was used to reclaim land later built on by Pirelli General Cable Works. One of the railway tracks leading to Town Quay was extended across the entrance of Royal Pier, and a temporary railway line laid in the roadway to reach the site. New railway lines were added so that the boat train could reach the new dock.

But these vast new liners not only needed longer quays and deeper docks, they also needed larger and deeper channels in Southampton water and in the swinging grounds in the river outside the docks as tugs turned them in and out.

The river was controlled not by the LSWR or the shipping lines but by Southampton Harbour Board. It was therefore, to the Harbour Board that Philip Curry, White Star's Southampton Manager, wrote on 18 December 1908 to ensure that all necessary dredging would be completed before the new liners arrived.

'It is with pleasure we have to inform you that with the object of bringing their Southampton–New York Service up to the highest standard of efficiency, and of developing to the fullest extent the traffic via Southampton, the Management of the Oceanic Steam Navigation Company Limited (White Star Line) are now having built at Messrs Harland and Wolff's shipbuilding yards at Belfast two steamships of the highest class, which will provide every attraction and comfort for travellers by the time and which will much exceed in tonnage any vessels now afloat or under construction.

It will be obvious to your Board that if the Port of Southampton is to derive full benefit from the advent of these steamers, it must be safeguarded against any possibility of reproach, or reflection upon its facilities, such as would arise were detention to be caused to the vessels in consequence of any deficiency in the draught of water in the channels and approaches to the port and docks.

We therefore deem it our duty to inform you that the builders estimate that these two vessels, when ready for sea in the Southampton Service, will draw approximately 35 feet of water, and it is expected that on their arrival at this Port from New York their draught will be in the neighbourhood of 32 feet 6 inches (less coal, less passengers by the end of the trip).

The steamers may be expected to take their places in the service in the spring of 1912, and we confidently hope to receive an assurance from your Board that whatever dredging may be necessary to enable them to sail promptly, and to land their passengers without detention will be undertaken and completed before they are delivered.'

This was the White Star's opening shot in what was to provide a long and complicated thrash with the Harbour Board over who was going to foot the bill for this essential work. Initially the Harbour Board's Works Committee, in the person of Commissioner A.J. Day, reported nervously on 4 February 1909.

'It does not seem necessary at the present time to do more than acknowledge this letter and state when the proper time arrives it will receive the serious consideration of our Committee. I cannot think that it is necessary to do more than this until we have the whole scheme (for the new wet dock) for South Western Railway before us, and until that Company has received parliamentary powers to carry out its proposals and made arrangements to proceed with carrying out of same.

As Mr. Curry states in his letter that these new steamers of the White Star Line will not be coming to Southampton before the Spring of 1912, there can be no great urgency in dealing with this most important question of further Dredging, and many things may possibly happen between now and then to alter the policy of the Railway Company and the White Star Line. When the time does arrive for the Board to deal with this question, I presume both the Railway Company and the International Mercantile Marine Company will be asked to guarantee that these new vessels of the White Star Line will not only come to Southampton, but will remain here for a term of years.'

The same day, a more alert Councillor and future Mayor, H. Bowyer (related, of course, to 'Uncle George' Bowyer) wrote to point out the problems of the alternative of merely mooring ever larger vessels in the river, given inadequate dredging, saying

'It would be impracticable for such large ships to swing to their own anchors in our river.'

Little progress over this thorny issue was made in 1909. White Star must have begun to worry! Their solution, in some desperation, appears to have been an official deputation on 6th January 1910, attended by no less a White Star grandee than its Director and General Manager, Harold Sanderson, the closest associate and personal friend of J. Bruce Ismay. He was accompanied by Philip Curry, the Assistant Local Manager E.W. Bond, their new Marine Superintendent Captain Ben Steel, Captain Haddock of the *Oceanic*, and their favourite pilot George Bowyer.

Onlookers watch the new *Olympic* arriving in
Southampton, summer 1911.

Southampton City Heritage Collections

'Well, gentlemen, I am sure we are very pleased to see
the deputation of the White Star Line this afternoon'

intoned the Harbour Board Chairman, Councillor
Oakley. He told them

'The Board as a whole hesitates to incur such a heavy
expense – some £100,000 – for the benefit of two vessels
which may or may not require more water than the 32 feet we
have now as it could not be considered a business proposition to
spend this large amount of money for the sake of two vessels
only, without securing a return to pay the interest to the
stockholders and provide for the sinking fund, we shall be glad to
hear what financial agreement you would enter into if the Board
would provide three feet more water the loan would be for 55
years.'

A doubtless startled, but by no means speechless
Sanderson, after first answering other points, retaliated

'I really think that is a question which surprises me very
much indeed, that we should be asked to provide improvements
at the ports the ships will frequent. I really think that such a
novel proposal would not have been made by any other port in
Great Britain. We are spending £1,500,000 on each ship,
and, ... you usually find extras ... in bringing two ships' trade
to Southampton we feel we are doing all that might be asked ...

purchases for the ships would be made at Southampton.

37 feet of water in the channel is the minimum for safe
navigation of these ships ... (under the present situation) in
1909, on 80 occasions the Olympic and Titanic could not have
sailed to time because of the low tide ... years before we came to
Southampton it was the boast of Southampton that ships could
arrive and sail without having to wait for water, as in other
ports. If you, gentlemen, come to the conclusion that this boast is
one which you do not agree to maintain, the value of our
argument vanishes ... it is for you gentlemen to decide, not for
me .... In Liverpool the people (passengers) are not willing to
put up with the delay ... (in unsuitable tides) we have to land
passengers at Holyhead. If a similar state of affairs prevails at
Southampton we shall have to put notices on our ships
recommending these people to leave at Plymouth, which will be
a reflection upon Southampton. You might not think that any
serious drawback, but do you not see any revenue to come from
this to meet your expenditure? Purchases are made at the port of
Southampton, that I think is a great point to bear in mind.'

Sanderson reminded the Committee of the vast
sums of money spent on dredging by the ports of
Fishguard, Belfast and New York before continuing

'These large ships pay large sums of money in wages
and it is not very hard to my mind to see that Southampton
derives some benefit in the large sum of money directly or
indirectly brought to the town by the crews and their dependants
and the men who work the ships in port. I do not think it is fair
that we should be looked harshly at for being the first people to
bring large ships to Southampton. We were not the first to
produce large ships, and we shall be followed in a short time by

others. The Germans will follow us in a very short time.'

Sanderson was referring to the *Imperator* and her sisters. Slyly he threw in the coup de grace

'How far you attach importance to shipping I do not know … if there happens to be a vessel leaving Hamburg drawing 35 feet, what can they do at Southampton to accommodate her? The Hamburg Company may desire to call, but would not think they should have to wait.'

In the event the *Imperator* and her sisters would not enter the docks until after World War I, when the Trafalgar dry dock was enlarged by LSWR to accommodate her and the Harbour Board had by that time improved the channels.

But after Sanderson's powerful speech, a somewhat thoughtful, even chastened, Committee began to consider how £88,650 might be raised to pay for a deeper channel from Thorn Knoll to Dock Head. The Councillors were confident of help from LSWR but soon threw the ball back at Sanderson, with Councillor W. Beavis, apparently locked in the past rather than the future, adding

'It is useless to compare Southampton to Liverpool which has five times as much shipping.'

Perhaps Sanderson's patience was beginning to run out.

'When we came to Southampton it was our intention we would do everything in our power to increase the trade, and make the line a very successful and excellent one. After this we produced these two ships, and there seems to be in the minds of some gentlemen resentment for having done it.'

'No, no,' chorused several Harbour Board Committee members, but Councillor Beavis was still hitting back *'You mention you would do all in the interests of Southampton, but you came in the interests of the White Star Line.'*

'At the same time' replied Sanderson.

The members still questioned the whole project very cautiously, apparently doubtful, or affecting to doubt, that White Star would still be in Southampton in ten years time. Councillor W.T. Hirst:

'Supposing in 10 years time the ships go elsewhere; where should we stand?'

Mr. Sanderson: *'That is not a reasonable thing to look at. Where will you be if you don't improve the Port?'*

Councillor W.T. Hirst: *'So far, so good, but is it really necessary to do the present work?'*

Mr. Sanderson: *'I hope you will think so.'*

Councillor W.T. Hirst: *'There is no proof at present.'*

Mr. Sanderson: *'We started with a little ship called the Oceanic 400 feet long, and we increased 10 feet at a time, each time feeling our way; undoubtedly a success. The last step was a big one, as you see we were willing to invest £3 million of money.'*

Councillor W.T. Hirst: *'We need to consider this matter closely and seriously. Was the work really necessary, where would the ships coal – at America in and out?'*

This last question was fair, and Sanderson assured them *'No, the Adriatic does, but these two do not have the accommodation (to fill two voyages' coal) and will coal at America and Southampton.'*

Captains Steel and Bowyer were on hand to calculate the tidal delays as Sanderson emphasised, *'We have to go to Cherbourg.'*

White Star was confident of LSWR support, particularly for the new wet dock, originally envisaged for ships drawing 32 feet, but soon deepened. It was a special situation. As Sanderson said *'We are confined to this question by the two ships, the Titanic and Olympic,'* adding *'they are the forerunners of other ships of a like capacity.'*

The Committee finally withdrew to mull it over, and White Star put on a friendly face. But the general reaction in the White Star office was exasperation, echoed in the shipping press. Philip Curry took dry pleasure in sending a damning cutting from *'Syren and Shipping'* to his friend the shipbroker and coal factor, George Washington Sandell, Southampton's Vice Consul for Russia and Norway.

'True to their parochial and cheeseparing methods the Southampton Harbour Board are displaying their accustomed ineptitude with the big ships of the White Star Line … Poverty can be excused, but not sheer downright tomfoolery such as the Southampton men are playing.'

In the end it was LSWR who made the necessary loans and grants to pay for the channel dredging. Public dissatisfaction with the performance of the Harbour Board eventually led to the formation of a new board of 26 members representing shipping interests, official bodies such as the LSWR with 3 seats, and for the first time organised labour. A particular spur for further dredging was ironically provided by the *Titanic* herself. When she set sail on her maiden voyage, as her propellers turned for the first time, as she began to move down Southampton water, some of the water displaced by her huge hull was pushed round another steamer, the American liner *New York* at berth, forcing her to break her moorings, sucked towards the *Titanic* in a near collision, until tugs and Captain Smith stopping the *Titanic*, averted it. The incident would be the subject of

Titanic on the stocks at Belfast, 1911.

Harland and Wolff

much pointed correspondence between the White Star Line and the Harbour Board immediately afterwards, and action was soon taken to further deepen the channel.

The same sort of problem concerned adequate swinging ground space in the river. George Bowyer remembered

'At first when we asked for a thousand feet of swinging ground, everybody concerned thought we were asking for something out of reason.'

White Star had an excellent relationship with LSWR from the start – their aims were partly shared – also J. Bruce Ismay was intimately involved with railways as a Director of the London North Western Railway, like his father before him. Work was proceeding well on the new wet dock, which LSWR agreed to name the White Star Dock, although it would be available for use by other companies. At the same time they turned their thoughts to a dry dock for the Olympic and Titanic. Not

even the Trafalgar Dock could take their great length. LSWR initially planned to build a new 1,000 feet long dry dock on the Chamberlayne estate on the left bank of the river Itchen, below Woolston, despite opposition by Southampton Corporation and the Harbour Board, but put this off when they found that the Trafalgar Dock could be enlarged at a fraction of the cost of a new one. Topham Jones and Railton again received the contract in May 1910. Excavation work began in October 1910 to enlarge it to 897 feet, but was not completed until spring 1913, so the new liners would initially dry dock back at their builders in Belfast. Olympic would first enter the Trafalgar Dry Dock on 16th July 1913.

But White Star Dock was nearing completion at the same time as the Olympic, launched sooner than originally expected on 20th October 1910. Titanic was by now fully framed, and would go down the ways on 31st May just before the Olympic's maiden voyage in 1911. The pair made an unforgettable impression on the stocks together shortly before Olympic's launch. Olympic's building berth could now be prepared for the third sister eventually named Britannic. Southampton awaited their arrival, one by one. The first ship to enter the new White Star Dock was the Teutonic, guided by 'Uncle George' Bowyer. Over the next few months several ships were

Onlookers watch the new *Olympic* arriving in Southampton, summer 1911.

Southampton City Heritage Collections

laid up in the dock, as work continued on the sheds, and the barrier was fully opened.

By June 1911, the *Olympic*, fitted out at breakneck speed, had completed her trials, picked up guests from the launch of the *Titanic*, called at Liverpool, and was ready for her first voyage to Southampton prior to her maiden voyage. Already her dimensions were knocking onlookers for six. George Bowyer recalled

'We could hardly believe our eyes there was such a ship!'

Captain Smith, previously of the *Adriatic*, told him

'Yes, but after you have been on board for some time her size will wear off.'

It took Bowyer some time. Special measures were still needed to cope with her alongside the new corrugated sheds, painted LSWR green in the White Star Dock. The official LSWR brochure describing the dock proudly informed the public

'Owing to the great height of the Olympic and her sister ship the Titanic, the passenger gantries are of the two decker type, in order that they may be available for passengers at different states of the tide.'

To enable easier access to ships *'the shed has a verandah 18 feet above the ground.'* Electric cranes at the far ends of the shed were the first electric quayside cranes to be introduced in Southampton Docks. Arc lights were also provided.

'Arriving on the morning of the 3rd June, the Ocean Dock was not completed – only her berth (No. 44), at the entrance to which two large dolphins were placed to protect the working of the two pier heads. We entered bow first between the dolphins, and got safely to our berth. On sailing day we had to go out stern first, pass between the dolphins and then on down

RMS *Titanic* on the stocks at Belfast, just prior to her launch in 1911.

Private Collection

THE LAUNCH OF THE S.S. TITANIC MAY 31. 1911

The launch of the *Titanic* recorded on this postcard sent to Mr. Watts, Highfield, Southampton.

Mike Petty Collection

to the entrance to the Itchen, where at that time was the only swinging ground then dredged.' **(George Bowyer)**

By the time Captain Bowyer piloted the *Olympic* into the almost complete White Star Dock for the first time on 3rd June 1911, Southampton was in a state of eager anticipation. Reports of *Olympic's* size, splendour, improvements in all classes, watertight compartments, which the *'Shipbuilder'*, the best known magazine recording the latest new ships, declared made her *'virtually unsinkable'*, were read out by Southampton fathers to their wives and children, while the public were allowed to view the ship, (the admission fee going to local charities) on 10th June 1911. *Olympic* finally sailed on her maiden voyage on 14th June. Summing it all up on 17th June, the Southern Daily Echo deemed her

'An unparalleled achievement. Southampton will soon be the home of three Olympic sized ships ... her twin sister Titanic will be ready at the end of the year; the third giant has yet to be built, but the triplets will represent a capital of £4½ million. The

town claims pride in the biggest ships in the world.'

No wonder that in Liverpool, deprived of this prize, some sailors were to be heard in pubs dismissing her sourly,

'a waste of money ... she's too big ... she'll bump into summat ... no ship's unsinkable ... no damn good to Liverpool ... she'll be sailing out o' Southampton.'
(From 'Tramps and Ladies' by Sir J. Bisset, first officer on the Carpathia).

Prophetically, the maiden voyage had been overshadowed by fears of a coal passers strike, but strike breakers, in the event, bunkered the *Olympic*. For the tugmen pulling her out, it was something of a trial run for the future, and it took them more than an hour to move her into the stream and point her bow down Southampton water. Although the Coronation of King George V was imminent on 22nd June, followed by a naval review at Spithead, dominating the national news, the *Olympic* dominated the port of Southampton. Her sister *Titanic* was keenly awaited, but was seen as another *Olympic*. The *Olympic* was an enormous success, and once established on her route, wealthy Americans flocked to her, as intended, along with her other second and third class passengers.

Olympic's Dr J.C.H. Beaumont, one of her several medical officers at the time, recalled the liner

'caused a sensation when she first appeared in Southampton ... she looked colossal and even 'uncanny' as she towered high above the waterline ... dwarfing all other craft within sight ... To prevent visitors getting lost or strayed, parties had to be formed and led around by guides who were by no means sure of the direct route.'

On her maiden voyage J. Bruce Ismay declared *'Olympic is a marvel'*. But observing closely her performance, he suggested modifications for the outfitting *Titanic*. Part of the enclosed 'B' deck promenade should be replaced with extra first class staterooms and suites, (two with their own private verandas or promenades) and an enclosed trellised café overlooking the sea, which would be known as the Café Parisien. An extra 100 first class passengers could now be carried by the *Titanic*, which would mean extra crew in the catering staff. An additional reception room was to be made outside the *à la carte* restaurant, so popular was the reception room outside *Olympic's* main dining saloon. Finally, very late in *Titanic's* outfitting it was decided to glaze over the forward third of her open promenade deck 'A' as *Olympic's* first class passengers complained of the spray from the wind and the sea. The effect of all these changes was to delay *Titanic's* completion, compounded by the sudden return to Belfast of the *Olympic* in October 1911 for hull replating after HMS *Hawke* collided with her in the Solent in a notorious incident, much discussed at the time.

A glimpse of life in the Belfast yard that autumn is given by a semi-anonymous shipworker, who sent a postcard of the launch of the *Titanic* to Mr C.L. Watts in Crown Street, Highfield, Southampton in November 1911.

Dear Ciss

How are you keeping. Hope you are quite well. Glad to be able to say I am alright. Am on the Arcadian now. Very soft job up here. Won't let you do too much. Worked all Sat. night on the Olympic. Drew 62/- last week. Saw the Arlanza launched last Thursday. Hope you are working. W.S. sends kind regards. Sincerely yrs Frank. Roll on Christmas!

(Courtesy Mike Petty Collection)

Olympic returned again in March 1912 for repairs to a propeller after mysteriously dropping a blade in the

Portside view of the *Titanic* fitting out at Belfast.

Southampton City Heritage Collections

North Atlantic. It was then that steward H.S. Etches met her designer Thomas Andrews later recalling *'I had met him several times at Belfast because I had been on the Olympic'*. It was Etches first opportunity to catch sight of the new sistership on which he would also serve.

The pressure was on in Belfast as the workforce was reshuffled to take on these extra jobs. *Titanic's* planned maiden voyage from Southampton on 20th March had fortunately not been made public, for this deadline could not be met. *Olympic* returned to Southampton on 6/7th March 1912, the port must wait a little longer for her sister.

The finishing touches were also being put at Belfast to RMSP Co's new liner *Arlanza*, which would arrive in Southampton on 10th June. RMSP Co itself was concluding negotiations in London to buy the Union Castle Line for £5,000,000. Ironically, RMSP Co's Chairman Owen Phillips, later Lord Kylsant, would eventually become Pirrie's successor as Chairman of Harland and Wolff, and also buy back the White Star Line from the IMM Co in 1927.

By 1st April *Titanic* was ready for her sea trials, but bad weather delayed this until the 2nd. Some 79 of her crew, a *'scratch'*, had come over from Liverpool and Southampton to bring her out, joined by numerous staff of Harland and Wolff. The trials were successfully accomplished in Belfast Lough and the Irish Sea to Board of Trade standards. Hand over papers were signed by Harold Sanderson of White Star and Thomas Andrews of Harland and Wolff. The *Titanic* sailed for Southampton at 8pm in order to cover the 570 miles to the port by the midnight tide the next day. The *Olympic* meanwhile set sail from Southampton for New York, and greetings were exchanged between the two ships by the recently invented Marconi radio. The Hampshire Independent reported they had passed each other, *'a short distance somewhere off Portland.'*

'My father, David Blair and his great friend and shipmate Commander Lightoller were on board when the Titanic was brought round from Belfast to Southampton for fitting out. They both remarked at the time on the small number of lifeboats provided.'

(MS of Miss E. Blair, published in Chart & Compass)

4th, Southampton
Arrived on 'Titanic' from Belfast today. Am afraid I shall have to step out to make room for Chief Officer of the Olympic who was going in command but so many ships laid up he will have to wait. Hope eventually to get back to this ship. Many thanks for parcel and letter, Nancy will be pleased and has already spotted the contents as she was too quick for us. So glad Winnie is coming, Nancy eagerly looking forward to her visit. You say she travels Thursday night. She said Friday so we are in doubt when she will arrive. I shall meet London trains tomorrow in case. Been home all day and down on board tonight on watch. This is a magnificent ship, I feel very disappointed I am not to make the first voyage.
Love to all from us. Affectionately
D.B.

(Letter sent by David Blair to Miss Mackness, Broughty Ferry, Scotland. Courtesy British Sailors Society)

The liner was almost certainly piloted into Southampton Docks by *'Uncle George'* Bowyer, who, so expansive on the *Olympic*, significantly avoids all reference in his memoirs to the *Titanic*'s week in Southampton, although he took her out as well. Her arrival, her portholes and windows glowing with light, coincided with high water. She must have been a beautiful sight. Waiting for her were six tugs of the Southampton, Isle of Wight and South of England Royal Mail Steam Packet Company, many years later known as *'Red Funnel'* – but in 1912 the funnels of their tugs and tenders were buff.

The tugs had nearly all been either built or engined or reboilered in Southampton. Although the *Ajax* had been built at Barclay Curle in Govan, *Hector, Neptune* and *Albert Edward* were built in Day Summers' yard at Northam, where *Vulcan* was reboilered in 1905. *Hercules* had been reboilered at Mordey Carney's yard in 1902-3. Dwarfed by the *Titanic*, but firmly in control of her, they warped her into the White Star Dock, stern first, under the firm commands of the tugmasters and their crews, alongside berths 43/44 just vacated by the *Olympic*.

The 'Hampshire Independent' recorded

'Quietly and unostentatiously without any blare of trumpets, the Titanic, the world's latest and biggest ship steamed up the silent waters of the Solent and docked at Southampton.'

Herbert Pitman, her 3rd Officer, said *'she was simply made fast in her berth.'* **(US Enq)**

Plymouth Harbour, 1910, by Norman Wilkinson (1878–1971). Painted for the First Class Smoking Room of *Titanic*, as one of a pair. The other painting, of New York Harbour, hung in the Smoking Room of the *Olympic*. (see page 188)

Rodney Norman Wilkinson Collection

"Ice skating - the latest craze"

High Street, Southampton. Early 1900s.

Southampton City Heritage Collections

One of the most important photographic developments in Southampton in 1912 was the arrival of a new newspaper. The age of the 'pictorial' had reached the town at last, and the old 'Southampton Amusements' was to be reformed as a 'penny weekly' called 'The Southampton and District Pictorial'. It would be 'bright, topical and copiously illustrated by a special staff of live photographers. Order at once from your newsagent – price one penny – don't forget Wednesday next', proclaimed the 'Amusement' on 6th April. One of the 'Amusement's' last issues solemnly recorded the recent whist drive of the Mercantile Marine League

'At the Avenue Hotel, Padwell Road, the LSWR representatives received a visit from the American and White Star Lines and the latter suffered a severe reverse by 23-13 ... one more engagement has to be fulfilled by the American and White Star Lines, who have to meet the Union Castle representatives, and they have won four out of thirteen matches.'

The new paper's first issue coincided with the maiden voyage of the *Titanic*, and the ship offered an exciting subject as it ran the following: *'We specially desire to draw the attention of the large army of amateur photographers to our weekly competition – a prize of half a guinea for the best local picture sent in. Preferably we should like something with a smile in it, but that is not essential.'* Who would have guessed that by the second issue, the subject of the *Titanic* would be associated with a calamitous tragedy. As well as the new Pictorial, illustrations had also begun to appear regularly in the Hampshire Advertiser and Hampshire Independent which included Southampton news.

'This is quite a new departure in local journalism, nothing on today's scale having hitherto been attempted... only possible by a very expensive plant which the proprietors have just had installed and their progressive policy had its reward in largely augmented sales... The same illustrations will never appear in both papers.'
(Echo, 13th January 1912)

Tudor House Museum, Bugle Street, Southampton. c1910.

Southampton City Heritage Collections

In early 1912, Southampton citizens had doubtless been following the much publicised Tharp-Studley divorce suit, in which Mr Tharp's house at Fawley, Eaglehurst, figured so prominently. As the result of the scandal Mr Tharp had put the house out to let, and in late February it was announced in the Hampshire Advertiser that 'Eaglehurst' had been taken by Signor Marconi, the wireless wizard, as a country residence.

What else was going on in Southampton in the spring of 1912? Here are a few random examples recorded in the local papers. Tudor House on Bugle Street had recently been acquired for the town by the Mayor, Colonel Bance, and was now *'being adapted as a museum of Hampshire antiquities, an old-world garden is being laid out to the rear.'* One of Tudor House's earliest exhibits would be the dress sword of Captain Smith of the *Titanic*, presented by his widow in 1913 as a memorial. The town's earliest maritime collections were displayed in Tudor House until a special maritime museum was set up in Wool House fifty years later.

Mayor Bance retired at the end of his third term in March 1912, and was presented with a silver gilt ceremonial casket featuring enamel plaques of Tudor House, the *Olympic*, and the Bargate, all prominent aspects of Southampton during his term. The Bargate's battlements had been restored under his aegis.

J.G. Swords, the doyen of local educationalists retired as headmaster of Woolston Boys School.

George Sandell had recently donated prizes for marine painting by students at Southampton School of Art.

William Burrough Hill, the auctioneer, and another town benefactor, was about to donate to Tudor House a series of watercolours of the fast vanishing *'old'* Southampton, commissioned by him from the artist W.M. Cooper over the years 1897 to 1912. The arrival of the big ships, the development of the docks and railways, the rise in some areas of business, and the beginnings of slum clearance were all altering Southampton bit by bit, as its population rose to 120,000.

The Southern Daily Echo (27 March) editorialised that *'the coming of the Titanic'* had *'a special significance. It sets the seal once again upon the future of Southampton... nothing, humanly speaking, can arrest the progress of the port...*

St. Mary's Street, Southampton. Early 1900s.

Southampton City Heritage Collections

the coming of the Titanic is a spur to our public men not only to keep the port, their sacred trust, up to present needs, but a little ahead of them.'

Cunard was making a cautious appearance in Southampton with sailings to Canada by the Ultonia, Ascania, Andania and Alaunia, having purchased the Thomson Line in 1911. But their express services to New York remained Liverpool based for the time being.

In March the annual dinner of Southampton Chamber of Commerce was held at the South Western Hotel, attended by E.W. Bond and E. Clibborn of White Star, Southampton. Bruce Ismay, Lord Pirrie and P.E. Curry amongst others sent apologies.

In February the *Hampshire Advertiser* ran a feature on the Sailors Home in Oxford Street. There had been a Southampton Sailors Home in the town since 1861 when three houses at the end of Canute Road were utilised. Movement to the new home in 1909 had seen the number of men accommodated on average leaping from 5,000 to a new high of 26,753 by 1911. As well as being a place for men to stay when they were ashore and work was scarce, the Superintendent was also involved in the recruitment of crews. Even this new increased capacity was not deemed enough and an appeal was being launched to add another storey to the building to provide an additional 52 beds. The cost was estimated at £2,000. Several of the *Titanic*'s crew were based here.

While Southampton Corporation debated the site of a new reservoir on Southampton Common, the town's theatres *(Hippodrome, Palace, New Grand, Royal Pier, Pavilion)* offered variety, sacred concerts, army

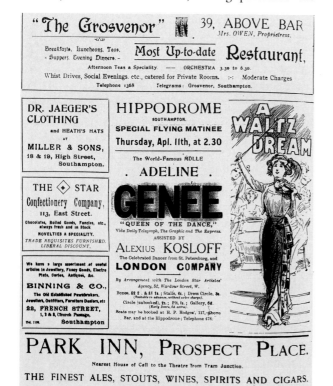
Southampton News

Southampton Local Studies Library

bands. Adeline Genée, the famous dancer, was expected for a special *"Flying Matinee"* at the Hippodrome on 11th April. On 9th April *Titanic*'s Purser McElroy and his wife sent flowers in the Danish national colours to Miss Genée. Mrs Langtry had recently appeared there. The New Grand was offering *'A Waltz Dream'*. Two of the new cinematographic theatres, the New Southampton Picture Palace in East Street and the Alexandra Picture Theatre, offered their own thrills, as the new medium began to gain respectability.

On the football fields the Saints' *'Custodian, W. Knight, is keeping goal very nicely just now.'* Indoor and outdoor skating was the latest craze at the Royal Pier and Shirley Road. The first cricket matches were being planned in the park. Millbrook Football Club had just enjoyed its annual supper and presentation.

Tyrrell and Green's store were advertising a *'Lady Expert'* to demonstrate in their dress material department, using Tyrrell's 'multiform skirt card coupon' on 11th and 12th April.

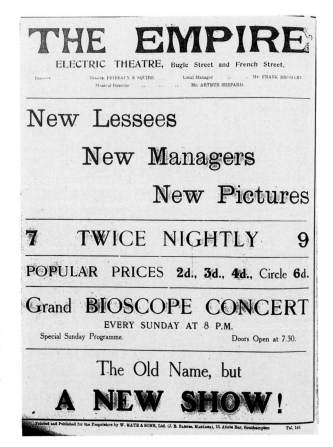

Back row (left to right): W.A.Hammock (director), I.Turner (trainer), J.Robertson, J.McAlpine, W.Knight, A.C.Brown, D.Gordon, E.Salway, D.Slade, G.Swift (secretary). Second row: G.Rainsley (asst trainer), E.Arnfield (financial secretary), A.Small, B.Penton, J.R.Eastham, S.Ireland, A.Lee, J.Curry, G.Smith, F.Grayer, H.M.Ashton (director), W.Bulpitt (director). Sitting: C.Sheeran, A.Gibson, H.Hamilton, G.S.Kimpton, H.Brown, J.Denby, G.Handley. On ground: J.Wilcox, S.Chalcraft.

The Saints 1911/12.

Ray Mursell collection

Palace Theatre, c1910.

Corbishley Collection

It was announced in the Southern Daily's social and trivia column that on Easter Monday a Master Felix Biet and Miss Nellie Biet of 'Edenholme', Darwin Road, would be entertaining *'sixty of their juvenile friends'* at an evening party in Kell Memorial Hall, *'entertained by Mr*

Tap room of Star Hotel, High Street. Early 1900s.

Southampton City Heritage Collections

Haye and dancing to Mrs Filsell's music.' What a contrast between this middle class world and that of the young in the town's dockland communities.

At the end of March a partial eclipse was visible over the town for *'all who cared to see it.'* Over the Easter weekend before sailing many of the crew were conducting their normal business such as W.A. Jeffrey of Highfield who on Easter Sunday was singing in the choir of Holyrood Church as he had done for the last sixteen years. Others no doubt were spending time with their families, or frequenting the local pubs, and of course many were already working hard to prepare the ship. Little did the people of this busy town realise what chaos and anguish would envelop them over the coming weeks.

★ PROVISIONING

"A ship full of flowers"

The *Titanic* had arrived in Southampton, but a black cloud had been looming since late February in the form of a national coal miners strike, for a minimum wage. Coal was not being delivered to the docks, forcing many companies to lay up their liners in ports all round the country. In Southampton several ships had to be tied up in pairs for lack of available berths. Over 17,000 men were out of work in Southampton as a result. The strike was not only in the newspaper headlines, but also the subject of church sermons. Many families were receiving the most basic monetary assistance *'on the Parish'* from the Corporation of Southampton, in order to survive. LSWR's Easter holiday excursion trains to Southampton and Southern regional spots remained cancelled, but the good news was that *Olympic*'s sailings and *Titanic*'s maiden voyage, now scheduled for 10th April, were not. Their speed would be reduced slightly if necessary to conserve coal. Apart from necessary reserves of coal taken in Belfast, *Titanic*'s holds would be filled with coal already stockpiled for, or else extracted from, the holds of other laid up liners of the I.M.M., namely White Star's *Oceanic* and *Majestic*, and American Line's *New York, Philadelphia, St Louis* and *St Paul*. Some of the *Philadelphia*'s passenger bookings were now transferred to the new *Titanic* including the Hart family. By 6th April the coal strike was settled, but it would be some time before the newly mined coal would be shipped to Southampton to replenish the laid up steamers.

March 14 1912

22 free meals given today. The distress is daily becoming more acute owing to stagnation caused by the coal strike.
(Northam Girls School Logs)

'We shipped coal, provisions, cargo was taken on board, passed the Board of Trade surveys.'
Charles Lightoller (US Enq)

Coal for the White Star Line was brought alongside the ships by the coal barges of their coal agents and shippers, R. & J.H. Rea. Rea's association with Southampton dated back to 1893; their barge capacity for coal in 1895 was 1,000 tons. By the time the *Olympic* arrived in 1911, Rea's could transfer over 4,000 tons of coal in 15 working hours, a world record for coaling a vessel of that size, and a source of much pride, but laborious and exhausting for the low paid coal handlers. Rea's repair yard was in Albert Road, Woolston. Their barges, some 100 in all in their heyday, were mostly built in Southampton, Woolston or Itchen Ferry yards like Fay's, Camper Nicholson, Day Summer. Others came from Portsmouth yards. Rea's offices were in Canute Road.

In 1907 James Rea had urged Southampton Harbour Board to ensure that passing ships from the Town Quay and Royal Pier slowed down while liners at berths 38 and 39 were being coaled by his men, so the work could be completed without loss or danger.

Rea's barges first tied up alongside one of the new special barge docks at 28 Berth where electric crane operators could hoist in coal packed by men in the bunkers from colliers and cargo ships on the other side, swing it across and load it into the waiting barges. The barges would then be moved to the dock alongside the liner, boomed out twenty feet from the quay, where Rea's men, known as *'coalies'* would shovel coal into buckets, hoisted or winched to more coalies suspended on winched platforms below the doors or *'coaling ports'* of the coal shutes in the liner's hull, just below the middle deck of *Olympic* and *Titanic*. Coal shute flaps were bottom hinged to take a temporary sheet iron scoop. Coal then poured down the shutes to coal bunkers between the decks and bulkheads.

Fred Vaughan and his brothers from Endle Street, Chapel, known as the street of tears because several of the crew who died lived there.

Southampton City Heritage Oral History

Rea's coalies at work on the Olympic, White Star Dock 1911.

Peter-Boyd Smith, Cobwebs

"My father was one who had a bath every day. But I do know…I do know for a fact that some of the chaps, some of the Coal Porters, used to come home and they'd have a type of a sleeping bag, as you'd call it today, with a draw-string at the neck and …coaling a boat would take about four days and during that four days they wouldn't bath. They couldn't bath for the simple reason there was no hot water laid on."
Frank Scammell (City Heritage Oral History)

"Always the men were out of work, especially in Chapel. My Dad was a Coal Porter, he used to coal the ships. There weren't many people had permanent jobs then — it was casual. You were picked up one day and dropped the next. There was no unemployment pay in those days. I don't know how we used to live, to tell you the truth."
Martha Gale (City Heritage Oral History)

After coaling, carpenters would seal up the coal ports with a buckram gasket, soaked in red lead. After coaling the ship had to be cleaned of the fine coat of dust inevitably accumulated in the open areas. As far as possible the interiors, public rooms and cabins had been sealed off, ventilators and air vent louvres covered or closed, but there was always plenty to do everywhere else.

Unless the coal from the laid up I.M.M. liners was already stockpiled elsewhere, it must have been an appalling job for Rea's men to bucket or bag up the coal that remained in their bunkers, and haul it all out, bit by bit, to gather enough for the *Titanic*. Luckily there was enough of it to top up the 1880 tons *Titanic* already carried after her trip from Belfast. During her week in Southampton she would use a further 415 tons of this for steam to power her cargo winches, her lights and her heating system. Coal left over from the *Olympic*'s last coaling was also added.

Other Southampton firms were involved in the supply, maintenance and provisioning of the *Titanic* and her crew. Messrs C.J. Smith were responsible for adjusting her compasses, which they did on her trials.

Oxford Street with the Docks Station in the background. The Grapes public house, still there today, where many of the crew had a drink on the morning of departure.

Southampton City Heritage Collections

Captain Smith; *Titanic* in drydock, Belfast.

Southampton City Heritage Collections

Miller's Naval Tailors of London, Tilbury and Southampton, with local premises in High Street and Canute Road, supplied uniforms to both the crew (and the officers) of the White Star Line and other companies.

"...oh yes, they would do private..but they had the contract for the shipping. Oh yes, they did private work and then they had a tailor's... I think the tailors used to do the private. Yes, it was quite nice there, but where I worked we had a man boss which was Mr Temple, and he died of cancer and Mr Saul took it on. And Mr Saul told us that they done all the uniforms for the Titanic, and he said they had to hurry to do it, and he said to one of the men 'I hope I shall never see this again'. Cos he thought they'd all bring it back, you know, and he said 'it was only a matter of speech because the work was so bad, where they had to do it so quickly.' And, he said 'little did I think that the Titanic was going down', and he didn't see it again."

Elsie Whitfield (City Heritage Oral History)

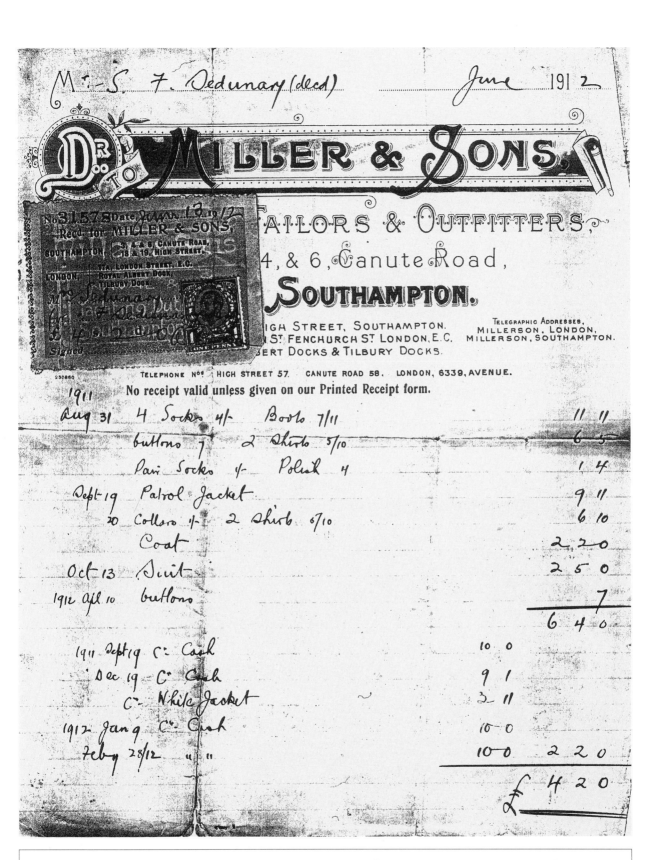

2nd Third Class Steward Sidney Sedunary's tailors bill.

Southampton City Heritage Collections

REGISTERED DESIGN
№ 375575

...congratulated on their new departure, which will doubtless be immensely appreciated by their patrons. The arrangements for the supply of the China have been made by Messrs. Stonier & Co., of 78 Lord Street, Liverpool, who have for many years supplied the whole of the Table Glass and China appointments of the magnificent White Star Fleet.

Advertisement brochure for Crown Derby china for first class passengers on *Olympic* and *Titanic*.

Southampton City Heritage Collections

White Star Line's china and glass supplier, J. Stonier and Co., although primarily a Liverpool firm, kept a store in Southampton Docks for replenishing the ships, particularly after stormy crossings when there were so many breakages. Most of the *Titanic*'s stock had been put on board the ship in Belfast, and had begun to be used by the White Star officials and guests, and Harland and Wolff staff, for the trials and crossing to Southampton. As well as manufacturing china, Stoniers were also agents, selecting and buying in designs from firms like Crown Derby for the china designs on the *Olympic* trio. The Stoniers mark would be added to that of Crown Derby on the base of each piece of china. Crown Derby took great pride in their service for the *Titanic*'s *à la carte* restaurant, issuing a special publicity leaflet advertising it. A sample plate of this china was given to the Chief Stewardess of the *Olympic* during her repairs at Belfast, alongside the *Titanic* in early 1912. After various adventures, this plate later passed to Southampton Maritime Museum, where it may be seen today.

Bottled beers for the *Titanic* were supplied by Charles George Hibbert & Co. of Southampton and London, export merchants, who held 'K' vault in the docks as stores for their beers. They appear to have been particularly proud of supplying the *Titanic*, for they made

A rare postcard showing part of the consignment of 15,000 bottles of beer about to be loaded on the *Titanic*.

Copyright S.B. Publications (*RMS* Titanic – *a Portrait in Old Picture Postcards*)

special bills or posters *'Bottled beer for the White Star liner Titanic, the largest vessel in the world'* and photographed the consignment, and three of their handlers, after it had been loaded in a goods train or carts and delivered to the new shed alongside White Star Dock. They were perhaps the only Southampton firm to have made anything of the *Titanic* connection in their advertising, this was also relatively rare among bigger firms like Crown Derby or Vinolia Otto soap. More publicity attached to shipbuilding, engineering, electrical fittings and ornamental metalwork for the ship.

It was the proud record of one Southampton firm supplying the White Star Line that *'we never advertised, we never needed to'*. This was the nursery and horticultural florist, F.G. Bealing and Son in Highfield, who supplied cut flowers, potted palms and other plants to decorate the liners. F.G. Bealing Snr., (died 1941) founded the nursery at Sholing in 1890. His grandson Raymond Bealing describes him as the firm's *'driving force, the towering genius, the backbone of the firm'*. He and his staff, which eventually numbered about twenty, were *'brave men (and later women) accepting the stress and pressure for very small returns'*. Their earliest main clients were the Union Line (after 1900 the Union Castle Line). In those early days first class male passengers might also find a Bealing *'buttonhole'* by their

place in the dining saloon. When the White Star Line arrived in Southampton in 1907, Bealings started to provide flowers for every White Star liner using the port. The contract came through Bealings' connection with Oakley & Watling, suppliers of fruit to the White Star Line. White Star became their most important client, and remained so until the Cunard White Star merger in 1934. They supplied Cunard liners from 1919, and finally the two *'Queens'* until the early 1960s. Because of the extra demand caused by White Star's arrival on the scene, F.G. Bealing moved his nursery from Sholing to a larger site at Burgess Road in Highfield, building his house *'Jesmondene'* alongside, where the Bealing family remained until the firm's closure in 1963. There were numerous glasshouses for different types of plants; thousands of plants were needed for the liners. Every time a White Star liner was in port, Mr Bealing, accompanied by his son Frank (Jnr) and his foreman Mr W.F. 'Bill' Geapin would load their mule drawn carts, usually in the evening, with flowers, palms and plants and drive them to the docks to the quay alongside each liner.

Frank Bealing Jnr. in the carnation beds at Burgess Road, c1914.

Southampton City Heritage Collections

The first class writing room of *Olympic* decorated with palms by Frank Bealing.

Southampton City Heritage Collections

Their loading system was somewhat haphazard in the early days, compared with their later practice on the *'Queens'*. Plants were normally just set down on a tarpaulin in one of the main foyers before the Bealings and Mr Geapin distributed them around the ship in their prearranged positions, partly dictated by the designers, partly by White Star staff, and partly by the Bealings themselves, in the public rooms, or in the case of cut flowers, in cool rooms for use the next day or later on the crossing.

"If the plant locations were similar to those on her sister ship the SS Olympic, then perhaps some 300 to 400 plants in 5 inch pots would have been required... I think that in those days small table plants were used as decoration on the restaurant tables."

Raymond Bealing (City Heritage Oral History)

The *Titanic* was no exception – her layout was familiar from the *Olympic*. Bealing palms were most in evidence above torchères in the First Class Writing Room, in fretwork containers in the Reception Room outside the First Class Dining Saloon, in pots in the *à la carte* restaurant, in the Verandah Café and the Palm Court. Smaller plants might stand in vases or pots on tables in some of the lounges. Bealing's may also have supplied the ivy climbing the trellised walls of the Café

Parisien, Palm Court and Verandah Café, although as some of this was photographed by Harland and Wolff's own photographer it is not clear if this work was already done in Belfast, or the photographer came to Southampton on the crossing from Belfast. Both Frank Bealing Jnr (died 1981 aged 91) and Bill Geapin in old age would often speak of having personally loaded the *Titanic* with old Mr Bealing (Snr) the evening before sailing day.

First class passengers on *Titanic*, Mrs Walter Douglas and Mrs Jacques Futrelle, recalled roses on the tables of the restaurant, but the best unconscious tribute to the Bealings comes from Lady Duff-Gordon in her memoirs **'Discretions and Indiscretions'**:

'I remember that last meal on the Titanic very well. We had a big vase of beautiful daffodils on the table, which were as fresh as if they had just been picked.'

Another of *Titanic*'s passengers, eleven year old Eileen Lenox Conyingham, (later Mrs Schefer) who crossed to Cherbourg, remembered *Titanic* as *'a ship full of flowers'*.

On *Titanic*'s sailing day from Southampton, Bealing *'buttonholes'* are thought to have been given to passengers. Some flowers were thrown down to the water as the ship pulled out.

Roland Southwell was taken to see the *Titanic* sail when he was 9 years old.

"All the people on deck were waving and throwing flowers down, they were all going into the sea."
Roland Southwell (City Heritage Oral History)

The *Titanic*'s sister ship *Olympic* remained a particular favourite of the Bealings until the end of her career in 1935. Grandson Raymond and his wife remember working on her. Raymond still remembers hearing of the fuss made by one of Harland and Wolff/Heaton's designers for *Olympic* and *Titanic*,

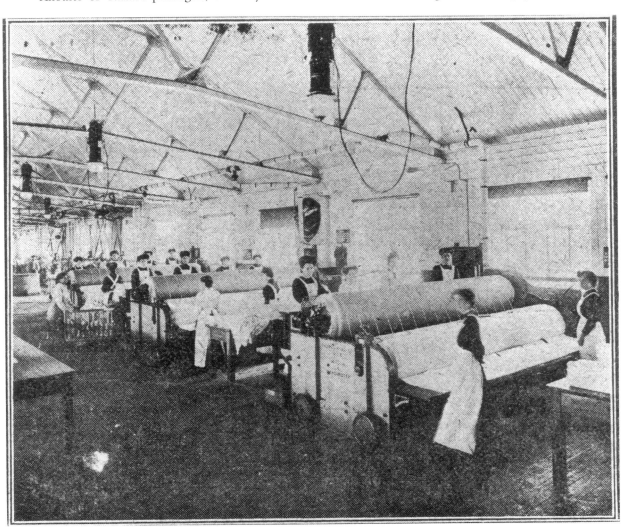

White Star laundry above Harland and Wolff works, Southampton docks.

Southampton Pictorial

White Star laundry.

Southampton Pictorial

possibly Edward Croft-Smith, when White Star decided to paint the waxed oak panelling and Honour and Glory Crowning Time of the first class staircase in the early 1930s.

"I think it was to give a more modern appearance but the designer was so appalled he said he would never design another companionway again."

J.C. Smith, the manager of W.H. Smith's newsagents in the docks would have supplied papers and sundries to White Star and *Titanic* crew and workers in the docks, as well as perhaps organising deliveries to the ship itself, as she lay in the port.

Perhaps some of *Titanic*'s crew were partial to 'John's Cough Lozenges' advertised for sale in Below Bar and Upper Prospect Place.

Cox and Sons in Bernard Street made razors and penknives, some engraved 'Southampton', as souvenirs perhaps. Steward F. Dent Ray possessed one on board

Titanic and preserved it as he left the sinking ship.

Edwin Jones' store (now Debenhams) is believed to have supplied some of the tablecloths used on board.

The laundering of the *Olympic* and *Titanic*'s linen was a massive challenge.

(But) 'above the noisy boilershop of Harland and Wolff is the extensive laundry of White Star and American Line'. **(Soton Pictorial 29.5.1913).**

Fifty laundry *'hands'* worked in the great corrugated iron buildings; servicing the *Olympic* once every three weeks was a useful preparation for repeating the operation the second week for the sister ship *Titanic*, and in time, the third of the trio. *Olympic*'s record landing of dirty 'linen, serviettes, sheets, bedspreads, towels and the like' **(Soton Pictorial 29.5.1913)** for a simple week was 75,000 items. An American Line steamer arriving the same week might land 23,000 pieces. Fresh quantities of clean linen had to be ready to replace it for the return trip, the dirty linen was laundered ready for the liner's next return. The laundry was fitted with the most modern electric equipment available in elevators, hydros, ironing machines, blanket drying

Southampton High Street. Oakley and Watling on the right.

Southern Daily Echo

horses, hand irons; it had its own water softening plant (vital with Southampton's hard water); a carpet cleaning machine was also available, as was a disinfecting machine – essential after stormy crossings! From the windows of the laundry rooms and boiler house the laundry hands could enjoy views of the ships in the docks (when they had a rare spare moment in the general bustle of a heavy inrush of linen). But the work was certainly different from the rest of the Harland and Wolff works. *'Docklands is full of contrasts'* as the Southampton Pictorial remarked of the White Star American laundry.

Some of the food supplies in a highly competitive market, would have been supplied by local firms such as Oakley and Watling, fruit importers, and Grey's (Grey and Co, store merchants) a small family firm founded in Liverpool in the 1880's, but recently with a local branch.

Advert for Oakley and Watling who supplied fruit and vegetables for the *Titanic*.

Southampton City Heritage Oral History

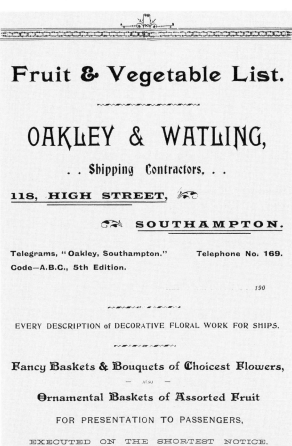

Fruit & Vegetable List.

OAKLEY & WATLING,

. . Shipping Contractors, . .

118, HIGH STREET,

SOUTHAMPTON.

Telegrams, "Oakley, Southampton."   Telephone No. 169.
Code—A.B.C., 5th Edition.

190

EVERY DESCRIPTION of DECORATIVE FLORAL WORK FOR SHIPS.

Fancy Baskets & Bouquets of Choicest Flowers,

— ALSO —

Ornamental Baskets of Assorted Fruit

FOR PRESENTATION TO PASSENGERS,

EXECUTED ON THE SHORTEST NOTICE.

'We did food, meat, poultry, tin foods for all the large ships. My father, Eric Grey, moved down to Southampton in 1911. We were in Queen's Terrace, later in Oxford Street. My father, who died in 1956, put food on the Titanic and he saw the ship off on her maiden voyage.'
Aubrey Grey

Some supplies were perhaps imported from the Channel Islands, and brought into the Inner Dock by steamers of the LSWR, before being taken by trains and trucks round to the sheds in the White Star Dock. 1,196 bags of potatoes were loaded on the *Titanic* by dockworkers and cargo loaders or crane operators. The *Titanic*'s own foremost derrick may have been used to hoist aboard a more spectacular item, a Renault motor car belonging to first class passenger W.E. Carter, which was then lowered into the hold, having first been carefully secured by men on the quayside.

The *Titanic*'s manifest lists *'everything under the sun'* in the way of items – anything from medical instruments, straw hats, linoleum, refrigerating machinery, delicatessen foods, hairnets, laces, velvets, periodicals, silver from Uppark House and a rare jewelled copy of the Rubaiyàt of Omar Khayyam. Perhaps 3,000-4,000 cases, bales and bundles were loaded on *Titanic* by the dockworkers, cargo loaders, porters and stevedores of Southampton Docks, under the watchful eyes of *Titanic*'s supervising crew and officers. Passengers' trunks, sent on ahead, would also be waiting to go on board.

A few Southampton postcard producers like Gertrude Pratt in Oxford Street may have managed to sell a few postcards of *Olympic* and a hastily photographed *Titanic*, but the bulk of postcards sold on board the *Titanic* in the barbers shop, were official *'company'* cards, from designs by artists such as Charles Dixon and Montague Black. Southampton's postcard producers had already made numerous cards of the *Olympic*, a popular subject in and outside the town, but their cards of *Titanic*, some obviously dubbed views of *Olympic*, would sell well immediately after sailing day, and then in mass numbers as *'memorial souvenirs'* after the sinking.

PROVISIONS

Southampton traders did well out of *Titanic*, although they would not have supplied all of what was needed to stock the ship:

Fresh meat	75,000lbs
Fresh fish	11,000lbs
Salt and dried fish	4,000lbs
Bacon and ham	7,5000lbs
Poultry and game	25,000lbs
Fresh eggs	40,000
Sausages	2,500lbs
Potatoes	40 tons
Onions	3,500lbs
Tomatoes	3,500lbs
Fresh asparagus	800 bundles
Fresh green peas	2,500lbs
Lettuce	7,000 heads
Sweetbreads	1,000
Ice cream	1,750qts
Coffee	2,200lbs
Tea	800lbs
Rice, dried beans, etc	10,000lbs
Sugar	10,000lbs
Flour	250 barrels
Cereals	10,000lbs
Apples	36,000
Oranges	36,000
Lemons	16,000
Grapes	1,000lbs
Grapefruit	13,000
Jams and marmalade	1,120lbs
Fresh milk	1,500gals
Fresh cream	1,200qts
Condensed milk	600gals
Fresh butter	6,000lbs
Ales and stout	15,000 bottles
Wines	1,000 bottles
Spirits	850 bottles
Minerals	1,200 bottles
Cigars	8,000

Once on board, the provisions had to be sorted, checked and stored. For the passengers to eat the food with, there were 57,600 items of crockery, 29,000 pieces of glassware and 44,000 pieces of cutlery.

In addition, there were 196,100 items of linen to be loaded, counted, listed in the inventory and stored.

★ SIGNING ON

"A job on the big 'un"

With the *Titanic* in Southampton at last, preparations could now be made to sign on her crew. Although the Captain and officers were already salaried, the rest of the crew were not – in fact there was no such thing as a real permanent crew on the liners in 1912 – they were paid for the voyage only, and had to re-offer their services each time, 'signing-on' before each voyage, and could not automatically depend on a job the next time.

"All the people around Chapel, it was a rough fighting area because they used to come home from their voyages, which were 'killer ships'; they all came home like walking skeletons, the stokers, and they had one glorious booze-up, which led to fighting and then off they went again."

"When a ship docked in those days the men...the crew were paid off. Well if that ship was in for 2 or 3 weeks they were put ashore and there was no unemployment benefit...so they couldn't afford to stay, they usually jumped in some other ship."
Alfred Fanstone (City Heritage Oral History)

Curiously, one officer, David Blair, who expected to automatically continue on the *Titanic* after the trip from Belfast, found he would not be going after all.

'The White Star Line thought it would be a good plan to send the Chief Officer of the Olympic, just for one voyage as Chief Officer of the Titanic, to help with his experience of her sister ship. This doubtful policy threw both Murdoch and me out of our stride, and apart from the disappointment of having to step back in our rank, caused quite a little confusion. Murdoch took over my duties as First, I stepped back on Blair's toes as Second, and picked up the many threads of his job, whilst he, luckily for him as it turned out, was left behind.'
Officer Charles Lightoller

David Blair wrote to his sister-in-law:

'This is a marvellous ship and I feel very disappointed I am not to make the first voyage.'

Belvedere Arms public house, Northam 1900's.

Southampton City Heritage Oral History

The new Liberal Club, Northam.

Southampton City Heritage Oral History

Titanic tied up at her berth. April 10th. Note the floating scaffolding at her bow.

Peter Boyd-Smith, Cobwebs

Joe Chapman as a boy outside his home in Portland Street, Southampton. Later was Boots on *Titanic*.

Southampton City Heritage Collections

His daughter Miss E. Blair later recorded:

'My father had to step out, much to his disappointment. In the rush to get his gear packed and taken off the ship he came away with the key of the crow's nest telephone in his pocket.'
(M.S. of Miss E. Blair, printed in 'Chart and Compass'. The key was left by her to the British Sailors Society)

At the same time the crow's nest binoculars, normally in the First Officer's care, and used on the trip down from Belfast, disappeared, apparently locked away by Blair in the rush. Perhaps he forgot to tell Lightoller where he had put them. The lookouts were indignant to find them missing.

'We asked for them in Southampton and they said there was none for us.'
Q. *'Whom did you ask?'*
A. *'They said there was none intended for us.'*
Q. *'Whom did you ask?'*
A. *'We asked Mr Lightoller, the Second Officer.'*
Fred Fleet (U.S. Enquiry)

(We) *'looked in the box on the crow's nest, but the glasses were missing.'*
Archie Jewell (British Investigation)

'I asked for the glasses and I did not see why I should not have them. I had them from Belfast to Southampton, but from Southampton to where the accident occurred we never had them ... I asked for the glasses several times.' **G. Hogg**

'They have glasses in all the other ships.' **G. Symons**

Each time the crew handed in their own discharge certificate book, which would be returned, normally stamped *'very good'* after each voyage, unless something had gone wrong. The situation was extremely insecure where short Atlantic voyages were concerned.

'Our contract lasted for that time we belonged to the ship'. **Joseph Scarrott (British Enquiry)**

Technically there was no such thing as a permanent crew. These seafarers could, as opportunity permitted, move from one ship to another, or to another shipping company, or to a privately owned vessel like a yacht. If they 'fitted in' on a particular ship or line, were keen to return, the company required them, and the signing-on officer knew and approved of them, they would return again and again, and occasionally even remain with one ship for many years. On 6th April 1912, the 'Southampton Times' approvingly quoted a recent comment in the 'Shipping Gazette' *'that the conditions of service on liners sailing from the Hampshire port are quite satisfactory from the sailors' point of view is frequently evidenced at the signing-on of crews. Only four days ago when the crew of the RMSP Co's Oruba were signing-on, there were practically no changes. The men who had made the previous voyage were re-employed for another trip!'* But it was more usual for them to serve on various ships and with different lines. This was true of several of the *Titanic*'s crew living in Southampton.

'I ran out of London on the P&O Line to Australia some years ago.' Steward **George Crowe**, (previously with the American Line) **(US Enq)**

'I do not generally come this way in winter time. I go on the Bombay route'. (i.e. with P&O) Able Seaman **George Moore (US Enq)**

First Class Steward **Edward Wheelton** said the crew were *'not only the White Star, but other ships.'* **(US Enq)**

Able Seaman **Frank Evans** was previously *'In the Tintagel Castle (Union Castle Line), in the Ferney an Admiralty Collier, and the Olympic.'* **(US Enq)**

Able Seaman **Frederick Clench**, at sea *'nineteen years now ... I have all the time been on steam boats. Different lines, you know ... well I done six voyages on the Olympic.'* **(US Enq)**

Quartermaster **Hichens**, had served on ships *'up about Norway and Sweden and Petersburg, and up the Danube.'* **(US Enq)**

'I had never crossed the Atlantic before – I was a stranger to everyone on board.' **Harold Lowe**, 5th officer **(US Enq)**

Interior of the Belvedere Arms. Many crew members were recruited through word of mouth in pubs.

Southampton City Heritage Oral History

Catering crew in the kitchen on board the *Titanic.*

Daily Graphic

Those crew who preferred to remain with one line on a more or less regular basis gave a continuity and appearance of permanence. Some waiters and stewards often became particular favourites of passengers who would alter their bookings to be looked after by them. These regulars also helped the ship to run more efficiently. Contemporary White Star Line publicity could in some truth point to

'the careful attention paid to all passengers by its well trained corps of servants, a large percentage of whom have been in its service for many years.'

This is borne out by the evidence of some of the surviving crew of the *Titanic*.

Samuel Hemming was at sea *'since I was fifteen years old, with the White Star Line for five years, Teutonic, Adriatic, Olympic.'* **(US Enq)**

'I had been with the White Star Line just four years.' Steward **C.E. Andrews (US Enq)**

'With White Star since the Navy – the Oceanic was the only other one (White Star liner) beside this one.' Seaman **Frank Osman (US Enq)**

'Fourteen years at sea. In the White Star Line service for twelve years past ... for the last seven years I have been Chief Steward, Second Class.' Chief Steward **John Hardy, (US Enq)**

'I have been with the White Star six years as First Class Steward ... I had sailed with quite a number of the men myself before that.' First Class Steward **Edward Wheelton (US Enq)**

'I was four years on the Oceanic, on the lookout ... I fetched Titanic around from Belfast on the lookout.' Lookout **Fred Fleet (US Enq)**

'I have been on the White Star Line six years ... on the Adriatic, Olympic and Titanic.' Steward **Alfred Crawford** – at sea since 1881 **(US Enq)**

'With the White Star Line five years this month.' Able Seaman **Ernest Archer (US Enq)**

Steward **Samuel Rule** had served on White Star liners under Captain Smith for the last thirty five years. **Joseph Chapman** served on the IMM/American Line *St Paul* in 1911.

'Seven to eight years previously only on Oceanic, otherwise only on sailing ships.' Lookout **Archie Jewell (British Investigation)**

Some of the *Titanic's* crew had begun their seagoing career with the Royal Navy, rather than the Merchant.

'This was my first trip, sir. I was just in the merchant service. I had just left the Navy' (after thirteen years). He purchased his naval discharge in favour of the more profitable Merchant Navy *'in order to better help his mother.'* Able Seaman **Edward Buley (US Enq)**

'I was in the Navy first, and then I came in to the Merchant Marine afterwards.' Quarter Master **Alfred Oliver (US Enq)**

'In the merchant service two years; previous to that fourteen years in the navy.' Quarter Master **George Rowe (US Enq)**

Titanic in Southampton, Good Friday April 5th 1912.

Southampton City Heritage Collections

SEAMEN ! JOIN THE BRITISH SEAFARERS' UNION !

The B.S.U. is out to secure HIGHER WAGES, SHORTER HOURS, BETTER FOOD, and DECENT SLEEPING and GENERAL ACCOMMODATION FOR SEAFARERS.

B.S.U. BENEFIT LIST.

Membership.

SHIPWRECK BENEFIT—6 months		-	-	£1	10 0
"	"	2 years	-	-	£2 0 0
"	"	3 "	-	-	£2 10 0
"	"	4 "	-	-	£3 0 0
DEATH BENEFIT (after 6 months' membership)			-	£5	0 0
ACCIDENT BENEFIT		-	-	8/- per week for 8 weeks	

DISPUTE PAY or STRIKE PAY.

LEGAL AID BENEFIT.—Members are entitled to legal assistance in all matters arising out of their employment.

Full information can be obtained at the following Offices:—

8, TERMINUS TERRACE, SOUTHAMPTON - - - - - -.	ARTHUR CANNON
GLASGOW BRANCH: 212, BROOMIELAW & 122, OLD GOVAN ROAD - - -	E. SHINWELL
ARDROSSAN BRANCH: 5, PRINCES STREET - - - - - - -	J. McHENRY
LIVERPOOL BRANCH: 59, SOUTH JOHN STREET - - - - -	GRIFF JONES

Advert from The British Seafarer Union magazine

University of Warwick Photographic Services. Courtesy R.M.T.

'Previously in Royal Navy for nine years then in the Merchant Navy.' Able Seaman **Frank Evans (US Enq)**

Not all the stewards, despite working on liners, had experience of navigation or basic practical seamanship. Mrs J. Stewart White recalled stewards Crawford and Hart and a cook in lifeboat number eight, asking her how to row, two saying *'I never had an oar in my hand before'*; the other gamely adding *'I think I can row.'* **(US Enq)**

There was particular demand for a job on the *Titanic* because of the recent coal strike laying up so many ships, with crews laid off. Also Southampton's general unemployment scene had another year to go before work could be described as plentiful.

One new development was working in the favour of Southampton's seafarers. By the end of the Edwardian era many unions had been formed and were campaigning for better conditions. Labour disputes became frequent as economic prosperity revived between 1910 and 1913. In August 1910 the Southampton branch of the Seamen's and Firemen's Union, discontented for some time, struck for an increase of 10 shillings a week, although their strike was not recognised by the union's central headquarters. White Star Line's *Adriatic* sailed late, relying on its engineers and the rest of the crew to stoke the boilers until she could pick up a 'scratch' crew of temporary firemen, hurriedly gathered from Leeds, Bradford and elsewhere. Eighty-nine of them had never been to sea before. The strike was soon settled.

In spring 1911, following a builders unions' strike, Southampton's shipwrights, coal porters, seamen, firemen, dockers, stevedores, bakers, plumbers and general labourers struck in turn. The coal porters had been ordered to coal the new *Olympic* at 6am, but had to wait until 11am before beginning. They were refused 'standing-by' money. The dispute spread, led by Councillor *'Tommy'* Lewis, and Harry Orbell of the Dockers Union. Nearly all the porters in the docks came out. *Olympic*'s seamen and firemen struck for extra wages citing 'the special difficulties' of working such an enormous vessel. The strike spread instantly to all the seamen and firemen of the port. Stewards made common cause with them. Shipping in the port was at a standstill for several days. All the strikes were orderly, the police were tactful, and Southampton Corporation arranged a conciliation committee and a swift settlement from the companies.

'A special meeting of members was held at the Southern District Schools on Tuesday April 2. The chair was taken at 8pm by the President who called upon the assistant

Southampton British Seafarers' Union Group.

University of Warwick Photographic Services. Courtesy R.M.T.

secretary.....the minutes of the last meeting which were passed as read.

The financial statement for the preceding week was also passed.

The President gave a report upon the Olympic test case after a lengthy discussion it was proposed by J Fanstone seconded by G Guard that the question be deferred and that the president and secretary be empowered to take legal advice upon the matter. Carried unanimously.

The subject of the arrest of Mr Tom Mann and others was next raised and the following resolution was proposed by the president and seconded.

That this meeting of members of the British Seafarers Union strongly protests against the action taken against Mr Tom Mann and others and demand their immediate release. It was also decided to forward a copy to the Prime Minister and Mr Tom Mann...

... Bro J Lock raised the question of members of the White Star Line who had applied for work upon vessels of other companies and who had been refused upon the grounds of having White Star discharges and after discussion it was decided that the matter be left in the hands of the officials to see to.

There being no further business the meeting closed.'

(British Seafarers' Union Records, April 1912. University of Warwick)

Shipping lines like White Star had not originally been keen to recognise unions or make concessions. But strike pressure was also on in Liverpool as well as Southampton, causing an extra dilemma. White Star found itself squirming uneasily between the two. By 21st June 1911 the Head Office in Liverpool was cabling J. Bruce Ismay, on the maiden voyage of the *Olympic*,

'The labour position Southampton very unsatisfactory, stevedores, coalies, crews all stopped work. Crews unwilling to accept Liverpool basis settlement. We think it is not desirable to

make any further concessions Southampton, as will inevitably result upsetting Liverpool settlement ... Informing Southampton (office) unless we get crew for Adriatic on Liverpool basis settlement, will blank round voyage. Think firm attitude necessary in order to clear position Southampton before Olympic returns. Do you agree?'

Ismay replied,

'Entirely share your views that Southampton steamers should not be given greater proportionate advance than crews Liverpool Steamers.'

But before long the Liverpool office was advising Ismay,

'Hopeful Southampton crews' wages difficulty may be settled satisfactorily, but demand is being made for full recognition of union here and Southampton, by allowing (union) officials on steamers. Believe Cunard Line and others have conceded, therefore our position greatly weakened.'

Accepting the inevitable, Ismay and the IMM Co, as well as various other shipping lines using British ports, decided to recognise the unions.

Millbank Street and Clarence Street, Northam 1912, during the annual flooding.

Southampton City Heritage Oral History

Although deck officers were likely to be members of the Imperial Merchant Service Guild and the engineer officers represented by the Marine Engineers Association, there were three main unions supplying the engine room, deck and victualling departments workforce. There was the National Sailors' and Firemens' Union of Great Britain and Ireland (with 5,000 members after the 1911 strikes, and shipping line recognition).

The Cooks were members of the National Union of Ships' Stewards, Cooks, Butchers and Bakers who opened their Southampton branch in 1909.

There was the Dock Wharf and Riverside Workers Union. *'A large number of the deck hands were members of the Dockers Union'* pointed out *Titanic* lookout R.R. Lee at the British Investigation into her sinking.

Then there was The National Union of Stewards, as well as *'slate'* clubs for stewards – one Southampton *'slate'* club had forty-seven members, of whom all but one would perish in the *Titanic* disaster. Arthur Paintin, personal steward to Captain Smith on the *Olympic* and *Titanic*, mentions in his last letter home to his parents *'I have been in a stewards' club since last August, and the benefits start after twelve months.'* **(Private Collection).**

But a new extra union had been set up in October 1911, called the British Seafarers' Union. Its secretary was 'Tommy' Lewis who described it at the British Investigation into the loss of *Titanic*.

Tommy Lewis. Secretary British Seafarers' Union.

University of Warwick Photographic Services.
Courtesy R.M.T.

'It is all Southampton men, my lord. It is at present a Southampton Union. It is called the British Seafarers' Union, but its headquarters are at Southampton and it has a membership of four thousand. Practically the whole of the seafarers' of the Titanic are members of our union.'

This *'Southampton Union'* was invited by the White Star Line's Southampton office to select and supply seamen and stokers, trimmers and greasers for the maiden voyage of the *Titanic*.

Whereas deck and engineer officers had joined their particular White Star liner by direct agreement with the line and the heads of their department, the rest of the crew were recruited by their unions in their halls and the White Star Line's own hiring hall. Recruitment began on Saturday 6th April, and the halls were soon jammed with applicants. 228 men signed on with the British Seafarers' Union, 100 with the National Sailors and Firemens' Union. More followed later. *'The pick of Southampton'* said fireman **George Kemish** of the *Titanic*'s crew.

Able Seaman **Ernest Archer**, *'signed on Monday, two days before she sailed.'*

Able Seaman **W. Brice**, *'I signed on Monday, two days before she sailed.'*

Steward **Frederick Clench**, *'I signed on Monday, sir.'* **(All at US Enq)**

After the jobless misery of the coal strike, most of the applicants, particularly those with families, were eager to join. Joseph Scarrott was an exception:

'I signed the "articles" as 'A.B.' on Monday 8th April, 1912 (note the total of numbers in the year). The signing on seemed like a dream to me, and I could not believe I had done so, but the absence of my Discharge Book from my pocket convinced me. When I went to the docks that morning I had as much intention of applying for a job on the Big 'Un as we called her, as I had of going for a trip to the moon. I was already assured of a job as a Q.M. on a Union Castle liner, also I was not in low water for "Bees and Honey". When I went home (36 Albert Road) and told my sister what I had done she called me a ......fool. Now this was the first and only time that she had shown disapproval of any ship I was going on. In fact she would not believe me until she found I was minus my Discharge Book.'
Able Seaman Joseph Scarrott (From Southend 'Pier Review' Number 8, 1932.)

Another doubter at this point was Harry Burrows, whose mother later told the Southampton Times' reporter

'My son Harry goes to sea, and he had stayed home for a month in the expectation of getting engaged on the Titanic. He went down to the docks to sign on, but at the last moment changed his mind and came away, for which we are very thankful. I can't explain why he changed his mind; some sort of

feeling came over him, he told me.'

Many of the *Titanic* crew were relative newcomers to Southampton. After the sinking, the Southampton Pictorial blithely reported what they called *'a touching little sketch'* by one Henry L. Marshall, of the Californian newspaper 'Corvina Argus'. Mr Marshall asked

'Who will write the epic of the Southampton man?' adding *'He was a Southampton man, and the crew of 800 men had been hand picked, everyone from the English town of seafarers, through many generations.'*

This romantic view is not entirely borne out by the crew's signing-on lists, which also record their birthplace. They show that perhaps 40% of the crew was even Hampshire born, the rest coming from all over Britain and Ireland. Inevitably many were Lancashire stock, following the White Star Line from Liverpool to Southampton in 1907, and the American Line in 1893. Two of the most famous crew participants in the drama, Frederick Fleet and Charles Lightoller were in this category. Lightoller was able to take on a large house at Netley. Captain Smith came originally from Staffordshire before moving to Liverpool to join the White Star Line. In 1907 he moved to Southampton, buying a large house in Winn Road, Southampton. Many of these newcomers settled in Southampton as it became the most important source of employment on the liners. A new *Titanic* steward, George Beedem from Harlesdon, spent his spare time going all over the place house hunting. He wrote to his wife to ask if it were possible to go right in for their own house, to think it over and see if anything could be

The cooling room in the Turkish bath, *Titanic*.

Daily Mirror

done. He said *'I shall be glad when we are all down in Southampton.'* Marriage often strengthened the bond with Southampton. As G.A. Hogg from Hull said,

'All my people are there, but my wife (and two children) is in Southampton. I make Southampton my home now. I married a Hampshire woman.' **(US Enq)**

First class second steward George Dodd had formerly served as J. Bruce Ismay's butler in Liverpool, but always hankered to go to sea. Ismay did not stand in his way, but arranged it, and Dodd moved to Southampton, living at 57 Morris Road. According to the Ismay family tradition, George Dodd was a great success on the liners,

'Everyone in the catering department relied on him. Whenever a problem arose it was always "ask Dodd, he knows".'

Left: Arthur Paintin (on right) in Oxford. Steward to Captain Smith of the *Titanic*.

Below: Titanic's surviving officers. Charles Lightoller lived at Netley, near Southampton.

Both Southampton City Heritage Collections

This would be borne out when he roused the crew of the sinking *Titanic*, although he did not himself survive.

By 1934 the White Star House Magazine could record the death in Southampton of 84 year old James Taylor, who had spent 58 years with the White Star Line service, their longest serving member who had originally been apprenticed in the Liverpool office of the Inman Line, going on to serve with various other lines before settling for his long run with White Star.

Able Seaman Joseph Scarrott originally came from Plymouth, where many liners tendered, including the White Star liners after 1907.

In signing-on for the *Titanic*, 699 out of the 898

Right: Fireman William Major (standing) with two friends. Studio portrait taken in Bernard Street, Southampton, before the disaster.

Private Collection

Below: First class stateroom, *Titanic.*

Harland and Wolff

Mrs McClaren nee Allsop, stewardess.

Peter Boyd-Smith, Cobwebs

crew gave Southampton as their current address, although some of these were citing their lodgings, as for instance in the case of Cornishman Archie Jewell, whose landlady was able to tell his father in Cornwall he had survived. A few were living in Southampton hotels and taverns like Marconi operator Harold Bride in Bannister's Hotel, or greasers W. Lake and J. McGinty in the Florence Hotel and Platform Tavern for instance.

Captain Smith's *'tiger'* Arthur Paintin's family came from Oxford. A journey home to see them was not always practical *'for we have now commenced the quick voyages all summer',* and speaking of a friend he wrote his parents

'You had better bring her down to Southampton for a day or two while we are there, for I don't see any chance of getting away.'
(Private Collection)

One part of the crew was ignored altogether in Mr Marshall's male oriented epic – the *Titanic's* 23 *female* crew, including the stewardesses. Nine of the women lived in Southampton. There were eighteen stewardesses, one third class matron, a masseuse, one attendant who worked in the Turkish baths and two women cashiers who were employed by the Ritz Restaurant. Of the crew members who lost their lives, there were three of the women crew, two of them from Southampton.

Mrs. M. Bennett, who survived the disaster, was a

Lucy Violet Snape from Shirley, Southampton. 22 year old second class stewardess on her first voyage at sea.

Daily Mirror

Kate Gold, stewardess, aged 42 from Bassett, Southampton.

Daily Mirror

30 year old stewardess who lived in Cranbury Avenue, Southampton, like many of *Titanic*'s crew she was transferred from the *Olympic*.

Mrs. Kate Gold, who survived the disaster, lived in Bassett, Southampton. She was born in London and had also lived in Staffordshire.

St. Annes on the Sea,
Express Newspaper article
19th April 1912.

'A Southport lady, who was on board the ill-fated *Titanic*, Mrs. K. Gold, stewardess, has been in three accidents. She was on board the *Suevic* when that vessel was wrecked returning from Australia, some two to three years ago. Her second experience was on the *Olympic* two or three months ago, when that vessel was in collision with HMS *Hawke* and now she has been rescued from the most appalling wreck in the history of mercantile marine. In spite of this experience, it is not expected Mrs. Gold will give up the life which she always declares she loves. She is a strongly nerved woman, and the two previous accidents did not deter her in the past from continuing in the service.'

Another stewardess, Violet Jessop, was also on the *Olympic* when it collided with HMS *Hawke*. Miss S. Stap, a native of Birkenhead, could even declare her birthplace 'at sea'. First class passenger Lady Duff Gordon later recalled her *'merry Irish stewardess with her soft Irish brogue and tales of timid ladies she had attended during hundreds of Atlantic crossings.'* But one stewardess Mrs Snape, who was lost in the disaster, had apparently secured her job on the *Titanic* through the intercession of her MP, Mr J. King, as she had a baby daughter to provide for. Another stewardess, Mrs McClaren, was the sister of *Titanic* saloon steward Frank Allsop, of Obelisk Road, Woolston. He was lost, but she was saved.

The liner's two masseuses, an innovation on a liner, Miss Caton and Mrs Maude Slocombe, were Londoners, and not perhaps typical of the bulk of the crew, nor were the cashiers in the *à la carte* restaurant. First Class Steward F. Dent Ray remembered there were *'Lady clerks for the Café.'* Stewardess Annie Robinson was from Belfast, and knew Thomas Andrews well. Pressed by J. Bruce Ismay to enter a lifeboat she said *'I am only a stewardess'*. He retorted, *'Never mind, you are a woman, take your place.'* She lived in Shirley Road, Southampton. She was called as a witness at the British Enquiry into the disaster. Twenty-seven year old stewardess Evelyn Marsden lived in West Marlands Terrace, Southampton. The Derbyshire Times of Saturday 20th April 1912 recorded:

Violet Jessop, *Titanic* stewardess, pictured while a nurse on *Britannic*.

The Only Way to Cross, John Maxtone-Graham

'Miss Marsden, the neice of Mr. George Robinson of Chesterfield, is among the rescued. Mr. Robinson had a telegram yesterday (Friday morning) announcing this fact.'

Miss T.E. Smith, aged 42, was another survivor. She lived in Cobbett Road, Bitterne Park, Southampton. She had also been transferred from the *Olympic*. Third class assistant matron Mrs. Catherine Jane Wallis of St. Mary's Street, Southampton, did not survive. Although born in Ireland, stewardess Miss Katherine Walsh had been residing in Church Road, Woolston, Southampton before, at 32 years of age, she became a victim of the disaster.

Scattered as they were around the vast liner, the eighteen stewardesses were still a relative minority on liners in 1912. First class steward Edward Wheelton was vague when asked about them at the US Enquiry, *'I could not tell you. There were stewardesses and Turkish bath attendants.'* Pressed to say if they even numbered 50, he admitted, *'I do not suppose they would.'* By the 1950s, at the apogee of Atlantic sea travel, one of Cunard's *Queens* would each carry about 100 stewardesses and female crew. Southampton's most famous stewardess was Mary Rogers, who perished in the LSWR's *Stella*, wrecked on The Casquet rocks in Guernsey in 1899. She gave up her lifebelt to another, saying *'Goodbye, goodbye'*. A photograph of her memorial, which stands under the

First class stateroom, *Titanic*.

Harland and Wolff

Town Walls, appeared, by a strange coincidence, under a photograph of the funnel of the *Titanic*, in the Southampton Pictorial on Good Friday 1912.

As we have already seen, many of the *Titanic* crew were 'old hands'. Chief baker **Charles Joughin** declared, *'It was practically a crew from the Olympic.'*

Able 'seaman **Thomas Jones**, a Liverpudlian, remarked, *'I know I had been shipmate with a few of these before … we had a good crew … I know a lot of the firemen.'*

Arthur Paintin, Captain Smith's 'tiger', had previously been 'in service' to Mr Justice North in Oxford, before joining White Star Line about 1907.

Others were described by **Steward Mackay** as *'strangers to the ship. They never came from the Olympic to the Titanic with us.'* **(US Enq)**

In fact some had transferred from the laid-up *Oceanic*, *New York* and other IMM steamers.

Chief Steward **John Hardy** said, *'I had great respect and regret for Officer Murdoch'* adding that he had confided *'I believe she is gone, Hardy,'* as *Titanic* sank lower in the sea.

Stewardess **Mary Sloane** spoke fondly of *'The dear old doctor (O'Loughlin).'*

One steward said of Captain Smith, *'This crew knew him to be a good, kind hearted man, and we looked upon him as a sort of father.'*

Charles Lightoller said *'He was a great favourite and a man any officer would give his ears to sail under. My first thought was I'll bet he's got a voice like a foghorn. As a matter of fact he had a pleasant quiet voice and invariable smile. A voice he rarely raised above a conversational tone; not to say he couldn't. In fact I have often heard him bark an order that made a man come to himself with a bump.'*
('Titanic and Other Ships', 1935)

Crew fellowship was useful in disaster as **Charles Joughin** found when swimming to an upturned collapsible lifeboat. He *'tried to get in, was pushed off, but I hung around. I got to the opposite side and cook Maynard recognised me and helped me and held onto me.'*

Many of the crew knew each other by their nicknames – 'Scooch' (George) Kemish, fireman, 'Gus Whiteman' (Augustus Weikmann), barber, 'Big Neck' (Nichols), bosun, 'Wally' (William) Major, fireman, or plain 'Jack' Hurst, fireman.

This was also true of the officers – 'Lights'

Three-poster bed in £870 apartment on the *Titanic*.

Harland and Wolff

Lightoller, *'Davie'* (David) Blair, and *'E.J.'* Smith, the Captain.

The officers knew some of the crew, but not all. **Lightoller** recalled *'Klein, who was a second class barber. That man is personally known to me.'* **(US Enq)**

Looking at the crew list, one cannot fail to be impressed by the variety of jobs on board the *Olympic* and *Titanic*. Apart from the Captain, the deck and navigating officers, engineer officers, pursers and doctors on one plane, there were among the crew Marconi operators, master at arms, quartermasters, boatswains mates, able seamen, nightwatchmen, look-outs, greasers, trimmers, stokers or firemen, lamp trimmers, leading hand engineer, boilermakers, electrician, carpenter joiner, storemen, firemen's messmen, all keeping the great machine going in one piece.

In the victualling department there were butchers and assistants, bakers, night bakers, Vienna baker, passenger cook, grill cook, fish cooks and assistants, sauce cooks, soup cooks, larder cook, roast cook, Hebrew cook, pastry cook and assistants, vegetable cook, cook and stewards messmen. Coffee man and assistant, assistant confectioner chefs, entrée cook, icemen, scullions, glassmen, plate washers, kitchen porter, carver, scullerymen, kitchen clerk, wine butler.

In the stewards department there were (dining) saloon stewards, pantry stewards and assistants, plate steward, reception room steward, lounge attendant, smoke room steward and assistants, verandah café stewards, deck stewards, library stewards, bedroom stewards (known as 'BRs'), bath stewards (for the bathrooms on all the decks – only a very few first class cabins had private bathrooms in 1912, apart from the suites). Hospital stewards, GH stewards, second and third class steward.

A la carte restaurant manager, *maître d'*, assistant waiters, and cashiers. Matron and stewardesses, telephone operator, boots, assistant boots, buttons, lift operators, clothes pressers and assistants, page boy, bell boys, ship's bugler (announcing meal times), barbers. Steerage passenger interpreter, store keepers, linen keepers. Masseuses, Turkish bath attendants, gym instructor, squash court attendant. Clerks, pursers' assistants, printer and assistant printer, stenographer. Post office clerks and finally an orchestra leader and band. These individual groups knew their worth and held their corner. **Joseph Scarrott** said *'There was a man in our boat who we thought was a sailor but he was not. He was a window cleaner.'* **(British Investigation) George Symons** deposed *'I was one of the men specially selected for lookout.'*

Some of the *Titanic's* crew have left us glimpses of their jobs on the ships. *'We have our own business and we attend to it. We look after it and attend to nobody else.'* Fifth officer **Harold Lowe (US Enq)**. *'Attending to all the passengers requirements, cleaning their rooms and everything …*

Mr McCawley demonstrates the rowing machine in the gymnasium.

Father Francis M. Browne, S.J. collection

I was on B deck forward.' Steward **Alfred Crawford (US Enq)**

'We are generally ordered below to attend to meals before leaving port.' First class saloon steward **Edward Wheelton (US Enq)**

'My duties were to be around the ship until 11 o'clock at night when I would see to the closing up of the rooms and the turning out of the lights.' Second class chief steward **John Hardy (US Enq)**

'Ordinary nights we should have been scrubbing the decks. Sunday nights we never had anything to do.' **A.B. Buley (US Enq)**

'To act in general and wait on tables.' Steward **George Crowe (US Enq)**

'usual routine of scrubbing the decks, working four hours on, four hours off.' A.B. **Frank Evans (US Enq)**

'To work from 6 to 5, keep it swept up and paint work clean. That was my duty on board that ship.' A.B. and 'alleyman' **Frederick Clench (US Enq)**

'to mix the paint and all that kind of thing for the ship, and to look after all the decks, trim all the lamps, and get them

in proper order ... to put the lamps in at night time, and take them off at daybreak.' He used 'Colza oil'. A.B. and lamp trimmer **Samuel S. Hemming (US Enq)**

Storekeeper **Frank Prentice** described himself as 'general dogsbody to the purser.' **(TV Times)**

For stateroom steward **Andrew Cunningham**, fire drill was 'getting the hose out, and seeing everything was alright.' **(US Enq)**

First class dining saloon steward **William Burke** was on duty 'during all meal hours, and about an hour before the meal and an hour after; breakfast, lunch and dinner.'

'Our duty does not take us on deck at all. We are entrusted with the passengers and that keeps us fully employed ... the bedroom stewards ... each have a set of rooms to look after ... a man has no more than twelve rooms ... the way we work on board ship, all unnecessary lights are out at eleven, and then there are four bedroom stewards kept on from eleven to twelve. That is only an hour. Then two bedroom stewards come along for the middle watch for twelve until four in the morning. Then they are relieved at half-past five by all hands for the day, until the following night.' Chief steward **Hardy**, bedroom

First class stateroom.

Harland and Wolff

steward **(US Enq)**

'Every morning at seven o'clock I went to his cabin. I used to take him some fruit and tea ...' He added, with some feeling, speaking of a suit Andrews wore visiting the boiler room, and presumably heavily soiled, 'I have seen that suit thrown on the bed when he had taken it off.' Thomas Andrews' steward **H.S. Etches, (US Enq)**

Stewardess **Annie Robinson** looked after 'Seven ladies, one maid and a governess.' **(US Enq)**

'I had charge of the bath on forward deck – on the forward section of F deck.' Second class bath steward **James Widgery (US Enq)**

'It was the custom for we firemen and trimmers to go up on deck (at Queenstown) and carry the mails from the tender to the mail rooms.' Fireman **John Podesta (Titanic Commutator)**

In an era of temperance and fear of the evils of drink, crew were officially forbidden it on all White Star liners, just as T.H. Ismay ordered it on his first ships.

'As for any intemperance you seldom saw anything on a boat like that ... I mean to say you cannot get anything to drink there, as you are bound to be a teetotaller there.' A.B. **Fred Clench (US Enq)**

'We never allowed it to be served on board the ship, sir.' **George Symons (US Enq)**

'I do not see where they could get it from.' **G.A. Hogg (US Enq)**

'In the first place the crew could not afford to buy drinks. There is no other means of getting it but to buy it so a man would not be in a position to do it if he drank ... there is no hope for him to get it, because he would not be served anyway.' Chief steward **Hardy (US Enq)**

Most of the stewards depended heavily on tips to augment their wage, especially if they had a young family, or a parent to support. They were keen to be taken on to wait at tables in the dining saloons. This was especially true in Southampton during the years of unemployment and strikes. Extras might be taken on after passengers boarded at Cherbourg or Queenstown. One steward, Jack Stagg, who perished in the sinking,

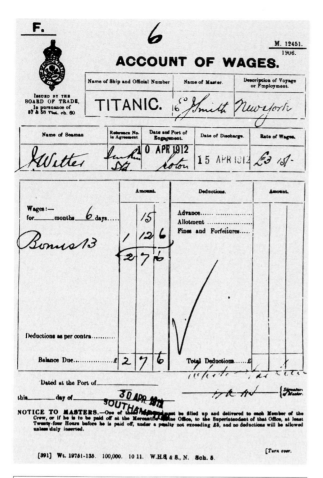

Account of wages of J. Witter, dining room steward.

Southampton City Heritage Collections

'I feel as if I were in a big hotel instead of on a cosy ship. Everyone is so stiff and formal. There are hundreds of help, bell boys, stewards, stewardesses and lifts.'
(Letter to her secretary Mr Shaw, reprinted in 'Her Name Titanic' by Charles Pellegrino)

On the tender at Cherbourg she saw

'The gang plank was held down by ten men on either side as it shook and swayed... Later, I stood aside and watched crowds of cooks, bakers and stewards carrying huge wooden boxes aboard and asked a steward what they were, and was told they contained tinned vegetables and provisions of all sorts for the trip over and return ... the process took fully two hours.' The steward told her, 'We have a pretty good crowd going over but it is nothing compared to what we shall have coming back, as I understand we are booked full.'
(From Diary of Edith Russell, quoted in 'Her Name Titanic' by Charles Pellegrino)

Edith Russell never forgot her dedicated and courageous steward Robert Wareham who retrieved her lucky mascot musical pig, or his final remark, 'I hope we get out of this alright. I have a wife and five little kiddies at home,' (46 Park Road, Southampton) and sadly recorded that he had been lost.

Colonel Archibald Gracie mentions his steward Cullen, a survivor, but particularly recalled Wright, the rackets attendant, and gymnasium instructor T.W. McCawley. (McCawley lived at 22 Camden Place, Southampton).

'One of the characters of the ship, best known to us all ... how well we survivors remember this sturdy little man in white flannels and with his broad English accent. With what tireless enthusiasm he showed us the many mechanical devices, and urged us to take advantage of the opportunity of using them, going through the routines of bicycle racing, rowing, boxing, camel and horseback riding, etc.'

Second class passenger Lawrence Beesley described a lift boy,

'He was quite young – not more than sixteen, I think – a bright eyed handsome boy, with a love for the sea and the games on deck, and the view over the ocean, and he did not get any of them. One day as he put me out of his lift and saw through the vestibule windows a game of deck quoits in progress he said in a wistful tone, 'My, I wish I could go out there sometimes.'

Second class passenger Selina Rogers remembered,

'We had a very nice stewardess and steward whose

gives a clear picture of this, and the hard work he did on board the White Star liner on sailing day, especially this brand new liner. Writing to his wife Beattie:

'It's been nothing but work all day long, but I can tell you nothing as regards what people I have for nothing will be settled until we leave Queenstown tomorrow. Anyhow, we have only 317 first and if I should be lucky enough to get a table at all it won't possibly be more than two that I shall have.'

In contrast to the crew's own accounts, we get an additional picture of them at work in the letters and accounts of some of the passengers on *Titanic*. Relatively few passengers cited the names of the crew, except their own steward. Regular White Star passengers were more familiar with some of them, many their favourite stewards, as well as, of course, the Captain. First class passenger Fred Hoyt told Archibald Gracie, 'I knew Captain Smith for over fifteen years.' But as so many passengers and crew were lost, this familiarity has not been so fully recorded as on other ships.

First class passenger Edith Russell (Rosenbaum) who preferred smaller ships, noticed, names were *Miss Walsh* and *Mr Petty*.' (57 Church Road & 26 Orchard Place, Southampton).

Later,

'I was feeling very sick. The stewardess was very kind and brought me a glass of milk. From 7.15 until 8.00pm the band played selections outside the library.'
(Titanic Commutator, Titanic Historical Society, Indian Orchard, Mass., USA 01151)

'The band played in the afternoon for tea' wrote first class passenger Adolph Saalfeld to his wife.

One second class passenger, Mrs I. Shelley, disappointed with her accommodation when she arrived on the ship at Southampton, observed some of the crew's difficulties on the new ship, not yet fully 'run-in', and unconsciously, their diplomacy.

'The stewardess was sent to the chief purser demanding transfer to the accommodation purchased. He replied that he could do nothing until the boat had left Queenstown, Ireland, when he would check up all tickets and find out if there was any mistake.' Catching a chill, nine trips to the purser, and a note to him warning a complaint to Captain Smith finally saw 'The arrival of four stewards to carry her (Mrs Shelley) to the room paid for, who offered apology after apology. The stewardess, on being asked what the purser had said, replied, 'He asked first if you were really so very sick, to which I answered there was no doubt about that … I also told him that the cabin was entirely too small and that it was impossible for myself or the steward to enter the cabin to wait upon the occupants unless both of them climbed into the berth. The purser then told me that he would have to act at once, or the company would get in trouble.' Although transferred to a new cabin, 'It looked in a half finished condition; that this room was just as cold as the cell from which we had been removed, and in asking the steward to have the heat turned on, he answered that it was impossible as the heating system for the second class cabins refused to work.'

Mrs Shelley noted,

'That although the servants on board were most willing, they had a hard time to do their work; that the stewardesses could not even get a tray to serve Mrs Shelley's meals and had to bring the plates and dishes one at a time in her hands, making the service very slow and annoying. The food, though good and plentiful, was ruined by this trouble in serving. That although both steward and stewardess appealed time and time again to the heads of departments, no relief was obtained; there seemed to be no organisation at all … in the ladies toilet room only part of the fixtures had been installed, some of the said fixtures being still in crates.'

But in the disaster Mrs Shelley thought

'No crew could have behaved in a more perfect manner.'
(Affidavit in the third person deposed to US Enq)

Many of the third class emigrants, too many for the one harassed interpreter L. Müller to look after at once, found as did one Scandinavian passenger,

'We did not understand what the ships' personnel said. They only spoke English.'

CREW PAY

> **In The Pit – Chant of the Firemen**
> This is the steamer's pit
> The ovens like dragons of fire
> Glare thro' their close-lidded eyes
> With restless hunger desire.
> Down from the tropic night,
> Rushes the funnelled air;
> Our heads expand and fall in;
> Our hearts thump huge as despair.
> 'Tis we make the bright hot blood
> Of this throbbing inanimate thing!
> And our life is no less the fuel
> Than the coal we shovel and fling.
> And lest of this we be proud
> Or anything but meek,
> We are well cursed and paid –
> Ten shillings a week!
> Round, round, round in its tunnel
> The shaft turns pitiless strong.
> While lost souls cry out in the darkness;
> "How long, O Lord, how long?"
> Francis Adams
> **From The British Seafarer**
> **(University of Warwick Modern**
> **Records. Courtesy RMT)**

'Five pound a month.' 'And your board?' 'Yes, sir.'
Able Seaman **Edward Buley (US Enq)**
'Five pounds a month, and five shillings extra, sir.'
Look-out **G.A. Hogg (US Enq)**

Captain E.J. Smith had a salary of £1,250 per annum (twice that of **Captain Rostron** of the *Carpathia*, and £350 more than a P&O Captain).

Radio operator **Harold Bride** was paid £48 per annum.

Steward **Sidney Daniels** was paid £3.15s a month.

Stewardess **Annie Robinson** was paid £3.10s a month.

A suite on the *Titanic* cost £870.

Albert Road, Chapel, 1912, Southampton dockland. Many of the crew would have used these six public houses.

Private Collection

The attitude of the crew to the passengers they worked among, was varied. But as we have seen, some of the regulars liked their passengers who took pains to seek them out, each voyage. F. Dent Ray, a steward, took particular pains to push his passenger, Dr Washington Dodge, into a lifeboat because the Dodge family had chosen *Titanic* because Ray would be on it. Steward Alfred Crawford lifebelted *'an old gentleman by the name of Stewart, and tied his shoes on for him.'* Others, either because of the nature of their job or because they were too new, did not have such a close relationship, saw them from the outside, in a more general way. Assistant storekeeper Frank Prentice recalled, *'It was one merry party – the best of food, the best of dinner, orchestras, dancing – oh, they had a fine time.'* **(Interview for TV Times, 1982)**

None the less the crew usually knew who the

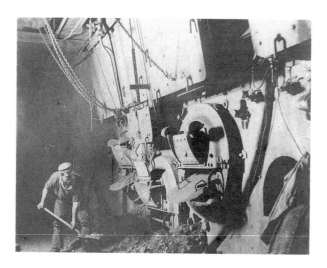

famous passengers were. Fireman George Kemish recognised the celebrated journalist W.T. Stead reading alone in the first class smoke room in *Titanic*'s last few moments.

Those crew who encountered the foreign emigrants in third class seem to have felt a mixture of puzzlement and exasperation, sometimes curiosity, *'At least this lot spoke English'* one said of the Irish emigrants in comparison to the others. Chief steward John Hardy recalled Syrians in his lifeboat *'chattering the whole night in their strange language.'*

Harold Lowe's famous view, as he searched for survivors and found one, *'There's others better worth saving than a Jap'* changed as having rescued him, he observed the man recover and begin to help rowing the boat, *'I'm ashamed of what I said. I'd save the likes of him six times over if I got the chance.'*

One of the two surviving third class stewards, John Edward Hart, freely conceded that third class male passengers were kept below decks as late as 1.15am as the ship sank and lifeboats were lowered.

On the other hand, one of only three stewardesses not saved was the third class matron, Mrs Wallis, who probably never left caring for her charges to the very end.

If the catering staff and deck officers were

The coal era … a stoker at work on the Union Line *Moor*, a tiny ship compared to the *Titanic*.

Southampton City Heritage Collections

The promenade deck on the *Titanic*.

Illustrated London News

inevitably encountered most by the passengers, the seamen were less close. *'We were away from the saloons altogether. We were in the forecastle head.'* A.B. **Edward Buley (US Enq)**

The below-decks crew, the firemen and trimmers in the engine room and outside the bunkers, were rarely glimpsed. Yet of course they were the crux of the ship – everything depended on their efforts. They worked in their own world, largely with their own rules, especially on the Liverpool ships and were handled warily by the rest of the crew, especially the officers. Charles Lightoller said of the older Liverpudlians *'A tougher bunch than the firemen on a Western Ocean Mail boat it would be impossible to find.'* By 1912 the Southampton firemen were considered less extreme than their Liverpool counterparts. With the newer ships Charles Lightoller found *'there was no call for the tough element, in fact it did not exist in Southampton.'* But they were still largely viewed with caution or distaste.

In 1912 most firemen's shore leave was their own, much of it spent in Southampton's drinking saloons. As *Titanic* fireman W.H. Taylor put it, *'The firemen never see a boat in Southampton.'* **(US Enq)**

Some stokers however had to remain on the *Titanic* in Southampton as a fire was smouldering in Number 10 coal bunker – they were working the coal, hosing water on it, and shovelling it away to try to get to the base of the pile, to keep the situation under control.

Fireman **George 'Scooch' Kemish** found *Titanic's* boiler rooms an improvement. *'Not what we were accustomed to in old ships, slugging our guts out and nearly roasted by the heat.'* but after the collision *'We certainly had one hell of a time putting those fires out.'* **(W. Lord, A Night to Remember)**

Some branches of the crew were considered outsiders professionally, even among the varied roles carried out by the rest of the crew. They were the musicians, the Marconi operators, the postal clerks and the staff of the *à la carte* restaurant. The *à la carte* was an innovation on the *Olympic*, and *Titanic*. White Star invited Luigi Gatti of the well known London restaurateurs, to run it as a concession. The elegant *'Mr Gatti in charge'* as first class passenger Mrs Douglas recalled him **(US Enq)** had recently managed the restaurant of the Ritz before adding Oddenino's Imperial Restaurant in London to his impressive record. When he accepted White Star's commission, he bought or rented a house in Southampton at Harborough Road, Polygon, naming it *'Montalto'* after his birthplace in Italy. He brought with him his young English wife Edith and their son Vittorio, who shortly before sailing day on *Titanic* gave his father a small teddy bear (made by the famous German toy maker, Bing) which was later found on his father's body and returned to the family.

Gatti also brought with him his own staff. Chefs, waiters, *maître d'*, manager, wine butler and glassmen

E. Roggi.

Rota.

v. Gilardini.

Valvasfore,

Alaria.

Crovello.

Crew members of the à la carte restaurant.

Daily Mirror

First class stateroom. *Titanic.*

Harland and Wolff

who were all French or Italian, living and previously working in London, unlike the majority of cooks and waiters in *Titanic*'s dining saloons. Some of Gatti's staff may have stayed at the International Club, then occupying Bowling Green House as a residential hostel. Their names stand out among those of the British crew, for instance Allaria, Crovelle, Gilandino, Perotti, Poggi, Rotto, Salussolia, Testoni, Vallasori, Zaracchi. Ten of Luigi Gatti's cousins were amongst the staff, and this was their first voyage. The feelings of the regular crew towards them were mixed. Steward **J. Johnson** recalled Luigi Gatti *'A nice little man, he was, like a Chief Steward in his own department'*, but said of the others *'Mostly Italians and French. I do not know. I never mix with them.'* **(US Enq)**

At this time Italians and foreigners generally were the butt of many a jingoistic tongue nationwide, as Europe's empires moved inexorably towards World War I two years later. On 19th June 1912 the Southampton Pictorial would record that the national pilots conference had protested against the granting of pilot certificates to foreigners. *'There are already enough foreign waiters in England to man an army corps, and it is absurd to train pilots, to show an enemy the way to our ports.'*

In the sinking and abandoning of the *Titanic* any misbehaviour, or boarding threat, or problem from passengers was nearly always attributed by the surviving crew to Italians or foreigners. Seaman **Evans** referred to *'a foreigner ... a crazed Italian'* **(US Enq)**. Later at the US Enquiry, the Italian ambassador to Washington objected strenuously to the crew's attitude, and men like Quarter Master Arthur Bright and Officer Harold Lowe were obliged to apologise. The apology, *'I did not intend to cast any reflection on the Italian nation'* was not a great success because he promised to instead substitute the words *'immigrants belonging to the Latin races'*. Southampton's postmaster referred to White Star third class passengers as *'mostly low class continentals.'*

Yet Gattis themselves prospered in Southampton, with the earlier opening of their restaurant near the Bargate, despite the loss of Luigi and all his cousins in the disaster. Of the *à la carte* staff, just one survived – the French *maître d'*, Paul Maugé.

Although Marconi operators John Phillips and Harold Bride were paid by the White Star Line, they were in fact employees of the Marconi company, and were effectively *'leased-out'* to White Star. Their role was still a great novelty on liners before the loss of the *Titanic* confirmed their importance even more definitely than that of the first seagoing Marconi operator, Jack Binns, when the White Star liner *Republic* sank following a collision with another vessel in 1909.

The musicians even sailed on a collective ticket as second class passengers under a contract by their agents C.W. and N.F. Black of Liverpool. Their E deck cabin contained a separate room for their instruments.

Then there were the postal clerks, who supervised the mails being carried by the White Star Line, as well as those letters written and posted by passengers on board. They were not employees of the line, but of the Southampton and New York branches of the British and US Post Offices, who managed what was called the *'Sea Post'*. This followed the Anglo-American postal agreement of 1905 allowing British and American clerks to handle mail on White Star and American Line vessels. Services began from Liverpool and Southampton that May. In 1907, when White Star arrived in Southampton, the postmark on the mails became 'British Sea Post Office, Southampton' but was soon changed to 'Transatlantic Post Office'. In 1908 a correspondent of the Southampton Postmaster commented,

'This service is looked upon as the best in the US Post Office ... they (the clerks) are paid much higher than their men,

minimum salary 1,200 (dollars) per annum ... hard and trying in winter ... only healthy men can stand the strain.' **(GPO Archives)**

A less serious problem reported by the London postal controller, Mr Bruce, in 1908, was *'the uniform provided for the sea post office staff on all British ships is sometimes mistaken for that of the ship's band and alterations are recommended.'* **(GPO Archives)** Their *'post horn'* badge was duly replaced by a crown.

By the end of 1912 there were sixteen sea post officials sailing out of Southampton and Liverpool, on the American Line and White Star combine ships. Four were employed on the maiden voyage of *Titanic*, two from New York, and two (James B. Williamson and John R. Jago Smith) from the Southampton Post Office. The headstamped postal number, 7, first used on *Titanic*, was allocated to the clerks themselves, and not to the ship. When the clerks were lost in the disaster, the number was never re-allocated to any of the other clerks in their service. Eleven numbers in all had been issued to the Southampton sea post.

On the *Olympic*, the clerks had complained of problems with their accommodation. On 9th April, the

day before *Titanic* sailed, Southampton's Postmaster W. James accompanied Head Office's Commander Foakes and Mr Parsons to inspect and report on the clerks' accommodation on the second ship. It was on F deck, the sorting room was on G deck and the mail room on Orlop deck. All had required certain modifications, most of which Mr James was able to report had been made by sailing day. The party also found

'Messrs March and Gwynn, US sea sorters, and Mr Rabley of the British service were on board, and they represented many features of the sleeping and dining quarters which they regarded as objectionable. Some of their representations were merely frivolous and may be disregarded, but their complaint regarding the noisy condition of their sleeping cabins should perhaps be brought to the company's (White Star's) notice.
The cabins are situated among a block of third class cabins, and it is stated that the occupants of these latter, who are mostly low class continentals, keep up a noisy conversation sometimes throughout the silent hours, and even indulge in singing and instrumental music. There is, too, a door on the other side of the inboard bulkhead of the larger cabin through which the steerage passengers are constantly passing and the sorting clerks complain that this door bangs at night and keeps them awake. These

First class dining saloon. *Titanic.*

Father Francis M. Browne S.J. Collection

80

remarks were prompted by their experiences in the Olympic where the accommodation is similar … if their work during the day is to be performed efficiently it is essential that they should enjoy decent sleep at night.

They complained about their dining room and desired to be established in the saloon with the passengers, but I consider that the mess room provided is suitable, convenient and in accordance with the understanding between the US Post Office, and the company, and no change is required. It might be suggested, however, that the doorway leading from the (passengers) 'valets and ladies' maids' dining room should be fitted with a door in order to prevent the present practice of using the mail sorters' mess room as a thoroughfare. The accommodation is far in excess both as regards size and fittings of any other British Packet carrying a sea post office on the Atlantic.'

(GPO Records Memorandum 11th April 1912, 355/768/11)

The Postmaster General duly approached Ismay and Imrie (the White Star Line) in Liverpool on 13th April over the issue. *Olympic's* clerks were soon moved to better cabins on E deck, particularly in the light of fears they expressed, after the *Titanic* sinking, of being trapped on F deck.

How were the regular crew accommodated when they boarded the ship in Southampton or Belfast or New York? Although their jobs meant they spent most of the day in their allocated duties all over the ship, on deck, in public rooms, or engine rooms, state rooms, kitchens, stores, the bridge etc, the bulk of their own accommodation was concentrated on E deck, below the first and second class dining saloons and galley, and above the third class dining saloons on F deck, where third class stewards, cooks, butchers and bakers were also placed. Extra accommodation was provided in the extreme bow on D, F and G decks, chiefly for firemen and greasers, linked by spiral staircases down to their main alleyway to the boiler rooms on the lowest 'tank top' deck. It is ironical that on a ship and in an age where class distinctions were the norm, and rigidly enforced, that, partly by the demands and complications of both naval architecture and a very big floating hotel, on this one E deck there were to be found, in unconscious (because barriered) democracy, not only cabins for all three classes of passengers, but also the cabins and dormitories of nearly 450 of the crew. There slept the master at arms, quartermasters, five musicians, sixteen printers, head waiter, wine waiter, cook and cooks, BRs, bakers, chef, pantrymen, pursers' clerks, bathroom stewards, first class cooks, first class stewards, restaurant waiters, saloon waiters, assistant stewards, second class stewards, twenty plate washers, scullions, the mate, seamen, and trimmers.

As many as 42 second class stewards filled one dormitory, 34 third class stewards might fill another, 38 saloon stewards in one of their three dormitories. There were 24 trimmers in each of three dormitories pressed into the bow. The crew accommodation 'The glory hole as we call it' said steward **William Ward (US Enq))** mostly took up five sixths of the port side of the ship. Third class passengers filled the stern, and part of the starboard bow. Second class filled a little more of the starboard stern, and first class cabins the greater part of the starboard side. A lady clerk was accommodated here, (far from the port side) and the 18 stewardesses, three to a cabin, were distributed amongst those of the passengers on A, C and D deck. Passengers' own maids and valets accompanying them had their own saloon on C deck, next to the postal workers. Engineers had their own mess. The other crew mess rooms and galley for seamen, greasers and firemen were on C deck in the bow.

Running alongside the crew accommodation on the port side of E deck adjoining the boiler casings leading to the uptakes or funnels, was the long working alleyway (already described by Frederick Clench) much wider than those in the passenger areas. It eventually twisted round into the bow. It was known by most of the crew as 'Scotland Road' but the officers, whose cabins were on the boat deck, liked, no doubt ironically, to dub it 'Park Lane'.

'That is what we call on the ship Scotland Road, the wide alleyway that leads from two or three sections of the third class. It opens into an emergency door leading into second class. It is a wide working alleyway.'

Titanic's chief baker Charles Joughin (British Investigation)

Many years later the crew on the *Queen Mary* would dub a similar working alleyway, 'Burma Road'.

Some of the crew have left other impressions of their quarters and the ship generally. Before joining *Titanic* able seaman **Joseph Scarrott** inspected her thoroughly *'from stem to stern … especially the crew quarters, and I must say she was the finest ship I had ever seen.'* **(Pier Review No. 8)**

George Kemish thought *Titanic* was *'a good job.'* **(W. Lord 'A Night to Remember')**

But the distances to walk or run between the deck and glory holes on the vast ship meant that for A.B. **W. Lucas** *'At times it took me longer … never knew my way. It was a new ship.'* **(British Investigation)** 2nd Officer **Charles Lightoller** found *'it took me fourteen days before I could find my way with confidence from one part of the ship to the other … a sailor does not walk about with a plan in his pocket, he must carry the ship in his head.'*

(I felt) *'as many others did proud to be selected for such a wonderful ship.'* **Sidney Daniels**

(Copy of letter sent to Richard Garrett from Sidney Daniels, supplied by R. Garrett to City Museums in 1986)

'Like the Olympic, yes, but so much more elaborate. Take the dining saloon – Olympic didn't even have a carpet but the Titanic – ah, you sank in it up to your knees. Then there's the furniture. So heavy you could hardly lift it. And that panelling … They can make them bigger and faster but it was the care and effort that went into her. She was a beautiful wonderful ship.' Baker **Reginald Burgess (From 'A Night to Remember' by Walter Lord)**

Then there was Captain Smith's personal steward Arthur Paintin (*'A man named Paintin I think it was, I am almost sure … he was last seen on the bridge standing by the Captain'*, remembered Steward F. Dent Ray at the US Enquiry). His feelings were justifiably mixed, writing to his parents

'Bai jove what a fine ship this is, much better than the Olympic as far as passengers are concerned but my little room is not near so nice, no daylight, electric light on all day, but I suppose it's no use grumbling.'

Olympic's doctor, J.C.H. Beaumont remembered the new liner's popularity in 1911 *'not less so with the crew, whose quarters were roomy, well ventilated, conveniently arranged, and altogether comfortable.'* **(See also Ward testimony US Enq page 601)**

Yet the misgivings or superstitious feeling of the crew experienced about the *Titanic*, men as diverse as AB Joseph Scarrott, chief engineer Bell and steward George Barlow, had apparently also been present when the *Olympic* came out the year before. They were just so big. *'The Big 'Un as we all called her'*, said Jo Scarrott of *Titanic*. Fifth officer Lowe's previous ship was the 10,000 ton *Belgic*. The *Titanic* was more than four times as large at 46,000 tons. He dubbed her 'The big Omnibus'.

Charles Lightoller reflected

'It is difficult to describe just where exactly that unity of feeling lies between a ship and her crew, but it is surely there in every ship that sails salt water. It is not always a feeling of affection either. A man can hate a ship worse than a human being.'

What did the wives and families of these crew think of the *Titanic*? The Daily Graphic's journalist visiting her in Southampton docks shortly before sailing, gave a patronising, almost insulting view,

'All these Southampton women were proud that their men had entered into service on the greatest vessel ever built by man. They prattled of the Titanic with a sort of suggestion of proprietorship … Rumours and legends and tales of her glories and luxuries and powers were banded about in every street in Southampton … in the phrase of the people she was 'the last word'.'

General view of Southampton, 1912. Lido can be seen bottom left.

Southampton City Heritage Collections

★ DEPARTURE

"There goes daddy's ship"

Now lying in Southampton Dock;
Her funnels towering high,
And proudly from her lofty masts,
The White Star did fly.
(From 'The Loss of the Titanic', Buxey's, Southampton, 1912)

A new ship the size of *Titanic* attracted much interest, although not as much as the *Olympic* the year before.

"Well the Titanic was just another ship to us at the time of course, she was one of a series of large ships … we were very interested in the Olympic and the Mauretania and the Lusitania, they came along about that time too. They were all wonders in their day and of course when the Titanic came she was just another wonder and we thought not an awful lot about her until the terrible happening."
John Wright, who saw *Titanic* from The Common. (City Heritage Oral History)

But many visited the docks to take a look at the new, even larger sistership, although few went on board.

To really appreciate the size and beauty of a liner in Southampton one needed to be on the water, as now, or one of the piers, or at a distance outside the town, as the immediate edge of town and docks is so low lying. Otherwise one must climb to the top of a high building. The Southern Daily Echo (9th April 1912) remarked,

'No better illustration of the Titanic's great size can be given than the fact that her masts and funnels can be plainly seen rising high above the trees and houses from the top of the Common and from the higher points of Portswood.'

This was a pleasure largely denied to boat train passengers who only caught a quick glimpse of part of the ship before they were pulled in along the other side of the dock shed.

Lawrence Beesley, although staying in Southampton the night before, found the next day that he did not get the chance

'to stand some distance away to take in a full view of her beautiful proportions, which the narrow approach to the dock made impossible.'

Titanic dressed with flags on Good Friday.

Southern Newspapers

Titanic in her berth, Southampton.

Ulster Folk and Transport Museum

He got his view in the middle of the Atlantic, rather than a New York skyscraper.

Workers arriving on board the ship for the first morning she arrived noticed the paint on the lockers was still wet. Because there was so much to be completed on the interior of *Titanic*, White Star reluctantly decided it could not open her to the general public in Southampton before the maiden voyage. *'Sightseers need not apply'* the Southampton Times sulkily informed the public on 30th March, four days before her arrival. But the Southampton Pictorial later noted in its first issue,

'Though the Titanic, the world's last word in shipbuilding construction, has not been open to inspection by the general public since her arrival at Southampton from Belfast, hundreds of sightseers have visited the docks to catch a glimpse of the leviathan as she lies moored in the new wet dock at the same berth occupied a week ago by her sister Olympic. Perhaps the most striking features of the great inert mass of metal, are the four giant funnels – huge tawny brown and black capped elliptical cylinders of steel which tower 175 feet from the keel plate, dominating the other shipping in the port, and dwarfing into insignificance the sheds on the quayside.'

The few visitors apart from crew, workmen and suppliers were privileged officials, friends and family of the crew, White Star office staff, and press representatives. Most came later in the week, as work was completed.

The sister of transferred officer David Blair, was one. Her niece (Blair's daughter) recorded

'My aunt (who) was expected on a visit to Southampton where we were living at the time. This aunt told me years later that my father took her on a tour of the ship the day before she sailed. This took several hours and the ship was still a hive of activity with carpets still being laid and decorators busy until the last moment.'

(MS by the late Miss E. Nancy Blair, reprinted in 'Chart and Compass' now bequeathed to British Sailors' Society Collection of Historical Artifacts)

At the same time Thomas Andrews continued busily on board.

'He himself put in their places such things as racks, tables, chairs, berth ladders, electric fans, saying that except he saw everything right he could not be satisfied. He was always busy, taking the owners around the ship, interviewing engineers, officials, managers, agents, sub-contractors, discussing with principals the plans of new ships, and superintending generally the work of completion.'

Looking at the new Café Parisien he noted a plan for staining the wicker furniture green – this idea was

later effected on *Olympic*, when a similar café was installed at her next refit.

Andrews' biographer goes on to record

'during his business career Andrews received many acknowledgements of a gratifying description … from the White Star Company, the Hamburg American company, and what I dare say he valued as much from the stewards of the Olympic.'

Several of those stewards would join him on *Titanic*. Steward **H.S. Etches**: *'I met him at different parts of E deck more often than anywhere else.'* **(US Enq)**

One of *Titanic*'s ill fated stewards, George Beedem, a protegé of John Bartholomew, the Victualling Superintendent, on board from early on, conveys his impression of the work in Southampton in letters he wrote to his mother and to his wife. At first they give an impression of quiet and monotony, with little about his work and more about family concerns and their plans to move to Southampton. But job frustration emerges over a pay failure, and the lack of dusters, perhaps still packed away or locked up, in the last minute rush as the new

Section of *Olympic* and *Titanic* with view of the proposed berthing position in the White Star Dock.

The Sphere. Peter Boyd-Smith, Cobwebs

A *Titanic* funnel receives some last minute attention.

Peter Boyd-Smith, Cobwebs

stowaway last trip but I told you all about it. I did not get your letter, that's on its way to America I expect. I have not got a stamp so shall not be able to post this till tomorrow. I should like to know how Uncle J is if you drop a line, don't forget 'Titanic' not 'Olympic'. I am quite well so goodbye with fondest love.
George
Mr B will come with us this trip I expect

Note: John Bartholomew did not accompany the stewards on the *Titanic.*

Southampton
5th April 1912
Titanic
Friday evening
Am enclosing card found in pocket

My Dearest Lill
Good Friday & I have been at work all day. I got on board yesterday about 9 o/c. The crowd here not started yet, they come tomorrow, there is very little difference between the two ships I have been 'standing by' today simply seeing the ship does not turn away, the others are not working, I signed on for rooms. It's been a lovely day today. Now how is your neck? Stick to that stuff my girl whatever you do. I cannot find any notepaper only this sheet in my bag so I must have another look. I have found a few sheets when I signed on. I found I had left my discharge book home on the dresser, please send it on to the Titanic. Now my girl I don't know what else to write about, I cannot get a stamp until tomorrow morning. I am going to take the pipe for a stroll somewhere or the other. I do like being here by myself so goodbye my little dears, hope Charlie sleeps alright now, so tata with love & kisses.
DaDa (George)

9th April 1912
On board RMS Titanic
Tuesday

My dear Lill & Charlie
This is the last night & thank goodness we are off tomorrow. I should never do another week along like I have this one. On Sunday I went all over the place house hunting. You had better let me know for certain at Plymouth what you are going to do in the way of coming down & going home. I don't suppose we shall leave the ship till 5 o/c on the Saturday night. I hope your neck is better, let me know all about it for certain at Plymouth. My cold has been rotten & I shall be glad to get away to have a good square meal. As usual I expect you will say I am wrong in my money. I have not been paid for Good Friday there were only 10 of us working & none have been paid through some fool leaving us off the list. I am sending 10/- that's 4/- short so I've managed to exist on about 8/- counting 2/- I had from

furniture and other surfaces were cleaned following their location under Andrews' directions.

On board RMS Titanic
don't forget

Dear Mother
I have done two days got back Thursday morning you can hardly tell the difference between the two boats. I have been standing by the ship today to see she doesn't run away. Nobody has been working on her being 'Good Friday' so I have a day's pay to come. Mr B keeps me in work. I have not seen him. I went to the office last Saturday but his head man told me I was to go on the Titanic on Thursday so I cleared off home straight away. Had a nice little time but all too short. Lill has not been very well I shall be glad when we are all down in Southampton I expect she will come down when I come home again to have a look around.
Am glad to hear Uncle is better hope he continues. I am signing on in Room ??? last trip was not above the average, nobody was travelling because of the coal strike. We came back practically empty but I think we are full up out & back this trip. I found a

Titanic is pulled away from White Star Dock by the tugs *Albert Edward* and *Ajax*.

Photo by H.G. Lloyd, Southampton Pictorial

you so it's a happy life. I have no news to tell you only the last 3 days. I've felt rotten & what with no dusters or anything to work with I wish the bally ship at the bottom of the sea. I heard from Mother today, Uncle John is a little better but cannot get up. Hope Charlie is having a nice holiday, so goodbye with love to both of you.

George

PS I have been thinking if it were possible to go right in for our own house, just think it over & see if anything can be done

Dad (George)

(Private Collection via British Titanic Society)

The Illustrated London News and the Hampshire Advertiser sent their press photographers to visit and record the ship on 6th April. The Southampton Times, after its own inspection, in its column reserved for maritime news 'Ship and Shore – Maritime Notes' editorialized that *Titanic* was

'*a wonderful ship ... in a port where the magnificence of the appointments of the Olympic are so well known, it seems scarcely necessary to say much about the Titanic. The privileged few who have had the pleasure of visiting the ship at Southampton have been at a loss to express their admiration. One person said that the Olympic was all that could be desired, and the Titanic was – well, something even beyond that! ...*

These gentlemen were quick to notice that several changes had been made in the Titanic and particularly was it noticeable that increased stateroom accommodation had been provided. The two private promenade decks were inspected with interest ... a delightful addition is the Café Parisien ... the deck space outside the restaurant has been utilised for it, and it represents an entirely new feature on steamers ... A reception room has been provided in connection with the restaurant ... itself increased in size ... all the magnificent decorations have been repeated (from Olympic) second class passengers have been very generously provided for ... the accommodation for third class passengers is also very good.'

Although so fascinated by the passenger accommodation, the Southampton Times was not remotely interested in the accommodation of the crew, unlike the press inspecting the new *QE2* in 1969, when social mores and business practices had changed to the point that crew comfort was a news item.

On the other hand the newspaper's maritime editor was well aware of the threat of the forthcoming Hamburg American Line giants being built at Hamburg, *Imperator* and *Vaterland*.

Although he crowed that the score '*Two to nil is held by the White Star Line ... with a third Olympic in Messrs Harland and Wolff's order list*' he reflected '*It will be* interesting to know whether she will be bigger than the *Imperator*.' (She would not, as it turned out, although *Britannic* was altered to a longer, wider and heavier version of her sisters.) He continued:

'The ultimate aim of the White Star Line is to have a weekly service of mammoth ships for Southampton and apparently they are to be challenged at every step by the Germans. For once in a way the Germans have been bested, and the White Star Line can take to themselves the full credit of having done something practical whilst the Germans were holding their hands.'

One feature the *Imperator* would briefly enjoy in the first year of her career, 1913, was a grotesque figurehead – an eagle on a globe inscribed 'Mein feld is die weld', Hamburg America's motto. It was swept away by a providential storm. But in 1912 the Southampton Times, looking at the clean sharp square bow of the *Titanic*, lamented the passing of figureheads on the British ocean liner as the nineteenth century clipper bow passed from favour. A few figureheads survived on older steamers of lines like the RMSP Co, and gilded scrollwork decoration, glinting in the sunshine would still be found on bow and stern of many liners, but the White Star liners made do with a plain thin gold painted band around the black hull.

'Those who have prided themselves on possessing an artistic eye have deplored the fact that the modern tendency of the ship designer has been to give a steamer a straight stem. Indeed the old custom of providing a figurehead has almost died out ... it was certainly a surprise to find the enterprising Germans are willing to revive it. Present day shipbuilding has no place for anything which does not serve a useful purpose."
(Southampton Times/Hants Express 6.4.1912. Maritime Notes.)

Among the visitors to the docks were a number of local amateur and semi professional photographers and distributors. Photographers like Courtney, Adolphe Rapp "Marine Photographers, 39 Bernard Street", S. Cribb, Willstead, Max-Mills (Wilfred Ashby). Other unrecorded *'snappers'* may even have been using the special *'Ensign'* roll film supplied by W.J. Dodridge in Victoria Road, Woolston. The grandest photographers were professionals like Debenham and Smith at Anglesea Place, Above Bar, but it was probably their Isle of Wight photographer who recorded the *Titanic* passing Cowes on 10th April. Several firms and printers made postcards of local ships – Thomas of Lordswood Avenue was one (*Olympic* was a favourite subject), Gertrude Pratt in Oxford Street was another. Few firms can have guessed how important the relatively few photographs taken of *Titanic* would later become. Some *'caught'* her dressed overall on Good Friday – a public relations gesture to compliment the town and

mitigate the disappointment of no public view.

Sailing day would provide the most attractive possibilities (few guessed what excitement lay ahead in the docks that day). Within weeks the Southampton Pictorial would be awarding a prize of ½ a guinea to H.G. Lloyd, son of Major Lloyd of Marchwood, for his shot, using a No. 2 'Brownie', of the departure

'a clever young amateur – gives the proper impression of the size but fills in the details of the departure so well'.

The print was developed by Burr's in Above Bar, and later made available to distributors such as Courtney.

Not many households in the dockland communities of Chapel, Northam and St Mary's, ran to owning a camera. But the opportunity to be photographed or obtain photographs or postcards with a personal connection was gladly taken if available at a cheap price, or given as a favour. Portrait photographers in the town had regular customers in the crews, including men from the *Titanic*.

Porters outside South Western Hotel.

Southampton Archives Service

88

60 SOUTHAMPTON. — South Western Hotel. — LL.

South Western Hotel.

Southampton Archives Service

There were also several artists in Southampton who took a good look at the ship before painting their own version. George Washington Sandell later showed her passing Calshot Castle, but George Fraser of Coleman Street, Chapel painted her as she prepared to leave on her maiden voyage. He had watched all the people going on board, painting some of them, but intended to add more of them later on when he got the next free moment. After the disaster he lost heart and turned the picture to one side – the forward superstructure of the *Titanic* remained largely devoid of the intended figures in the painting which he never resumed.

A young electrician but keen watercolour artist, Walter Dane Bryer, son of a Northam master baker and brother of future famous Naval aviator 'Peter' Bryer, portrayed the ship at sea in crisp April weather.

More prosaic painting was done on *Titanic* herself, as seamen, suspended from the funnels, gave them a last coat of pinky buff paint.

SOUTHAMPTON HOTELS

Although the majority of *Titanic*'s passengers arrived on sailing day on the boat train from London, a few were already in Southampton. The most wealthy or 'important' stayed at the South Western Hotel, leased by LSWR to Spiers and Pond Ltd, and managed by Arthur Banks. Porters in red uniform would meet them from their train, or at the ship, or from their car at the door. One of these was really a working passenger, Thomas Andrews, one of *Olympic* and *Titanic*'s designers; he was testing the new liner, looking to make improvements, and had come over on her from Belfast, staying all week at the hotel while he oversaw the last touches to the not quite complete liner.

'Throughout the various days that the vessel lay at Southampton, Mr Andrews was never for a moment idle. He generally left his hotel at about 8.30 for the offices (Harland and Wolff's) where he dealt with his correspondence, then went on board until 6.30, when he would return to the offices to sign letters' remembered his secretary, Thomas Hamilton.

The day before sailing Bruce Ismay and his family motored down from London to spend the night at the South Western, where they were met by Ismay's valet Richard Fry, who had arrived ahead of them. Ismay's secretary W.H. Harrison, joined them to make a trio on the voyage. (Ismay's wife and children were only seeing him off this time although Mrs Ismay and J. Bruce's

Atlantic Hotel opened for the emigrant trade in 1894 in Albert Road by John Doling whose daughter and daughter-in-law were second class passengers on the *Titanic*.

A.G.K. Leonard Collection

brother James had gone with him on the *Olympic*'s first crossing.) This time J. Bruce Ismay wanted *'to see how she works, and with the idea of seeing how we could improve on her for the next ship which we are building'* (the *eventual Britannic*). **(US Enq)**

White Star officers occasionally met up in the South Western to dine, including the doctors. J.C.H. Beaumont recalled Dr O'Loughlin of the *Titanic*

'Whether he had any premonitions about the Titanic (I think it is known that (purser) McElroy had) I cannot say, but I do know that during a talk with him in the South Western Hotel he did tell me that he was tired at this time of life to be changing from one ship to another. When he mentioned this to Captain Smith the latter chided him for being lazy and told him to pack up and come with him. So fate decreed that 'Billy' should go to the Titanic and I to the Olympic.'

One young lad in Southampton, Harold Campbell from St Mary's Road, Newtown, had left school as soon as possible and was working as a *'boots'* at the Star Hotel, where a head steward from the *Titanic* offered him a recommendation to join the ship, as Campbell wanted to go to sea. But in the event he did not take it up. Later he served as a steward on the *Homeric* but mostly with RMSP Co, relieved that he had never

gone on *Titanic*.

The manager of one hotel in Southampton, probably the Oriental, was a friend of Chief Engineer Bell. As a special treat Bell showed the manager's son around the *Titanic*'s engine room the evening before sailing day.

The night before sailing, one of White Star Line's Southampton office ticket clerks went on board and enjoyed a meal on the ship.

Second class passenger Lawrence Beesley also stayed in Southampton the night before, possibly in Queens Terrace or Canute Road.

'It is pathetic to recall that as I sat that morning in the breakfast room of an hotel from the windows of which could be seen the four huge funnels of the Titanic towering over the roof of the various shipping offices opposite, and the procession of stokers and stewards wending their way to the ship, there sat behind me three of the Titanic's passengers, discussing the coming voyage and estimating among other things the probabilities of an accident at sea to the ship. As I rose from breakfast I glanced at the group and recognised them later on board, but they were not among the number who answered to the roll call on the Carpathia on the following Monday morning.'

The boat train leaving Waterloo for Southampton.

Father Francis M. Browne, S.J. collection

'Left and right stretched a wall of steel that towered high above the roof of the station… 40 feet above the quay level, yet scarce more than half way up the side of the ship. Below us the people looked tiny… 120 yards aft we could see the second class passengers crossing the gangway to their portion of the ship.'

Father Francis M. Browne, S.J. collection

Crowds of onlookers, photographed by First Class passenger Father Browne, bid *Titanic* farewell from White Star Dock.

Father Francis M. Browne, S.J. Collection

SAILING DAY

'Out from the docks of Southampton
Steamed on her maiden trip
The magnificent *Titanic*
The mighty modern ship ...
And the people standing on the quay
Cheered as the ship went by.'
(From poem **'Be British'**, 1912)

"Captain John Smith he lived in Winn Road. Well, in those days, I was 11 years old and I used to do a paper round from Smith & Sons bookstall on St. Denys Station... my round was all Winn Road and I used to serve nearly every house and I used to stop at the top and come down one side and up the other. I used to do that round before I went to school in the week, when I got up to the last house before where Captain Smith lived, he was just coming out. And I always remember him saying to me, 'alright son, I'll take my paper' and I gave him his newspaper and he was just going down to the docks to join the Titanic. That would be, near enough, 7 o'clock in the morning because he would have to be down there for what was

the recognised Board of Trade muster at 8 o'clock, when all members of the crew had to be there from the Captain right down to a bell boy."
Albert 'Ben' Benham (Lee Raymond Collection)

'At last sailing day arrived and from end to end the ship which for days had been like a nest of bees, now resembled a hive about to swarm'. **Charles Lightoller.**

'The weather was very fine – perfect weather, summer weather.' **Officer Herbert Pitman. (US Enq)**

'We sailed from Southampton April 10th. Two days previous to that I was working aboard ship, in and out, to the dock.' **Steward George Crowe. (US Enq)**

The first to arrive on the ship shortly after sunrise were the crew in small groups.

'I was under orders to join the ship at 7am. Wednesday, April 10th, the time of sailing being 12.0 that morning. The trip was to be a 'speed up' trip, meaning that we were to go from Southampton to New York, unload, load, and

Spectators on the *New York* watch as *Titanic* is pulled round the knuckle at the entrance to White Star Dock. The tug *Neptune* is at her bow, but will soon move.

Ulster Folk and Transport Museum

back again in 16 days. Although it was unnecessary to take all my kit for this short trip, I did not seem to have the inclination to sort any of it out, and I pondered a lot in my mind whether I should join her or give her a miss. Now in the whole of my career of 29 years of going to sea I have never had that feeling of hesitation that I experienced then, and I had worked aboard the Titanic when she came to Southampton from the builders and I had the opportunity to inspect her from stem to stern. This I did, especially the crew's quarters, and I must say that she was the finest ship I had ever seen.
Wednesday 10th. I decide I will go, but not with a good heart. Before leaving home I kissed my sister and said 'Goodbye', and as I was leaving she called me back and asked me why I had said 'Goodbye' instead of my usual 'So long, see you again soon'. I told her I had not noticed saying it, neither had I. On my way to join the ship you can imagine how this incident stuck in my mind. On joining a ship all sailors have much the same routine. You go to your quarters, choose your bunk, and get the gear you require from your bag. Then you change into your uniform by that time you are called to muster by the Chief Officer. I took my bag but did not open it, nor did I get into uniform, and I went to muster and Fire and Boat Drill without my uniform. 11.45am. Hands to stations for casting off. I am in the Starboard Watch, my station is aft, and I am still not in uniform. My actions and manners are the reverse of what they should be.'

Able Seaman Joseph Scarrott (City Heritage Collections)

'We joined the Titanic on Wednesday at 6 o'clock.'
A.B. Frank Evans. (US Enq)

'I arose on the morning of April 10th 1912 and made off down to the ship for 8 o'clock muster (an affair which usually takes about an hour).'
Fireman John Podesta (Titanic Commutator, December 1964)

Captain Smith arrived at 7.30, but the officers had spent the night on board. Before the boat trains arrived the crew would find their quarters, change into uniform, attend crew muster at 8 o'clock and medical clearances and a few would take part in the lowering of two boats in a brief drill.

'All the able seaman participated' said 51 year old Able Seaman **George Moore**, 'about 30-40 ... We lowered two boats in the water.' Asked if they knew Titanic's boats would not carry all on board he replied, 'I suppose they did.' **(US Enq)**

'We had the first muster, and had an inspection by the officers and went to boat drill. There were two boats. We went away in one of those boats. There were nine in each.' **A.B. Frank Evans (US Enq)**

Few stewards were among them.

Captain Smith on boat deck of the *Titanic*.

Illustrated London News, 20th April 1912

'*Speaking of Captain Clarke we call him a nuisance because he is so strict ... he makes us fork out every detail*', confided Second Officer Charles Lightoller at the beginning of the US Enquiry.

There were other visitors, less official than Captain Clarke.

"*My father was a mariner... at one time he was in the Royal Mail Steam Packet Company, that was before I was born. Previous to that he had been the master of the steam yacht Latona which was owned by the Baron von Knoop. My father just simply said to me I'm taking you down to see the Titanic... he thought it would be a good thing for me to see it and he knew Captain Smith... I remember we got on the tram car which passed our house in Shirley Road and away we went down to the docks... as we went through the gates we could see the Titanic on the right hand side in the distance... We went up a covered gangway into the ship, it was huge, I was very overawed, it was magnificent, big grand staircase was right in front of me. My other impression I got then was of a tall man completely bearded and he was wearing a frock coat, he had on a peaked cap and the thing that struck me was that it was not like the ones that are worn today, it had a small brim and small top. I remember my father speaking to him. Captain Smith didn't speak to me but he bent down and shook me by the hand, there was a tremendous bustle going on and Captain Smith was surrounded by people.*"

Roy Diaper (City Heritage Oral History)

A chance visitor to *Titanic* was marine artist Norman Wilkinson, on his way to Devon. He remembered that

'*On reaching the jetty at the top of Southampton water I saw the new White Star liner Titanic. She was to sail on her maiden voyage that afternoon. I said to my friend, 'What a bit of luck. I know the Captain. We will go aboard and look round the ship.'*
The quartermaster at the head of the gangway said that Captain Smith was on board and took us along to his cabin. He was nearly sixty years old with forty years service in the Line and radiated Edwardian confidence. He gave me a warm welcome but said that he was extremely busy and would hand us over to the Purser, who would show us round. We made a thorough tour of the splendid ship. Over the mantlepiece in the smoking room was a painting I had done as a commission for Lord Pirrie of Harland and Wolff of Belfast, who had built her. The subject of the picture was Plymouth Harbour. There was a companion picture of mine in the SS Olympic of New York Harbour. Both were made from sketches drawn in the respective harbours. And so on April 11th (sic) Titanic sailed for New York ... none of us had the slightest fear for her safety; she was the last word in modern efficiency and was said to be literally unsinkable.'

(From A Brush with Life, Norman Wilkinson, 1969.)

'*If we would all go to drill meals would not be ready for the passengers .... So many firemen, so many sailors, so many quartermasters and so many stewards were assigned to the lifeboats*'. **Edward Wheelton, a first class steward. (US Enq)**

In charge was Officer **Harold Lowe**,

'*We were lowered down in the boats with a boat's crew. The boats were manned and we rowed around a couple of turns, and then came back and were hoisted up and had breakfast and then went about our duties.*' **(US Enq)**

Some of the stokers were free to go back on shore before returning by noon. Board of Trade clearance certificates, signed by Captain Smith were now handed by him to Captain Steele, White Star's Marine Superintendent, and Captain Clarke of the Board of Trade.

So many visitors, so many last touches. Steward Arthur Paintin had hoped to post a letter to his parents before leaving Southampton, but as he wrote a few hours later, *'There did not seem time for anything.'*

Mrs Smith and her daughter boarded the ship briefly, visiting the bridge before leaving again. The Ismay family toured the ship before saying goodbye to Bruce Ismay and returning to the quay to wave as the ship left.

PASSENGERS AND LOCAL PASSENGERS

The boat train carrying second and third class passengers had arrived from Waterloo alongside the White Star Dock at 9.30. Passing through the new shed, and clearing immigration formalities (and medical checks for third class passengers) they boarded the liner and were directed to their cabins by the stewards. The second class purser's clerk reassured passenger Mrs Becker, fretful at the new untried status of a ship on its maiden voyage.

'You don't have to be afraid at all. If anything should happen to this ship the watertight compartments would keep it afloat until we did get help.'
(Titanic Commutator and Titanic Historical Society, Indian Orchard, Mass., USA 01151)

A deck hand carrying up luggage was asked by second class passenger Mrs Albert Caldwell *'Is this ship really non-sinkable?' 'Yes, lady',* he answered. *'God himself could not sink this ship.'*
(W. Lord, A Night to Remember)

All these passengers needed much more time to be handled than those first class passengers on their own boat train which arrived as late as 11.30am, following a slight delay on the line.

Some of the press caught W.T. Stead, the famous journalist, social reformer and spiritualist, and he told them he had not intended making the trip, but President Taft had asked him to speak at the World Peace Conference at Carnegie Hall.

Although so many of the *Titanic's* passengers came from all over Britain, Europe, the United States and even Japan, most of them travelling down on the boat train from London, a few passengers came from the Southampton area or became connected with it.

Travelling in second class was *'Mr H.P. Hodges, the well known Southampton musical instrument dealer who was a passenger on the Titanic.'* **(Southampton Pictorial, 17th April)**.

His firm supplied music for the Harbour Board's events at Royal Pier. His business premises were 117 Above Bar with other branches (see advert and photograph of showroom in Southampton Pictorial, 24th

Advert for the return journey that never took place.

Southern Daily Echo

April 1912). He was to visit a relative in Boston. *'Little did I think when I saw Mr Hodges about 10 minutes to 12 on the morning of sailing it was the last occasion on which I would shake him by the hand. We talked about the Newtown Ward Association, and Mr Hodges showed he had its interest at heart.'*
(R.W. Jesson, Hants Advertiser, April 27, 1912)

Some of his stock was sold off soon afterwards (sale advert in Southampton Pictorial, September 18th 1912)

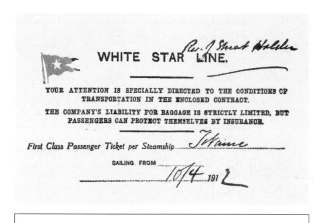

First class baggage ticket.

Merseyside Maritime Museum

Second class passengers Harvey Collyer, his wife Charlotte and their baby daughter Marjorie were recent residents (25, Church Road, Mount Hill) of Bishopstoke, near Southampton, now emigrating to the United States.

"The day before we were due to sail (our neighbours) made much of us, it seemed as if there must have been hundreds who called to bid us goodbye and in the afternoon members of the church arranged a surprise for my husband. They led him to a seat under the old tree in the churchyard and then some of them went up

Lawrence Beesley and a friend cycling in the gymnasium.

Father Francis M. Browne, S.J. Collection

into the belfry and, in his honour, they rang all the chimes that they knew. It took more than an hour and he was very pleased. Somehow it made me a little sad. They rang the solemn old chimes as well as the gay ones and to me it was too much of a farewell ceremony."

Charlotte Collyer (American semi-monthly magazine, 1912)

Also in second class was the Brown family who knew Southampton well as a port in their regular commutings between London and South Africa where they lived for many years. Their fifteen year old daughter Edith, who survived with her mother, spent much of her married life in Southampton and lives there today.

In third, the Dean family was connected with Woodlands (Mrs Dean's parents lived there). She would lose her husband in the *Titanic*, and returned with her two infant children to make a new life in Southampton. Her son Bert would marry Dorothy Sinclair, whose father had bought part of the H.P. Hodges business at the sale. The firm, Gale and Sinclair, would distribute *Titanic* memorial music sheets in aid of the *Titanic* fund.

"My father worked for a Mr Hodge... he went over to America on the Titanic and he was drowned... he had a piano shop and my father took it over. He bought it for a £1,000, that was the living accommodation and all, he used to sell sheet music for 3d... as the business got bigger he had a manager in Becketts of Southampton, that was our manager."

Dorothy Dean née Sinclair (City Heritage Oral History)

Some of the descendants of *Titanic* victim Samuel Hocking, travelling in second class, whose letter to his wife gives a vivid picture of being on the *Titanic*, would grow up in Southampton.

A large number of passengers from all classes joined some of the crew at Divine Service on Sunday 14th April, in the first class dining saloon, conducted by Captain Smith who used the White Star Line's own published prayer book.

The Daily Graphic's correspondent was in Southampton for the occasion and waxed lyrical about,

'The happy start. The air was busy with the clatter, with goodbye for the present and good wishes. We lived that morning in an atmosphere of pride ... we who had come to take temporary parting from dear ones and friends were shown a new and latest marvel in the Prom Deck – it was called the Café Parisien ... some of us looked at the suites ... the delicate glass and napery and the flowers and the fruit ... no one looked at the boats.'

Early passengers were also keen to explore,

'Between the time of going on board and sailing, I inspected in the company of two friends who had come from

Tugs *Hector* and *Neptune* at *Titanic*'s bow as *New York* is moved to a new berth.

Father Francis M. Browne, S.J. Collection

Exeter to see me off, the various decks, dining saloons and libraries, and so extensive were they that it is no exaggeration to say that it was quite easy to lose one's way in such a ship. We wandered casually into the gymnasium on the boat deck and were engaged in bicycle exercise when the instructor came in with two photographers and insisted on our remaining there while his friends as we thought at the time, made a record for him of his apparatus in use. It was only later that we discovered that they were the photographers of one of the illustrated London papers. More passengers came in, and the instructor (McCawley) ran here and there, looking the very picture of robust, rosy cheeked health, and 'fitness' in his white flannels, placing one passenger on the electric 'horse', another on the 'camel'. While the laughing group of onlookers watched the inexperienced riders vigorously shaken up and down as he controlled the little motor which made the machines imitate so realistically horse and camel exercise.'

Lawrence Beesley (The Loss of the SS Titanic)

"Just before sailing time I rushed aboard with the last of a consignment of new typewriters and delivered same to the Purser's Office. Realising that the Titanic was the last word in ocean travel, I took the opportunity of having a good look round.

I saw the beautiful swimming bath - which was something new to transatlantic liners - and I was soon caught up and entranced with the physical culture gymnasium. There I was invited to take exercise of various mechanical machines, electrically controlled. I had a camel ride, a cycle ride and a donkey ride. At the will of the instructor in charge I was subjected to all the inconveniences that can apply to the camel and the donkey and in the case of the cycle I was subjected to riding up steep gradients; all controlled from a switch.

Suddenly, I was switched out of the gymnasium and told hurriedly to leave the ship, as the whistles and bells had gone. I hurried along the companion ways, through the milling throng of passengers, not knowing which was port or starboard side. However, I eventually reached the gangway. The two officers and ABs had already loosened the ropes and a foot gap lay between the gangway and the side of the ship. Amid protestations on my part and vocabulary which was unprintable, the officers instructed the ABs to pull in the gangway. I ran down that gangway full speed, glad to reach terra firma. I had the feeling that I nearly sailed on the Titanic.

My task completed and also my little excursion, I walked to the end of the quay and watched the unsinkable

Titanic leaving Southampton April 10th 1912. *New York*'s bow projects from Dock Head. *Vulcan* is now taking off departing workers and officials.

Private Collection

E.L.P. Pearson and his cycling cups. Shirley, Southampton 1912.

Private Collection

mammoth liner glide past me and down Southampton water, until she became a mere speck on the horizon.

That is my memory of the Titanic just fifty years ago. I was sixteen years of age ..."

R.C. Lawrence, Freemantle. (Echo 17/04/1962)

At a late stage in the preparations, one sailor, Joe Mulholland, had a row with one of the Engineer Officers. *'I walked off the ship at Southampton just before she sailed'* he later told Bill MacQuitty, maker of the film 'A Night to Remember' (see Stage & Sound, 1957).

Among the crowds on the quay were six year old Bert Lester and his father, Mrs Lightoller and her two sons, Philip Moberley (who later served on the *Olympic* as an Officer) with his father, 15 year old E.L.P. Pearson on his bike.

"...I had the pleasure of going down to see the Titanic...from the dock, on her maiden voyage. That's the first time I ever seen the water.....bar the Floating Bridge. But, apart from that, to see the ships going out, that was a great delight of mine, you know..... ....I remember the tugs was... ...blowing their whistles and everything. It was quite a sight, very interesting. But little did I know I was going on the ships afterwards. Yeah, I went to sea at seventeen."

Albert Shute (City Heritage Oral History)

'Six of us left (the Grapes public house) *about 10 minutes to 12 and got well into the docks and towards the vessel. With me and my mate were three brothers named Slade (Bertram, Tom and Alfred). We were at the top of the main board and a passenger train was approaching us from another part of the docks. I heard the Slades say, Oh let the train go by,*

Titanic leaving with tugs.

Southampton City Heritage Collections

but Nutbean and myself crossed over and managed to board the liner. Being a rather long train, by the time it passed the Slades were too late, the gangway was down – leaving them behind,' (with a trimmer, Mr Penney, who lodged with the Slades.)
John Podesta (Southern Daily Echo)

There were also three brothers called Pugh in a similar last mad run – one turned back, but Alfred and Percy made it onto the ship.

Lawrence Beesley noticed

'Just before the last gangway was withdrawn, a knot of stokers ran along the quay with their kit slung over their shoulders in bundles and made for the gangway with the evident intention of joining the ship. But a Petty Officer guarding the shore end of the gangway firmly refused to allow them on board; they argued, gesticulated, apparently attempting to explain the reasons why they were late, but he remained obdurate and waived them back with a determined hand, the gangway was dragged back amid their protests, putting a summary ending to their determined efforts to join the Titanic.'

'12.00 noon. The order to "let go" is given.'
Joseph Scarrott

Finally, with pilot George Bowyer to guide her out, *Titanic* cast off, aided by the tugs and began to move away. *'She made an impressive picture as she quietly glided in brilliant sunshine down Southampton Water, quite dwarfing all the adjacent shipping'* said one journalist.

Salvation Army Bandmaster Buckingham from Marlow would later relate *'how he had witnessed the departure of the Titanic from Southampton and waved adieu to those on board the doomed ship.'*
(The War Cry, April 27, 1912)

'I saw the Titanic leave Southampton Dock from her berth and the Dock Head, on my cycle. I heard the band playing', remembered Edward 'Lance' Pearson, on Easter holiday from Hurstleigh School. He was soon to become apprenticed with the RMSP Co. following the failure of his father's agricultural engineering business in Shirley. At one time the firm had a contract to sell hay for the horses which drew Southampton's trams.

"My father was a motor man on the trams and he said, 'I'll pick you up this morning about 11 o'clock and take you to the Pier... he dropped me off at the end of High Street, where the Town Quay is today, where the Hythe boat used to run from, just on that corner. And I remember standing on those rails, 12 o'clock on Wednesday the 10th of April – 'cos White Star boats always sailed on a Wednesday midday, Cunard boats midday Saturdays. Well I remember seeing the Titanic coming out, swung round stern first – her stern up towards the town... The Pier before they straightened her off and away she went down the river. That was on a Wednesday. And I remember hearing on the following Monday morning that she'd sunk... I remember going home and saying to my father, 'I've just heard up the Post Office that the 'Titanic sunk' and he caught hold of me and shook me. He said, 'Don't you talk like that', he said, 'that boat's unsinkable!' but, of course, it was true."

Albert 'Ben' Benham (Lee Raymond Collection)

"I can remember, it hardly seems credible to me, but it stuck in my mind somehow, we walked down the end of Swift Road to look towards the Docks and watched the Titanic go out. I must have only been, I don't know whether I was three or just over two, but I suppose you can remember as long as that, for some reason that stuck in my mind a four funnel steamer going out, you know".

"I also well remember at eight-years-old watching the Titanic leave on her maiden voyage never to return. We were standing together on the shore outside Woodcock's boatyard at Millbrook. I and six children, the name of them; Wormald. There was Jackie, Joe, George and Fred and Mick, the other one I forget. They were saying: 'There goes Daddy's ship,' and waving their arms to the distant vessel.

He was a baker (sic) aboard the Titanic. His body was picked up out of the water by the vessel that warned the Titanic, the Carpathia.

The widow with her six children boarded the Olympic, a White Star vessel, shortly after the sinking of the Titanic and set out for Nova Scotia to see her husband's grave. She was, of course, turned back at Ellis Island and they all trooped home, six weeks after setting sail.

Her house had been in the meantime let. My parents had stored her furniture in one room until they came back to Southampton."

G.W. Eustace (Echo 4/05/1970)

THE NEW YORK INCIDENT

As the Titanic, pulled and pushed by the tugs Neptune, Hector, Vulcan, Hercules, Albert Edward, and Ajax, came out of the White Star dock, the waving crowds

The near collision with SS New York (swinging out from RMS Oceanic) Titanic immediately stops.

Peter Boyd-Smith, Cobwebs

The *Vulcan* has a line on the *New York* while *Titanic* drifts safely astern. *Hercules* is towing *New York* to Dock Head.

Private Collection

Collision averted, *New York* moved to dock head. *Titanic* resumes her departure from Southampton.

Peter Boyd-Smith, Cobwebs

SS *New York* is towed to safety at dock head. Crowds watch and look up at the *Titanic*. *Oceanic*'s bow is on the left.

Photo by Miss May, First Class passenger on the *Titanic*. Private collection

began to run down towards the Ocean Quays and to Dock Head. The tugs turned her to point into Southampton Water.

'She had got underway beautifully. It is doubtful whether the Olympic has ever cleared the new dock in such a splendid manner as the Titanic on this occasion.'

'A few of the people standing by began to move homeward some of them being heard to make exclamations of surprise at the ease with which a 46,000 ton steamer could be shaped for the sea.'
(Southampton Times and Hampshire Express)

'The Titanic moved slowly down the Dock, to the accompaniment of last messages and shouted farewells of those on the quay. There was no cheering or hooting of steamer whistles from the fleet of ships that lined the dock … the whole scene was quiet and rather ordinary. The Titanic, which had just begun to move her propellers, moved majestically down the dock, the crowd of friends keeping pace with us along the quay.'
Lawrence Beesley

'The liner was pulled out of her berth soon after twelve o'clock towards what we call "the swinging ground" off the dock head. I was still on deck and heard the telegraphs ring up to start up engines. In berth 38 off the dock head, there were two liners moored abreast to each other. While the Titanic's engines were in motion the ropes of the two ships snapped like cotton and they drifted from the wall. That is a thing I never saw before, or after (and I kept sea going until 1923 when I packed up altogether).'
John Podesta (Echo)

When the liner passed the laid up *Oceanic* and *New York*, at berth 38, tied alongside each other (an old system still in use in the late 1960's when Cunard liners were laid up at berth 101, or as in the Seamens' Strike of 1966) the force of the water displaced by the *Titanic's* underwater hull pushed under the laid up ships. Churned by the *Titanic's* propellers, it caused the *New York* to break her moorings with a loud snap and swing out towards the *Titanic* and it seemed a collision. The ropes snapped 'as easily as a grocer snaps a piece of twine with his fingers'.
(Southampton Times and Hampshire Express)

'*There came a series of reports like those of a revolver
and in the quayside of the New York snaky coils of thick rope
flung themselves high in the air and fell backwards among the
crowd, which retreated in alarm to escape the flying ropes. We
hoped that no one was struck but a sailor next to me was certain
he saw a woman carried away to receive attention. And then, to
our amazement, the New York crept towards us, slowly and
stealthily. There was shouting of orders, sailors running to and
fro, paying out ropes and putting mats over the side where it
seemed likely we should collide.*'
Lawrence Beesley

Captain Smith immediately stilled the *Titanic's*
propellers, while the tugs *Vulcan* and *Hercules* swiftly
intervened. Among the many accounts (see Woolner,
Beesley, Gracie, Haismann, Hart, Lenox Conyingham)
given of this, one of the most knowledgeable was given
by Captain Gale of the *Vulcan*.

'*I assisted the Titanic out of the new dock in the first
place and had hold of her aft. We let go by the starboard quarter*

Titanic off Hythe.   '*Passing ships seem to sail right across the grass.*' Degna Marconi.

Titanic proceeds down Southampton Water.

Southampton City Heritage Collections

and dropped astern in order to get alongside and pick up a number of workmen who were about to leave the Titanic. I sung out to the Officer of the liner and he told me to go to the port side. When I got to the port side we followed up behind the liner whose port engine was working astern all the time. The Titanic was drawing about 35 feet of water. There was a young flood and she was near the ground. As soon as she got abreast of the New York, the latter's ropes began to go. It may have been due to the backwash of the liner, on the pressure of the water, but all her ropes gave way and she began to move. Someone sang out to me to get up and push the New York back, but such a thing was impossible. Had I got between the two ships we would almost certainly have been jammed and goodness knows what might have happened, but instead of that I turned the Vulcan round and got a wire rope on the port quarter of the New York.

Unfortunately, that rope parted but our men immediately got a second wire on board and we got hold of the New York when she was within four feet of the Titanic. Had the New York touched the outward bound liner she would have hit her abreast of the after funnel. The Titanic stood a chance of fouling the starboard screw of the New York and of knocking in the latter's starboard quarter, but the American Line steamer was

checked just in time and we got her clear of the Titanic.'

Captain Gale added that it was one of the closest things he had seen for a long time … the broken ropes of the *New York* were lying in the water and the tug might easily have picked them up on her propellers and been rendered helpless. *'It was a narrow squeak'*. The *Vulcan* was no stranger to collisions having witnessed one between RMSP Co's *Atrato* and the paddle steamer *Princess Beatrice* in Outer Dock in 1897.

As seen from the *New York*

'An unusual number of sightseers had assembled on the quays … and some who were anxious to get a better view climbed the gangway of the Oceanic whence they joined the decks of the American liner New York which was moored alongside.'

'At once all was in a state of commotion, and it seemed inevitable that a collision must occur. Vast crowds of people, including many photographers and police officers, could be seen on the quay sides.'

'The over ambitious sightseers were however unable to land until the New York was again moored alongside the

Oceanic. A hastily constructed gangway was then thrown across, and the 'enforced voyagers' were glad to regain 'terra firma'.'
(Southampton Times and Hants Express)

On *Titanic*, Harland & Wolff electricians George Ervine and Alfred Middleton *'were on the top of the after funnel, so we saw everything quite distinctly. I thought there was going to be a proper smash because of the high wind, but I don't think anyone was hurt.'*
(Letter published in Eaton & Haas, Triumph & Tragedy)

Chief Engineer Bell wrote *'No one was hurt, but it looked like trouble at the time.'*

Titanic's crew were astonished by the *New York* incident. Joseph Scarrott still unhappy: *'I said to a chum of mine "I am going to get my bag and if the New York drops alongside I'm going on this one", but I didn't get the chance as she did not come close enough.'*

'Perhaps another warning' thought Steward Arthur Lewis.

The *Titanic* headed down Southampton Water past Hythe (where a member of the Malet family photographed her, perhaps from the Westcliffe Hall Hotel, or Mount House) and Fawley, where two waiting spectators had a special connection with the ship.

Beatrice and Degna Marconi were the wife and daughter of Guglielmo Marconi, the Italian developer of radio at sea, in use since 1899 on the American Line but first earning world acclaim in 1909, when White Star Line's *Republic* sank after a collision with the *Florida*. All her passengers and crew were rescued following the swift arrival of the wireless alerted *Baltic*.

Henceforth Marconi's system was adopted on most steamships, including *Olympic* and *Titanic*.

Following an accident and eye operation, and partly to alleviate domestic stress resulting from his busy public life, Marconi was advised to live for a while in the English countryside.

'Mother accordingly found, rented and furnished a romantic, if impractical, house looking across Southampton Water, Eaglehurst at Fawley. One of those wonderful lawns only to be found in England lay like a carpet between house and shoreline. From the French windows passing ships seemed to sail right across the grass.

What we youngsters enjoyed about Eaglehurst, beside our pony cart and the sheltered pebbly beach, was the tower. This was a curious and entertaining eighteenth century architectural folly. Father came home so seldom, and when he did, spent so much time in the laboratory he had set up in the tower.

The tower stood on the lawn above the water's edge and my mother climbed up it with me on the morning of April 10, 1912 to watch the Titanic sail by. I was only three and a half years old, and yet I still recall how tight she held my hand and I sensed that she was sad. When I was older I knew why. She wished she were on board.*

She and Father were invited by the White Star Line to be guests on the maiden voyage of the Titanic but their plans went awry. Father switched his passage to the Lusitania. Mother expected to follow on the Titanic. Then Giulio (Degna's brother) spoiled everything by coming down with one of those alarming baby fevers.

Together we waved at the ship, huge and resplendent in the spring sunlight, and dozens of handkerchiefs and scarves were waved back at us. As the Titanic passed from our view over the calm water we slowly descended the steps. It was a long way down.'
Degna Marconi ('My Father Marconi')

OMENS

'The night before sailing I asked my wife to put my White Star in my cap and while she was doing it, the star fell all to pieces. With a look of dismay she said, I don't like this.'
Steward Arthur Lewis (Echo)

'You may not believe in dreams, but Mrs Slade I am telling you the truth when I say that one of my boys had a dream about the boat the night before sailing day and he afterwards said he had a dread of her. I knew they were not very keen on going, but nevertheless they went down.'
(Conversation reported in Soton Times 20.4.1912.)

"My father was so excited about it and my mother was so upset … The first time in my life I saw her crying … she was so desperately unhappy about the prospect of going, she had this premonition, a most unusual thing for her …"

"We went on the day on the boat train … I was 7, I had never seen a ship before … it looked very big … everybody was very excited, we went down to the cabin and that's when my mother said to my father that she had made up her mind quite firmly that she would not go to bed in that ship, she would sit up at night … she decided that she wouldn't go to bed at night, and she didn't."
Eva Hart (City Heritage Oral History)

"My father, when we arrived, he went straight away to book our passage and when he got there he wanted first class but it was full up so they said they only had three berths of the second class for us so we took the three berths and that's how we managed to get on the Titanic".

"Then we went up the gangway and then my father took the bag like, you know, so my mother turned round and asked if he was ill and he said no he was quite all right. Because he had a presentiment before he left South Africa, but he wouldn't tell my mother what it was and of course when we got our cabin we took all our things off and put them there, then we went up on deck and saw the people, you know, looking over the Titanic".

"On sailing day it was really, well everybody was so happy and saying goodbye to everyone, you know, we had nobody to say goodbye to coz we said goodbye in South Africa you see, but , because then there was a boat called the New York and she nearly went into the Titanic..... ..... My father said, when he saw that, he said that's a bad omen"

Edith Haisman née Brown (City Heritage Oral History)

"We were let out of school for the half day to see her, I lived in Woolston and that's where we could see the docks from where we were standing. Teacher was in control of us and we watched the Titanic come out so far and then there was a delay and it was drawn back in again to the wharf and so we waited and waited and finally they started again and that time she went down out of sight in the Southampton waters and that was the last we saw of her."

Q. I understand you figured it was bad luck when it backed up...?

A. "Well, that's what an old gentleman mentioned alongside me, that it was, that was a sign of bad luck, let's hope not he said."

Mrs Lois Jacobs, née Brown (City Heritage Oral History)

"He always took a little revolver, only a small thing, always beautifully oiled in a little box. He took it on all his voyages to protect himself abroad, but this particular time he told my grandmother to keep it because he wouldn't be needing it on this voyage and my grandmother felt it was an omen. She used to keep it locked in her trunk and when the Second World War broke out she took it to the police station when the call went out for firearms."

Mrs Jean Fagin, grand-daughter of Jack Stagg (City Heritage Oral History)

"Mother would never go and see my father off and this particular day she went and she always swore that that was the most unlucky thing that she ever did".

Mrs Molly Adams, daughter of John Stewart, Verandah Café steward. (City Heritage Oral History)

"Although only a kiddie coming up to eight years old when the Titanic sailed from Southampton, I well remember that day. My father and his brother were both on her and both were lost. It was the only time my mother had gone down to the docks to see my father off, as he always said it was reckoned to be unlucky in the sailor's world.

Apart from our own personal tragedy, two things stick out in my mind during this period. The first was at the dockside - while watching the Titanic start to move, my mother started to cry. On asking her why, she replied: 'That boat will never reach New York, dear.'

I can still see the people round us and hear their remarks about a 'silly woman.'

The second thing was a few days later when after a day or two, waiting to hear if my dad and his brothers' names were on the survivor lists, my mother at breakfast said: 'Your father will not be coming home any more children; in this morning's paper it says there are some children lost and your father would never leave a child behind, no matter what happened.' That to me seems to have been a wonderful thing for a wife to say of her husband."

W.A. Hawkesworth, (Echo May 1970)

"When the Titanic sank, I was a small child. My father had been posted to the Olympic, bitterly disappointed because all his friends were to sail on the Titanic. They were all lost in the disaster.

On April 14, a large picture in our home descended to the floor with a crash. In those days among the wives of sea going men this was believed to be an ill omen. My mother's remark was 'My goodness a ship will go down tomorrow' never thinking of the Titanic which was considered to be unsinkable.

The memory stays in my mind, as does that of the Echo boys running through the streets at mid-day calling 'Titanic sunk....Titanic sunk."

C.L. Daughtrey (Echo Dec 1970)

"On Sunday night, at about the hour when disaster befell the liner, Mrs Gatti had a strange presentiment of danger and throughout the night she was unable to sleep. This feeling had such an effect upon her that the next morning she came to London and remained with a sister. Mr Gatti held a similar position (Restaurant Manager) on the Olympic at the time of her collision with the Hawke, to that he occupied on the Titanic."

(Daily Mirror 19th April 1912)

'I once asked my grandmother why my grandfather was not on the Titanic. She told me he was to have been, but had very serious pneumonia so was at home. She then added that on the night of the Titanic disaster, he suddenly came out of the coma and said:
"Bruce is in trouble, Bruce is in trouble."

A grandchild of James Ismay. (His grandfather was Bruce's younger brother.)

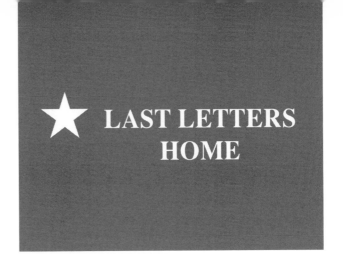

★ LAST LETTERS
HOME

"My dear little treasures"

CHERBOURG 10.4.1912.

"Our first port of call was Cherbourg and before we arrived there I had resigned myself to the inevitable and had settled down to my proper routine. After embarking continental passengers and mails we left for Queenstown which was our last call before crossing the Atlantic which we hoped to do at record speed."

(J Scarrott, Pier Review No 8. 'The sailing of the Titanic').

From Southampton the *Titanic* steamed to Cherbourg, where she arrived an hour late at 6.30 pm because of the New York incident. Among the 22 cross channel passengers leaving here was 11 year old Eileen Lenox-Conyngham, who had whiled away part of the crossing writing this letter to her nanny, Louisa Sterling.

The voyage was to be a special treat for Eileen and her brother Denis, 10. *"We were going on holiday in France with my mother and Aunt Alice. We were all of us very bad sailors. Mother wanted the largest, safest, steadiest ship afloat. She chose the Titanic".*

On board RMS Titanic
Wednesday 10 April 1912

Dear Lusia

The Titanic is the biggest ship in the world there is a swimming bath a gymnation Turkish baths in it. the ship started at about 12.15 then we had a long delay because this ship broke the ropes of another ship the Oceanic as it went flotting about and knocked into this ship but they got it allright after a bit. This is the first long voyage the Titanic has ever made, it is quite calm.

Yesterday we went in a boat on the river Denis and I rowed a lot, yesterday morning we motored to the sea. Last Monday Denis went out fishing with a little boy, Denis did not catch anything but found an eel which we had for breakfast the next day.

It is quite calm now nobody has been sick so far. We should arrive in Cherbourg at five but I do not think we will get there till six.

Please write soon to me

Love from Eileen

(Private Collection)

"I was born in Edinburgh July 11th 1900. My father was a classical scholar, teaching at Fettes College, there were four of us. I was the second, my sister was older than I was, and then a brother (Denis) the one who came with me on the Titanic, was very close in age and then a much younger brother who was still a child, a baby then and so the letter that I wrote to Louisa, she had been my nurse and she now was a nurse of my younger brother Alwyn. We were very very fond of her.

My grandmother, my father's mother, lived in Ireland, in Northern Ireland, and then later when her husband died she went to live in Dublin. We used to go every year and visit her and all the family, my father was one of eleven children who grew up and they were scattered around the world but they would gather when they could in the summer at a seaside place to be near my grandmother and of course going across all four of us were frightfully bad sailors and were always seasick the moment we got on board. That was one of the reasons we went on the Titanic, my mother thought if she took us on something as big as the Titanic we wouldn't feel the channel's waves and of course we didn't and the second reason more important was it was one of the wonder ships of the world and she thought it would be a marvellous experience for us.

Titanic in Southampton Docks, April 10th 1912.

Southampton City Heritage Collections

Letter from Eileen Lenox-Conyngham to her nursemaid Louisa.

Private Collection

They decided that year that two should go with my father to visit my grandmother and the other two should go with my mother to France and my father's youngest sister came too, so we were a party of four. She thought we would learn some French and study architecture.

We travelled by train and went to stay with my godmother a Miss Burrell who had a house, (Fairthorne Manor, at Botley) near Southampton and we stayed with her. She had a car and she sent us in to Southampton...

And then we went in the morning to Southampton and we were absolutely staggered at how enormous the Titanic was because we'd been used to the small cross channel boats, and her size and the beauty of her lines she was absolutely lovely! Unbelievably lovely!! I just remember the sight of her when we came on board. Just the enormous size and the beauty of the lines and then we were able to go all over the ship ... and we had I remember a lovely luncheon in the dining room with its arched staircase and things.

We had lunch and tea on board and then when we got to Cherbourg the tender came out because of course she couldn't dock at Cherbourg or at Queenstown and so a tender came out with the Americans who had been touring in France and the French people who were going over to New York and then the tender that brought the Americans and the French on board took us on shore.

It was so lovely, all the fittings were so lovely ... the glass and the china and the flowers, everything was brand new.

We just walked around you see ... we didn't have a cabin because we weren't sleeping on board. It was only a four hour crossing and we wandered round the ship. We had seats to sit on deck and we watched when we were going off when it went into another ship.

After we had lunch we were both very excited. My mother, to calm us down, said 'You can sit down and write letters', and so of course we wrote letters and postcards to people and this is the only thing that has survived, just by chance that Louisa kept the letter.

Oh, there was a writing room.

We went to the different desks and sat.

I remember vaguely the enormous dining room and of course it was all very exciting for us because in those days children led a very nursery life we didn't have our meals with our parents we had them in the school or the nursery and it was generally very plain food milk puddings and rather dull things like that ...and so it was very exciting to have this elaborate food offered us.

We saw a Turkish bath, we didn't have one ...there was a swimming pool but it wasn't filled ...they never fill it till they get right out at sea because the water's too dirty ... so we saw the swimming pool we saw the Turkish Baths we played with the gymnasium things.

I remember watching the tender coming up from Cherbourg and then climbing into it and then we stood and we watched the Titanic sail out. We stayed that night in a small hotel at Cherbourg because we were not going to Paris. We went to Paris eventually. We went first to Bayeaux and saw the tapestries there and I remember we went to Châtres to see the cathedral and then we got to Paris and it was in Paris that we heard about the sinking.

Titanic Gymnasium

Harland and Wolff

It was quite a shock to think that the lovely ship had been lost because it was so beautiful. But we didn't realise at first there had been this loss of life. We took it that they had been picked up and put into lifeboats and things and then gradually it came out that there was this fearful loss of life.

When we were walking out we saw this poster which said 'Blesse au mort le Roi des vessaux' and we said 'That can't be the Titanic' but of course it was.

Eileen Schefer (City Heritage Oral History)

274 Passengers boarded at Cherbourg by the White Star Line's new tenders *Nomadic* and *Traffic* specially built at Belfast in 1911; 42 first class passengers like Denver millionairess, Mrs J J Brown, the Ryerson family, Ben Guggenheim, couturier "Lucile" (Lady Duff Gordon, and her husband, Sir Cosmo), Edith Russell (Rosenbaum), a fashion correspondent and buyer for a clothes store, 30 second class passengers and 102 continental, in fact Syrian Armenian, middle Eastern and Croatian emigrants. The crew had to see them all safely on board the ship from the tender. As Edith Russell noted

'the gang-plank was held down by ten men on either side, as it shook and swayed and pulled in every direction.'

Thomas Andrews wrote this note to his wife in Ireland from Cherbourg.

'We reached here in nice time and took on board quite a number of passengers. The two little tenders looked well, you will remember we built them about a year ago. We expect to arrive at Queenstown about 10.30 am tomorrow. The weather is fine and everything shaping for a good voyage. I have a seat at the Doctor's table.'

(From 'Thomas Andrews, Shipbuilders' by Shan Bullock, 1912.)

More mail was posted and taken off the ship and other bags taken on. At 8.10 pm the *Titanic* set sail, a superb sight, by now lit up against a dark Spring night as she headed for Ireland and Queenstown.

Bedroom Steward George Beedem wrote this letter to his wife and son and posted it at Queenstown on 11th April 1912. He did not survive the disaster.

On board RMS Titanic
Thursday morning
My dear little treasures
Just for a bit of luck I am on watch from 12 to 4. I received your letter and am very glad you are going to the hospital, the lump is bound to hurt with the iodine, perhaps it might be drawing gradually to a head, let's hope so.

We have a more decent crowd on board this time although no so many. There is a lot to come on at Queenstown I think, the more the merrier. If you are not well enough don't come down this time but be sure and let me know at Plymouth. As we left today the American boat New York broke her moorings and drifted right across our bows, missed the Oceanic by about a foot. We had to reverse engines sharp and one of our tugs went and got her under control before any damage was done. Anyhow, it was a narrow squeak for all of us.

We have a lot of new faces this time everywhere on the boat. I have just had a shave etc and shall be glad when 4 o/c comes and I turn in till about 7.30. Now I don't know what to write about only my chest is not so sore today. I did not go to Mother's although I should have liked to: now I'll finish, don't forget, don't come down if you don't feel well enough, it would only be a waste of time and would not do you any good whatever.

Now tata, glad you liked the pictures and I suppose those chocolate eggs have all disappeared down that great big hole.

With fondest love to both of you.

Dada

I suppose you got the hospital ticket?

(Private collection, via British *Titanic* Society)

"All the White Star boats and Cunard liners outward bound called here to pick up mails and passengers by tender and it was the custom for we firemen and trimmers to go up on deck and carry the mail from the tender to the mail room. A fireman whom I knew very well (John Coffee) - I was in the S.S. Oceanic and Adriatic with him - said to me, 'Jack, I'm going down to this tender to see my mother'. He asked me if anyone was looking and I said no and bid him good luck. A few seconds later he was gone! (Coffee hid under mail bags in the returning tender, arriving safely in Queenstown undetected.)"

John Podesta (Echo)

As John Podesta said, Queenstown was the traditional last call, principally for emigrants and mails before crossing the Atlantic, originally coming down from Liverpool. The call was maintained after the move to Southampton, but White Star's Southampton liners returning home called at Plymouth instead of Queenstown.

Titanic arrived at 11.30 am, having come up St George's Channel, passing Daunt's Rock Light Vessel and anchored two miles off Roche's Point. 113 Third class passengers and Irish emigrants, 7 second class passengers and 1385 sacks of mail were transported on the tenders America and Ireland. 7 passengers including

Thomas Andrews, a managing director of Harland and Wolff. He drowned in the disaster.

Ulster Folk and Transport Museum

the future Father Brown, celebrated for his photos of the *Titanic* during that first part of her voyage, along with the Mays and Odells, left on the same tender as John Coffee deserting. Immigration Officer E.J. Sharpe certified the number of passengers aboard. '*At least this lot spoke English*' recalled another seaman.

The very last letters posted on board by passengers and crew of the *Titanic* before continuing the voyage were landed here and would arrive at their destinations some while before news of the *Titanic's* sinking followed. Those letters that have survived in the hands of descendants or collectors are our last poignant link with those who were lost, although in some cases they are records of lives of survivors, in which the *Titanic* was but one experience.

This letter was written by first class bedroom steward Richard Geddes to his wife Sarah Ann at their home in Grove Road, Freemantle. Richard did not survive.

Above: Sarah Ann Geddes. *Below:* Richard Charles Geddes.

Private Collection

On board RMS Titanic

My dearest Sal

We got away yesterday after a lot of trouble. As we were passing the New York and Oceanic the New York broke her ropes and very nearly ran into us but we just happened to avoid a collision. I could see visions of Belfast it must have been a trying time for the Captain.

Well sweetheart there is none of us got much of a show and there won't be much made on the outward journey but it wont matter as long as we get something good on the homeward one. well it cannot be helped we might be luckier next trip, now I hope you are feeling good and not worrying, because I think you needn't. how is my little sweetheart getting along I guess she misses me a wee bit, what do you think;

This ship is going to be a good deal better than the Olympic at least I think so, steadier and everything up till now.

If we get in on time on Wednesday and there happens to be a boat I will write from New York but you see if there isn't it will come by ours and that won't be any good.

I will drop a letter card to… you had better write too. I will close now dear I haven't any news. I am feeling pretty good.

With fondest love and kisses to my dear wife and kiddies.

Your affectionate husband Dick xxxxx

(Private Collection)

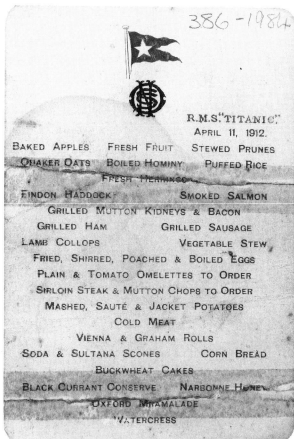

Southampton City Heritage Collections

Another crew member who did not survive was Edward Hendy, a dining room steward, who pencilled a hurried note to his wife Sophia in Southampton on a used breakfast menu card. (see left)

Queenstown, April 11, 1912.

Dearest,

We got away all right at last.

We thought there was going to be a collision when the New York broke all her ropes as we were passing her (in Southampton Docks) suction from this ship. But everything went off all right, I'm glad to say. I'm feeling pretty good and hope you are; also the dear little ones.

Heaps of love xxx from your loving hubby Ted.

(City Heritage Collections)

Second class passenger Harvey Collyer wrote this letter to his parents in Surrey. Travelling with his wife Charlotte and daughter Marjorie, they were emigrating to America to buy a fruit farm, partly also for a better climate for Charlotte who had consumption. They had been living in Bishopstoke, Hampshire where Harvey ran a grocery store.

Titanic April 11th

My dear Mum and Dad

It don't seem possible we are out on the briny writing to you. Well dears so far we are having a delightful trip the weather is beautiful and the ship magnificent. We can't describe the tables it's like a floating town. I can tell you we do swank we shall miss it on the trains as we go third on them. You would not imagine you were on a ship. There is hardly any motion she is so large we have not felt sick yet we expect to get to Queenstown today so thought I would drop this with the mails. We had a fine send off from Southampton and Mrs S and the boys with others saw us off. We will post again at New York then when we get to Payette.

Lots of love don't worry about us. Ever your loving children Harvey & Lot & Madge.

(Private Collection)

Due to a shortage of crew bedroom steward Fred Simmons was transferred from the *Oceanic* at the last minute. He wrote this letter to his wife at Staple Terrace, Millbrook, Southampton. Fred did not survive and left a young wife and five month old son.

On board RMS Titanic, Queenstown

Just a line in great haste to let you know I am feeling fine and rather pleased with the ship. Of course I don't know if I shall have a show or not but I hope to. How are you going on I hope you and baby are keeping very well. I expect I shall be comfortable here. When you write please address F.C. Simmons as there are two more of that name in the ship. Well darling I have no more to say now as I am in a hurry, love to all at home and heaps of it and kisses for you and Teddy.

From your everloving husband Fred.

(Private Collection)

Winifred Simmons with her son Edward.

Private Collection

Fred Simmons, c1910.

Private Collection

Captain Smith's steward Arthur Paintin, who was also lost, wrote to his parents in Oxford.

Arthur Paintin, steward to Captain Smith.

Private Collection

On board RMS Titanic, Queenstown 11/4/1912.
My dear Mother and Father
Many thanks for your nice long letter this morning received before leaving. I intended writing before we left, but there did not seem time for anything. I cannot realise that I had ten days at home, and am very sorry I could not get to Oxford, for we have now commenced the quick voyages all the summer (bar accidents). I say that because the Olympic's bad luck seems to have followed us, for as we came out of dock this morning we passed quite close to the 'Oceanic' and 'New York' which were tied up in the 'Adriatics' old berth, and whether it was suction or what it was I don't know, but the 'New York's' ropes snapped like a piece of cotton and she drifted against us. There was great excitement for some time, but I don't think there was any damage done bar one or two people knocked over by the ropes.
Now as regards the Hearts of Oak, I should like to join if you will tell me how to get about joining, and I will do so at once. I have been in a stewards club since last August and the benefits start after 12 months.
Please let me know how to set about the Hearts of Oak if you are not too busy with the Thames St affairs, what an awful business it must be settling everything. I hope it will turn out better than you expect.

My cold is still pretty bad, but nothing like it was last week. We spent Easter very quietly for Henry could not get away.
I hope the cyclists had a good time of it, and I hope Mr Barker made a good impression.
Bai jove what a fine ship this is, much better than the Olympic as far as passengers are concerned, but my little room is nothing near so nice, no daylight, electric light on all day, but I suppose it's no use grumbling. I hope to make up a bit for last voyage for I saved nothing to think of.
I wonder if I shall see Nellie before she leaves home, I think you had better bring her down to Southampton for a day or two while we are there, for I don't see any chance of getting away. Do you think she has enough money to go on with? If not, let her have some from Elsie's account, for no doubt she wants a lot of extra things. Alice was very pleased with book and I told her to return it when she has finished.
Now I think I must say au revoir once again.
With best love to all from
Your ever loving son Arthur
(Private Collection)

A letter written by Samuel James Metcalfe Hocking, second class passenger. He did not survive.

On board RMS Titanic April 11 1912.
My Dear Ada
Just a few lines as I hear we are calling for passengers at Queenstown, Ireland and they will also take letters and we are just off there now. 7.30am. It is a lovely morning with a high wind but no heavy seas, in fact it has been like a millpond so far but I expect we shall get it a bit stiffer in the Bay of Biscay if this wind continues. This will be the ship for you, you can hardly realise you are on board except for the jolting of the engines that is why it is such bad writing. I am longing already for you to have a trip. I wish it had been possible for us to all come together, it would have been a treat. I have fallen in with a young couple from Liskeard named Chapman. He has been home for 6 months holiday and got married and they are now going out together. He like myself worked for his father but could not get on with him, so I am pleased I have met someone nice, in fact you don't meet anyone rough second class. I have a bunk to myself which is pretty lonely but still I would rather be alone than have a foreigner who I could not talk to. There are two beds in a bunk and a couch so when you come out, and I hope it will not be long, you will be able to manage with the two children splendid. I hope you are keeping all right, also the kiddies. I suppose they ask for me? You must get out a good bit and the time will pass quicker. Tell Penn his fags are my only comfort and I am smoking a few! Write me a few lines to 98 Liberty Street, Middletown, Conn., USA and I shall get it when I get there.
I turned in at 10 o'clock last night but could get no sleep owing to the rattle of water bottles, glasses and other things too numerous to mention, so I was glad to get up at 6 o'clock, but I suppose I shall soon get used to it.

Don't forget to address letters J. Hocking c/o Mr. I. Hocking. Now dear Ada I must draw to a close as we are getting pretty close to Queenstown and I am afraid of missing the post, so with heaps of kisses to you and the children, and best respects to Mabel and all at home.
I am your ever loving husband
Jim.
xxxxxxxxxxx x
divide these between the three.
Everybody tells me I shall not regret the step I have taken so buck up and we shan't be long.
(Private Collection)

Saloon Steward Jack Stagg, another crew victim, posted this letter to his wife at Queenstown.

> *On board RMS Titanic*
> *Queenstown, 1912*
> *Dear Beatie*
> *Just a few lines to let you know I arrived on board all right, but what a day we have had of it, it's been nothing but work all day long, but I can tell you nothing as regards what people I have for nothing will be settled untill (sic) we leave Queenstown tomorrow, anyway we have only 317 first, and if I should be lucky enough to get a table at all it won't possibly be more than two that I shall have, still one must not grumble for there will be plenty without any.*
> *I expect you will have heard about the New York breaking away from her moorings through the suction of our ship it look (sic) as though there was going to be another collision but happily the tugs got hold of her in time. Now darling you must excuse this short note for it's getting late and we have to be up again by 4.30 in the morning and I expect there will be another rosy time with stores and baggage of course I don't find any ship so bad excepting the food and that we have to scramble for like a lot of mad men but that won't last for long when things get straightened out a bit.*
> *Well goodnight dear, and mind you don't spend all your money. I hope Mrs Hack will soon be well enough to relieve you of your Charges so that you may have plenty of room to sleep at night.*
> *Love to all xxxxxx Jack*
> *I made sixpence today. What luck.*
(City Heritage Collections)

This card was send by Ettie Dean to her mother, Mrs G. Light, at Bartley Farm, Netley Marsh, Southampton.

Jack Stagg and his wife Beatrice at the time of their marriage.

Private Collection

White Star Liner "Titanic."

Front of postcard sent by Ettie Dean to her mother.

Ken Marschall Collection

Dear Mother
Just a card to say we are enjoying ourselves fine up to now.
Little baby was very restless. With best love, Ettie.
(Ken Marschall Collection)

Posted at Queenstown, and received by Mr Hector Young, secretary of the Newtown Conservative Association. The writer, Mr H.P. Hodges, was a second-class passenger.

"We've had a fine time up to now. You don't notice anything of the movement of the ship. OK on top deck there are twenty boys marching round and singing. Others are playing cards and dominoes; some reading and some writing. Everything is quite different to what we thought to see at sea."
(City Heritage Collections)

Mr. H.P. Hodges, the well known Southampton musical instrument dealer.

Southampton Pictorial

BOATS WHICH RESCUED SOME OF THE PASSENGERS—SEEN TO THE LEFT OF PROMENADE DECK

From left: Elsie Doling, her sister-in-law Ada Julia Doling, with Frederick Wheeler, valet to Alfred Vanderbilt, Queenstown. Both women survived but Frederick was lost. Elsie's father ran the emigrants home in Albert Road, Southampton.

Daily Mirror

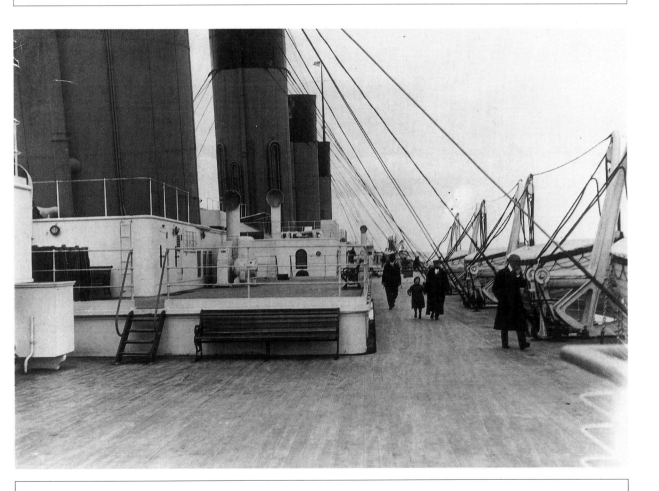

Titanic at Queenstown. Second class passengers on the boat deck.

Cork Examiner/Southampton City Heritage Collections

Saloon Steward E.A. Stroud of 167 Shirley Road did not survive, nor did his relative A. Stroud.

SS Titanic, Queenstown.
Dear Ma
Just a line hoping all are quite well. Having pretty easy time. Five ladies and eight kids.
From your loving son, Ted.
Mrs E. Stroud, 120 Malmesbury Road, Shirley, Southampton, England.
(Private Collection)

The *Titanic* raised anchor at 1.30 pm, Officers Murdoch Boxhall and Lightoller, with three able seamen, closed the gangway door and set sail, turning round and heading out towards the Atlantic, leaving behind her very last sight of land. She had 2,208 passengers and crew on board, settling down for the normal routine of the Atlantic crossing.

'*I still don't like this ship....I have a queer feeling about it.*' Chief Officer Wilde in a letter to his sister posted from Queenstown.

First Officer Murdoch and Second Officer Lightoller with other members of the crew. Photographed from the tender at Queenstown, April 11, 1912.

Cork Examiner/Southampton City Heritage Collections

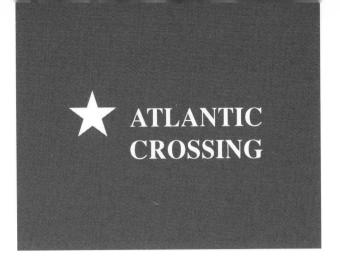

ATLANTIC CROSSING

"Iceberg ahead"

During the uneventful crossing the ship received numerous ice warnings. Their significance was not fully appreciated by Captain Smith, not least because ice was normally further north. Two particularly important warnings were sent. One, from the *Amerika*, was not delivered to the bridge. Another, from the *Californian*, was blocked out by harassed operator Harold Bride, busy sending passengers' wires, before *Californian* could complete hers. *Titanic*, by now off the Grand Banks of Newfoundland, sailed on towards the ice field.

7.30 p.m. *"42o 3'N. 49o 9'W. Three large bergs 5 miles to the southwards of us."* (**Californian to Antillian, overheard by** *Titanic*)

9.40 p.m. *"42o to 41o 25'N, 49o to 50o 30' saw much heavy pack ice and great number of large icebergs, also field ice, weather good, clear"* (**Mesaba to** *Titanic*)

That last message never reached the bridge. The lone Marconi operator on duty was too busy sending passengers' messages to the USA, via Cape Race. Later ...

10.30 p.m. *"We are stopped and surrounded by ice."* (**Californian to** *Titanic*)

SUNDAY 14 APRIL 1912

The day began with continued fair weather, the sea was so calm it appeared like glass. A morning service was held for all passengers in the first class dining room, and the day progressed as normal.

9.00 a.m. *"Bergs, growlers and field ice in 42oN, from 49o to 51oW"* (**Caronia to** *Titanic*)

11.40 a.m. *"Much ice"* (**Noordam to** *Titanic*)

1.42 p.m. *"icebergs and large quantities of field ice in 41o 51'N, 49o 52'W ... wish you and Titanic all success."* (**Baltic to** *Titanic*)

By 5.30 p.m. passengers had noticed that the temperature on deck was dropping rapidly.

This message was interrupted by *Titanic*'s operator replying:

"Keep out! Shut up! You're jamming my signal. I'm working Cape Race." (meaning he was sending ship to shore messages for passengers.)

Near mid-night on Sunday 14th April one of the look outs, Fred Fleet, spotted an iceberg and immediately rang the bridge, 'Iceberg ahead', 'Thank you', said First Officer William Murdoch, who ordered the watertight doors to be shut and instinctively turned the ship to port to try to dodge the berg. Unfortunately it scraped alongside, fatally opening six of *Titanic*'s compartments to the sea. Orders were given to lower the lifeboats. Only 650 of her passengers and crew took to them, although another 400 could have been taken. A few men jumped or swam to join them. They tried to row towards a mystery ship on the horizon and awaited rescue, or hopefully even return to the ship if all was well. But at 2.10 pm the liner, which had been tilting lower and lower into the water, took a plunge, and broke in two just below the water. The forward section then sank followed a little later by the stern section which had remained above water. Most of her passengers and crew went down with her, but several hundred remained on the surface, buoyed up in their lifejackets until they died of cold. One third class woman passenger, Salvationist Rosa Abbott, thrown with her sons (both lost) in the water from the stern section, reached Collapsible Boat A and safety.

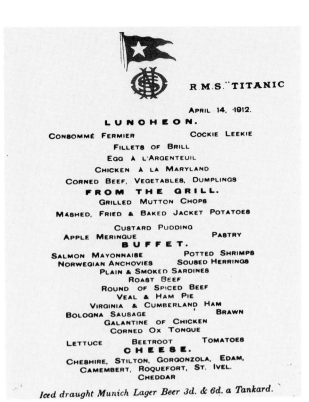

Third class deck space.

Cork Examiner

Thirty survived on an upturned lifeboat launched at the last minute. A few more were picked up by lifeboat 14, which, unlike the others, returned to the scene after the cries of the drowning and dying subsided.

Some of those who survived recall the voyage, such as Edith Haisman:

"I was born in South Africa, it was during the Boer War … my father had the Masonic Hotel in Worcester … 1896 I was born. My mother's sister out in America, in Seattle, said 'Why don't you come out here, things are booming out here …"
"We stayed a few months in London … my father bought a lot of bedding like sheets and blankets for the new hotel he was going to open in Seattle … he went straight away to book our passage … and that's how we managed to get on the Titanic. It was a great big ship … it was really a floating palace."
Edith Haisman née Brown (City Heritage Oral History)

Millvina Dean, at 9 weeks old was the youngest passenger on board. Her brother Bertram was 2 years old.

Edith Brown aged 20 in 1916 with her mother Catherine Elizabeth, taken in South Africa. Both survived the *Titanic* disaster.

Southampton City Heritage Oral History

Bertram Dean Senior (on right) shortly before he sailed on *Titanic*.

Private Collection

"We were emigrants, my parents had a public house in London ... we were going to Kansas, my father was going to buy a tobacconist's shop."

"My grandfather and grandmother came to see us off at the docks in a horse and trap and he said 'Oh it's a wonderful ship. You'll have a wonderful time.'"

"It was very brave of my mother, because we were so very, very small and she didn't know really what was going to happen out there. She didn't know if my father was going to make the shop pay or anything."

Millvina Dean (City Heritage Oral History)

"I was born in Ilford Essex January 31st 1905, my father was a master builder ... he had a friend who had gone to Canada and was doing remarkably well as a builder ... and he tried to persuade my father to join him ... it was all decided in the space of one night."

"It was a 4 berth cabin ... we had the 3 beds and my mother had a table she used to sit at to do her knitting or sewing ..."

Eva Hart (City Heritage Oral History)

"She felt this little 'bump' as she always described it, because we were a very long way from it. We were on the port side of the ship and the collision was on the starboard side of the ship, and had she been asleep it wouldn't have wakened her ...

she immediately awakened my father ..."

"My father went away and spoke to one of the sailors and came back and said 'We've hit an iceberg ... they're going to launch the lifeboats but you'll all be back on board for breakfast.'"

"They started to lower the boats and my father put my mother and I in without any trouble at all ...

"I never saw him again ... he told me to hold my mummy's hand and be a good girl, that's all he said."

"The panic seemed to me to start after the boats had gone, we could hear it ... after we were rowing away from the ship ... then we could hear the panic of people rushing about on the deck and screaming and looking for lifeboats ... I was terrified ... it was dreadful ... the bows went down first and the stern stuck up in the ocean what seemed to me like a long time ... but it stood up stark against the sky and then keeled over and went down, you could hear the people screaming and thrashing about in the water."

"... and finally the ghastly noise of the people thrashing about and screaming and drowning, that finally ceased. I remember saying to my mother once, 'How dreadful that noise was' and I'll always remember her reply and she said, 'Yes, but think back about the silence that followed it ... because all of a sudden the ship wasn't there, the lights weren't there and the cries weren't there."

Eva Hart (City Heritage Oral History)

Eva Hart with her parents shortly before they sailed on the *Titanic*.

Private Collection

↓ 15 FEET FROM BOAT DECK TO WATER.

A contemporary representation of *Titanic's* lifeboats being lowered. Drawn by C.J. De Lacy. The distance from the Boat Deck to the water was actually 60 feet.

The Sphere/Southampton City Heritage Collections

Copy of drawing of sinking of the *Titanic* - lifeboat in foreground. By William Müller.

Southampton City Heritage Collections

"My mother didn't talk about the disaster very much. She only said one or two things ... I don't think she wanted to think much about it."

"She told me of one or two episodes, that my father heard something had happened, and came back down and said 'You'd better put something on the children and get dressed because we have apparently struck an iceberg.' So we hurried on deck and my mother was put in a lifeboat, and my brother, and I of course went in a sack and went over ... that was the last my mother saw of my father."

"I remember her telling me in the lifeboat was a Chinaman and the other women there were so annoyed that a Chinaman was in there when their own men couldn't get on that they said they would thrown him overboard, but they didn't, they thought better of it."

"Another woman whose husband was left behind was only concerned that she'd lost her feather bed ... she didn't say anything about her husband, just that her feather bed had gone."

Millvina Dean (City Heritage Oral History)

"I was in my cabin at the time when it struck the iceberg ... asleep ... but the vibration was so great when she struck, she was going so fast she struck the iceberg and was thrown back.

"Being young ... I didn't realise we might be drowned ... because when I stood on the boat deck my father was talking to Reverend Carter, I turned round and said to my father, 'Look, there's a ship over there, see the lights', and then the lights went out."

"You could see the ice for miles across the sea ... nobody worried about it, some of the people came up playing with the ice on deck and they wouldn't believe it, they said 'No, she's unsinkable, they went back to bed ... I thought it was wonderful to see the ice like that, you know ... just wondered what happened, like everybody else."

"My father never said anything ... he was smoking a cigar ... he put my mother and me into a lifeboat ... then he walks away, they wouldn't believe that the boat was sinking.

126

Well you couldn't notice it, you couldn't feel the boat was going because, until you were out in the lifeboat you could see her lights going down ... and you could see her lights disappearing all the time 'til it got to the boilers and then a most terrible explosion. She went down slow ..."

"It was terrible, lots of shouting and people crying as she went down, people were so upset, never heard anything like it, you could hear the screams of all the people that was left on deck, it was really terrible."

"Our lifeboat was number 14 ... we had quite a lot of people on our lifeboat ... mostly women ... but there was a man dressed as a woman, he jumped into the lifeboat as it was going down ... and the officer said 'I've a good mind to shoot you, you might have capsized the boat ...'"

"... Nearly 6 hours we must have stayed in that lifeboat ... freezing it was, terribly cold ..."

Edith Haisman née Brown (City Heritage Oral History)

Contemporary newspaper reports went into rapture about the role of some women during the disaster.

Lifeboat 14 under the command of Fifth Officer Lowe towing collapsible D approaches rescue ship *Carpathia*.

Southampton City Heritage Collections

> **Heroic Conduct of Women Survivors**
> **Thrilling Narratives**
> **Ladies Pulling Oars**
> **Suffragists' Claim "Women braver than men."**

Special Cable from our own Correspondent New York, Sunday.

Instances accumulate here that womanhood will never find anything for which it need blush in the *Titanic* disaster. Every virtue shown by the men had its duplicate many times in the women, and the manifestations are numerous. I collected today from the survivors enough evidence to prove that if bravery is essential to suffrage, many women who landed from the *Carpathia* on Thursday should have not one vote, but a dozen. The world now knows of the devotion of Mrs. Isador Strauss, who would not forsake her husband, and, likewise of Mrs. Allison, of Montreal, who was joined by her daughter. *"I won't go without you,"* said Mrs. Strauss to her husband, and she resolutely fought off the efforts of the crew to put her into a boat. *"No,"* said Mrs. Allison bravely, and she eluded those who would have saved her and her daughter. Physical force got Mrs. Astor into the boat, as it did Mrs. Walter Clark, of Los Angeles; Mrs. George Widener, of Philadelphia; Mrs. Jacques Futrelle, Mrs. John Thayer, Mrs. Turrell Cavendish *(sic, actually Mrs Tyrrell Cavendish)*, and many others,

English and American alike. The heroism of Edith Evans, who gave up her own life that another might be saved, stands out conspicuously. Miss Evans was nearly 30 years old, and, independently well-to-do, she spent much of her time in travel. She was a passenger on the *Titanic*, travelling with her aunts, Mrs. Cornell, Mrs. Appleton, and Mrs. Brown. The signal came for the women and children to go, and Mrs. Cornell and Mrs. Appleton secured seats in one of the lifeboats. Mrs. Morgan and Miss Evans sought another. It was one of the last boats to go. They

Collapsible D approaching *Carpathia*.

Southampton City Heritage Collections

Lifeboat number 6 approaching *Carpathia*.

Southampton City Heritage Collections

'Safe at last' – A step ladder is lowered from the *Carpathia*.

Southampton City Heritage Collections

found places, but as the boat was about to be lowered it was seen to be overcrowded. One person would have to get out. Miss Evans arose, although her aunt put out a restraining hand, announcing she would go. *"I must be the one to go,"* declared the young woman. *"You stay; you have children at home; I have nobody."* She jumped out and the lifeboat was lowered. That was the last seen of her.

One able-bodied seaman, who shipped aboard the *Titanic* when she left Southampton, is tired and a little listless and subdued from the things he lived through last Monday. But his eyes light up and his speech becomes animated when you ask him what part the women played in the trying hours after the *Titanic* sank.

"There was a woman in my boat as was a woman," he told The Daily Telegraph representative yesterday. *"She was the Countess of Rothes. I was one of those who was ordered to man the boats, and my place was in No. 8 boat. There were thirty-five of us in that boat, mostly women, but some men along with them. I was in command, but I had to row, and I wanted someone at the tiller. When I saw the way she was carrying herself, and heard the quiet, determined way she spoke to the others, I knew she was more of a man than any we had on board, and I put her in command. I put her at the tiller, and she was at the tiller when the Carpathia came along five hours later."*

"And there was another woman on board who was strong in the work we had to do. She was at the oar with me, and though I never learned her name she was helping every minute. It was she who suggested we should sing. 'Sing?'

you say! I should think we did! It kept up our spirits. We sang as we rowed, all of us, starting out with 'Pull for the shore,' and we were still singing when we saw the lights of the Carpathia. Then we stopped singing, and prayed."
(City Heritage Collections)

Woman Saves Sailor

Of Miss Bentham it is related that she was sleeping soundly when the stewards came for her. She arose, dressed herself warmly, and was handed into a boat. This was very crowded; so much so that one sailor had to sit with his feet dangling in the icy-cold water. As time went on, the sufferings of the man from cold became apparent. Miss Bentham arose from her place and had the man turned round while she took his place with her feet in the water. Miss Marie Young showed her spirit by compelling

those in command of one boat to take on more passengers. When her boat got away it was found there was room for many more. There were twenty-six aboard when Miss Young thought forty could be carried safely. *"Twenty-six is the limit,"* said one sailor. The young woman declared more should be taken, and she was so emphatic that they picked up several who were swimming in the water.

The lives in many of the boats were imperilled because they took from the water more people than the craft could safely hold. Mrs. Joel Swift was another woman who took her turn at the oars. There were twenty-four persons in her boat, four of them men, all members of the crew. *"Let me help,"* she said; and she did. She induced other women to join in, saying it would warm them up.

Miss Marie Young, who taught music to the children of President Roosevelt, was another oarswoman. She was in a boat which she said was marked to have a capacity of eighty persons, although there were only twenty-eight in it. Miss Young, finding only four men to do the rowing, took her seat at the rowlock and went to work. She was very cool, and even reproved a sailor for puffing strong tobacco.

Mrs. Marvin could not row, but she helped by taking care of a little brown-eyed French girl who was handed into the boat as it was being lowered. There was no one to claim the youngster, and she still carried the child in her arms nearly five hours later, when the *Carpathia* had come to the rescue. The youngster is now in the care of the Women's Relief Committee.

Miss Jessie Leitch, of London, a second class passenger, came ashore with the six-months-old infant of her cousin, the Rev. John Harper, of London, who was drowned. Mr. Harper handed the child to her, kissed the little one goodbye, and remained to perish. Miss Leitch wrapped the child in her own clothing, and stoically endured the cold until help came. Six or seven little babies, all orphans, are now nestling in cots provided by the relief committee. All are doing well.

Mrs. Fred Kenyon got into a boat in which three men, not members of the crew, were at the oars. Mrs. Kenyon discovered that none of these men could handle an oar. She and several of her sisters in the boat contemptuously ordered the men out of their places, and picked up the sweeps. They and one sailor handled the boat until help came.

(City Heritage Collections)

"The worst thing really during the night was the lifeboat that I was in which was number 14 was so hopelessly overcrowded that in the night they started taking people out of it and putting them in other boats ... I got separated from my mother ... when the dawn came up and we were being picked up by the Carpathia I wasn't in the same lifeboat with her ... I spent the rest of the night screaming for her ... and I found her on the Carpathia."

Newspaper photograph taken on the *Carpathia* shows Gus Cohen 3rd class passenger asleep in deck chair and Ettie Dean (right) with baby Millvina in her arms.

Private Collection

Q. How did you get on board the *Carpathia*?

"... *in a sack, winched up in a mail bag because the children couldn't climb up rope ladders, so we were each one of us put in a mail sack and that was terrifying, swinging about over the ocean.*"

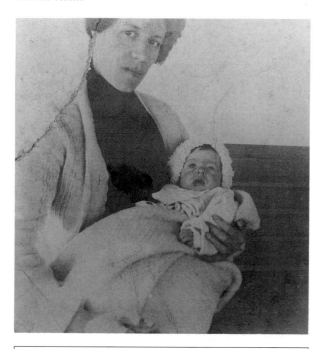

Ettie Dean with nine-week old Millvina returning to England aboard the *Adriatic*.

Private Collection

"*I was taken to hospital when I got to New York because I was still so sick and then in a very short space of time we came back. My mother's greatest thought was to get back to England and I was the one in trouble coming back, I was terrified, she wasn't at all nervous coming back ... she had no more fear ... she had such a job to get me on to. the deck to get some air, I was terrified.*"
Eva Hart (City Heritage Oral History)

"*We went on to America, stayed in a hospital for 6 weeks and then came home again ... we came back to my grandfather's place, a big, old place in Woodlands, the New Forest.*"
"*My mother got a pension for us until we were 18 ... they paid also for my brother to go to King Edwards and I went to Greggs School, they paid for our schooling.*"
Millvina Dean (City Heritage Oral History)

"*After we were picked up on the Carpathia my mother came to me 'cos every time a lifeboat came I went to see if my father was on it you see, and he wasn't, so my mother turned round and said 'You've lost your father, you won't see your father any more ... he's gone'.*"
"*And the next morning you'd never believe when daylight came that the iceberg could do that damage to a ship...*"
"*When we got to New York there were crowds of people at the docks, I think that the whole of New York must have been there ...*"
Edith Haisman née Brown (City Heritage Oral History)

A Suffragist's Claim

And so one could enlarge the list by the score. Apropos of the women's heroism, as developed in the tragic story of the *Titanic*, several of our most notable women suffragists are declaring that *"women are naturally braver than men,"* and should refuse to go first into the lifeboats.

This novel view was expressed yesterday by Miss Lida Stokes-Adams, a prominent Suffragist, of Philadelphia, who declares that women lost one of the greatest chances ever presented in the cause of female suffrage, when they did not assert themselves even more, and prove they were on a superior plane to men from the point of view of personal courage.

"Of course," she conceded, *"it is hard to answer whether the women and children should have had the preference in such a disaster, but I don't think they should have had. I think the women should have insisted that the boats be filled with an equal number of men and women, or that the men should have had an equal chance of saving themselves, even though in brute strength they are stronger. It would have been a wonderful thing for the suffrage cause if this had been done. Years from now there will be similar accidents, and I venture to say men and women will share the disaster alike, and women will endeavour to save the men."*

After making this prediction Miss Adams praised the men of the *Titanic* for their heroic conduct.

(City Heritage Collections)

Survivors being cared for aboard *Carpathia*.

Deathless Story of the Titanic/Southampton City Heritage Collections

Shortly after the disaster Charlotte Collyer from Bishopstoke near Southampton, related her experiences to an American womens' magazine:

Survivor's True Story

The next morning we went to Southampton and then my husband drew from the bank all his money, including the sum he had received for our store. The clerk asked him if he did not want a draft, but he shook his head and put the notes in a wallet which he kept to the end in the inside breast pocket of his coat.

It came to several thousand dollars in American money. We had already sent forward the few personal treasures that we had kept from our old home so that when we went on board the *Titanic* our every earthly possession was with us.

We were travelling second cabin and from our deck which was situated well forward, we saw the great send off that was given to the boat. I do not think that there had ever been so large a crowd in Southampton and I am not surprised that it should have come together.

The *Titanic* was wonderful, far more splendid and huge than I had dreamed of. The other crafts in the harbour were like cockle shells beside her, and they, mind you were the boats of the American and other lines that a few years ago were thought enormous. I

Drawn for 'The Sphere' by G. Bron.

The Sphere/Southampton City Heritage Collections

remember a friend said to me 'Aren't you afraid to venture on the sea?' but now it was I who was confident. 'What on this boat!' I answered. 'Even the worst storm could not harm her.' Before we left the harbour I saw the accident to the *New York*, the liner that was dragged from her moorings and swept against us in the Channel. It did not frighten anyone, as it only seemed to prove how powerful the *Titanic* was.

I don't remember very much about the first few days of the voyage. I was a bit seasick and kept to my cabin most of the time. But on Sunday April 14th I was up and about. At dinner time I was at my place in the saloon and enjoyed the meal, though I thought it too heavy and rich. No effort had been spared to give even the second cabin passengers on that Sunday the best dinner that money could buy.

After I had eaten, I listened to the orchestra for a little while, then at nine o'clock or half past nine I went to my cabin. I had just climbed into my berth when a stewardess came in. She was a sweet woman who had been very kind to me. I take this opportunity to thank her for I shall never see her again. She went down with the *Titanic*.

'Do you know where we are' she said pleasantly, 'we are in what is called the Devils Hole'. 'What does that mean' I asked. 'That is a dangerous part of the ocean', she answered. Many accidents have happened near there. They say that icebergs drift down as far as this. It's getting to be very cold on deck so perhaps there is ice around us now. She left the cabin and I soon dropped off to sleep, her talk about icebergs had not frightened me, but it shows that the crew were awake to the danger. As far as I can tell we had not slackened our speed in the least. It must have been a little after ten o'clock when my husband came in and woke me up. He sat and talked to me for how long I do not know, before he began to make ready to go to bed. And then the crash! The sensation to me was as if the ship had been seized by a giant hand and shaken once, twice then stopped dead in its course. That is to say there was a long backward jerk, followed by a shorter one. I was not thrown out of my berth and my husband staggered on his feet only slightly. We heard no strange sounds, no rending of plates and woodwork, but we noticed that the engines had stopped running. They tried to start the engines a few minutes later but after some coughing and rumbling there was silence once more.

Our cabin was so situated that we could follow this clearly. My husband and I were not alarmed. He said that there must have been some slight accident in the engine room and at first he did not intend to go on deck. Then he changed his mind, put on his coat and left me. I lay quietly in my berth with my little girl and almost fell asleep again. In what seemed a very few moments my husband returned. He was a bit excited then. 'What do you think', he exclaimed. 'We have struck an iceberg, a big one, but there is no danger an officer just told me so.' I could hear the footsteps of people on the deck above my head. There was some stamping and queer noises as if ships tackle was being pulled about. 'Are the people frightened', I asked quietly. 'No' he replied. 'I don't think the shock woke up many in the second cabin, and few of those in the saloons have troubled to go on deck.'

I saw the professional gamblers playing with some of the passengers as I went by. Their cards had been jerked off the table when the boat struck, but they were gathering them up and had started their game again before I left the saloon.' The story reassured me. If these people at their cards were not worried why should I be.

I think my husband would have retired to his berth without asking any more questions about the accident but suddenly we heard hundreds of people running along the passageway in front of our door. They did not cry out, but the patter of their feet reminded me of rats scurrying through an empty room. I could see my face in the mirror opposite and it had grown very white, my husband too was pale and he stammered when he spoke to me. 'We had better go on deck and see what's wrong', he said. I jumped out of bed and put over my nightdress a dressing gown and an ulster. My hair was down but I hurriedly tied it back with a ribbon. By this time although the boat had not made any progress, it seemed to have tilted forward a little. I caught up my daughter just as she was in her nightgown, wrapped a White Star cabin blanket around her and started out of the door. My husband followed immediately behind. Neither of us took any of our belongings from the cabin and I remember that he even left his watch lying on his pillow. We did not doubt for an instant that we would return. When we reached the second cabin promenade deck we found a great many people there. Some officers were walking up and down, but I want to say that at that time no-one was frightened. My husband stepped over to an Officer, it was either Fifth Officer Harold Lowe or First Officer Murdock (sic) – and asked him a question. I heard him shout back 'No, we have no searchlight but we have a few rockets on board. Keep calm! There is no danger.'

Our party of three stood close together. I did not recognise any of the other faces about me, probably because of the excitement. I never went near the

Labels within the image: First Class | Lounge | Promenade | Private Suite | Promenade | Corridor | Bath Rooms | First Class Dining Saloon | Companionway Stairs | Second Class | Third Class Dining Saloon | Water Line | Boiler Room | ICEBERG From 50 to 100 feet according to various accounts | ← Starboard port holes

'Through the portholes we saw ice rubbing against the ship's sides.' Lawrence Beesley.

The Sphere/Southampton City Heritage Collections

first class cabin deck so did not see any of the prominent people on board. Suddenly there was a commotion near one of the gangways and we saw a stoker come climbing up from below. He stopped a few feet away from us. All the fingers of one hand had been cut off. Blood was running from the stumps and blood was spattered over his face and over his clothes. The red marks showed very clearly against the coal dust with which he was covered. I went over and spoke to him. I asked him if there

was any danger. 'Danger', he screamed at the top of his voice, 'I should just say so!' 'It's hell down below, look at me. This boat will sink like a stone in ten minutes.' He staggered away and lay down fainting with his head on a coil of rope. At this moment I got my first grip of fear – awful sickening fear. That poor man with his bleeding hand and his speckled face brought up a picture of smashed engines and mangled human bodies. I hung on to my husband's arm and although he was very brave, and not trembling, I saw that his face was as white as paper. We realised that the accident was much worse than we had supposed, but even then I and all the others about me of whom I have any knowledge did not believe that the *Titanic* would go down. The Officers were running to and fro and shouting orders. I have no clear idea of what happened during the next quarter of an hour. The time seemed much shorter, but it must have been between ten and fifteen minutes. I saw First Officer Murdock (sic) place guards by the gangways to prevent others like the wounded stoker from coming on deck. How many unhappy men were shut off in that way from their chance of safety I do not know, but Mr Murdock (sic) was probably right. He was a masterful man, astoundingly brave and cool. I had met him the day before when he was inspecting the second cabin quarters, and thought him a bull-dog of a man who would not be afraid of anything. This proved to be true, he kept order to the last, and died at his post. They say he shot himself. I do not know.

Those in charge must have herded us toward the nearest boat deck for that is where I presently found myself, still clinging to my husband's arm, and with little Marjorie beside me. Many women were standing with their husbands and there was no confusion. Then above the clamour of the people asking questions of each other, there came the terrible cry 'Lower the boats!' 'Women and children first.' Someone was shouting these last few words over and over again. 'Women and children first! Women and children first!' They struck utter terror into my heart and now they will ring in my ears until the day I die. They meant my own safety but they also meant the greatest loss I have ever suffered – the life of my husband.

The first lifeboat was quickly filled and lowered away. Very few men went in her, only five or six members of the crew, I should say. The male passengers made no attempt to save themselves. I have never seen such courage, or believed it possible. How the people in the first cabin and the steerage may have acted I do not know, but our second cabin men were heroes. I want to tell that to every reader of this article. The lowering of the second boat took more time. I think all those women who were really afraid and eager to go had got into the boat. Those who remained were wives who did not want to leave their husbands or daughters who would not leave their parents. The Officer in charge was Harold Lowe. First Officer Murdock (sic) had moved to the other end of the deck. I was never close to him again.

Mr. Lowe was very young and boyish looking, but somehow he compelled people to obey him. He rushed among the passengers and ordered the women into the boat. Many of them followed him in a dazed kind of way, but others stayed with their men. I should have had a seat in that second boat but I refused to go. It was filled at last and disappeared over the side with a rush. There were two more lifeboats at that part of the deck. A man in plain clothes was fussing about them and screaming instructions. I saw Fifth Officer Lowe order him away. I did not recognise him but from what I have read in the newspapers it must have been Mr Bruce Ismay, the Managing Director of the Line.

The third boat was about half full when a sailor caught Marjorie in his arms and tore her away from me and threw her into the boat. She was not even given a chance to tell her father goodbye! 'You too!' a man yelled close to my ear. 'You're a woman, take a seat in that boat or it will be too late.' The deck seemed to be slipping under my feet. It was leaning at a sharp angle for the ship was then sinking fast, bows down. I clung desperately to my husband. I do not know what I said but I shall always be glad to think that I did not want to leave him. A man seized me by the arm then another threw both his arms about my waist and dragged me away by main strength. I heard my husband say 'Go, Lotty, for God's sake be brave and go! I'll get a seat in another boat.' The men who held me rushed me across the deck and hurled me bodily into the lifeboat. I landed on one shoulder and bruised it badly.

Other women were crowding behind me, but I stumbled to my feet and saw over their heads my husband's back as he walked steadily down the deck and disappeared among the men. His face was turned away so that I never saw it again, but I know that he went unafraid to his death. His last words when he said he would get a seat in another boat buoyed me up until every vestige of hope was gone.

Many women were strengthened by the same promise or they must have gone mad and leapt into the sea. I let myself be saved because I believed that he too would escape, but I sometimes envy those whom no earthly power could tear them from their husbands' arms. There were several such among those brave second cabin passengers. I saw them standing beside their loved ones to the last, and when the roll was called the next day on board the *Carpathia* they did not answer.

The boat was practically full and no more women were anywhere near it when Fifth Officer Lowe jumped in and ordered it lowered. The sailors on deck had started to obey him when a very sad thing happened. A young lad hardly more than a schoolboy, a pink cheeked lad, almost small enough

The boats of the *Titanic* hanging on the *Carpathia*'s side.

Southampton City Heritage Collections

to be counted as a child, was standing close to the rail. He had made no attempt to force his way into the boat though his eyes had been fixed piteously on the Officer. Now when he realised that he was really to be left behind his courage failed him. With a cry he climbed upon the rail and leapt down into the boat. He fell among us women and crawled under a seat. I and another woman covered him up with our skirts. We wanted to give the poor lad a chance, but the Officer dragged him to his feet and ordered him back onto the ship. We begged for his life. I remember him saying that he would not take up too much room but the Officer drew his revolver and thrust it into his face. 'I give you just ten seconds to get back onto that ship before I blow your brains out', he shouted. The lad only begged the harder and I thought I should see him shot where he stood. But the Officer suddenly changed his tone. He lowered his revolver and looked the boy squarely in the eyes. 'For God's sake be a man!' he said gently. 'We have got women and children.' The little lad turned round eyed and climbed back over the rail without a word. He was not saved. All the women about me were sobbing and I saw my little Marjorie take the Officer's hand. 'Oh, Mr Man don't shoot, please don't shoot the poor man!' She was saying and he spared the time to shake his head and smile. He screamed another order for the boat to be lowered, but just as we were getting away, a steerage passenger, an Italian I think, came running the whole length of the deck and hurled himself into the boat. He fell upon a young child and injured her internally. The Officer seized him by the collar and by sheer brute strength pushed him back onto the *Titanic*. As we shot down towards the sea I caught a last glimpse of this coward. He was in the hands of about a dozen men of the second cabin. They were driving their fists into his face and he was

bleeding from the nose and mouth. As a matter of fact we did not stop at any other decks to take on other women and children. It would have been impossible I suppose. The bottom of our boat slapped the ocean as we came down with a force that I thought must shock us all overboard. We were drenched with ice cold spray but we hung on and the men at the oars rowed us rapidly away from the wreck.

It was then that I saw for the first time the iceberg that had done such terrible damage. It loomed up in the clear starlight, a bluish white mountain, quite near to us. Two other icebergs lay quite close together, like twin peaks. Later I thought I saw three or four more, but I cannot be sure. Loose ice was floating in the water. It was very cold. We had gone perhaps half a mile when the Officer ordered the men to cease rowing. No other boats were in sight and we did not even have a lantern to signal with. We lay there in silence and darkness in that utterly calm sea. I shall never forget the terrible beauty of the *Titanic* at that moment. She was tilted forward head down with her first funnel partly under the water. To me she looked like an enormous glow worm for she was alight from the rising waterline clear to her stern – electric light blazing in every cabin, lights on all her decks and lights to her mast head. No sound reached us except the music of the band which I seemed strange to say to be aware of for the first time. Oh those brave musicians! How wonderful they were! They were playing lively tunes, Ragtime, and they kept it up to the very end. Only the engulfing ocean had power to drown them into silence. At that distance it was impossible to recognise anyone on board, but I could make out groups of men on every deck. They were standing with arms crossed upon their chests and with lowered heads. I am sure that they were in prayer. On the boat deck that I had just left perhaps fifty men had come together. In the midst of them was a tall figure. This man had climbed upon a chain or a coil of rope so that he was raised far above the rest, his hands were stretched out as if he were pronouncing a blessing.

During the day a priest, a certain Father Byles, had held services in the second cabin saloon and I think it must have been he who stood there leading those doomed men in prayer. The band was playing 'Nearer my God to Thee'. I could hear it distinctly. The end was very close. It came with a deafening roar that stunned me. Something in the very bowels of the *Titanic* exploded and millions of sparks shot up to the sky. This red spurt was fan shaped as it went up but the sparks dispersed in every direction in the shape of a fountain of fire. Two other explosions followed dull and heavy, as if below the surface the *Titanic* broke into two before my eyes. The fore part was already partly under the water. It wallowed over and vanished instantly. The stern reared straight on end and seemed poised on the ocean for many seconds, they seemed minutes to us. It was only then that the electric lights on board went out.

Before the darkness came I saw hundreds of human bodies clinging to the wreck or jumping into the water. Cries more terrible than I have ever heard rung in my ears. I turned my face away but I looked round the next moment and saw the other half of the great ship slip below the surface of the water as easily as a pebble in a pond. I shall always remember that last moment as the most hideous of the whole disaster. Many calls for help came from the floating wreckage but Fifth Officer Lowe told some women who asked him to go back that it would certainly result in our being swamped. I believe that some of the boats picked up survivors at this time, and I was told afterwards by more than one trustworthy person that Captain E.J. Smith of the *Titanic* was washed against a collapsible boat and held on to it for a few moments. A member of the crew assured me that he tried to pull the Captain on board, that

he shook his head, cast himself off, and sank out of sight.

For our part we went in search of other lifeboats that had escaped. We found four or five and Mr Lowe took command of the little fleet. He ordered that the boats should be linked together with ropes so as to prevent any of them drifting away and losing itself in the darkness. This proved to be a very good plan and made our rescue all the more certain when the *Carpathia* came. He then, with great difficulty, distributed most of the women in our boat among the other craft. This took perhaps half an hour. It gave him an almost empty boat and as soon as possible he cut loose and we went in search of survivors.

I have no idea of the passage of time during the balance of that awful night. Someone gave me a ship's blanket which seemed to protect me from the bitter cold and Marjorie had the cabin blanket that I had wrapped around her but we were sitting with our feet in several inches of icy water. The salt spray had made us terribly thirsty and there was no fresh water and certainly no food of any kind on the boat. The suffering of most of the women from these various causes was beyond belief. The worst thing that happened to me was when I fell, half fainting

"There were ice fields and ice floes all around us" – A French cruiser traversing an ice floe off Newfoundland.

The Sphere/Southampton City Heritage Collections

against one of the men at the oars, my loose hair was caught in the row-locks and half of it was torn out by the roots.

I know that we rescued a large number of men from the wreck, but I can recall only two incidents. Not far away from where the *Titanic* went down we found a lifeboat floating bottom up. Along the keel were lying about twenty men. They were packed closely together and were hanging on desperately but we saw even the strongest amongst them were so badly frozen that in a few more moments they must have slipped into the ocean. We took them on board one by one, and found that of the number four were already corpses.

The dead men were cast into the sea. The living grovelled in the bottom of our boat some of them babbling like maniacs. A little further on we saw a floating door that must have torn loose when the ship went down. Lying upon it face down was a small Japanese. He had lashed himself with a rope to his frail craft using the broken hinges to make his knots secure. As far as we could see he was dead.

The sea washed over him every time the door bobbed up and down and he was frozen stiff. He did not answer when he was hailed and the Officer hesitated about trying to save him. He had actually turned the boat round, but he changed his mind and went back. The Japanese was hauled on board and one of the women rubbed his chest while others his hands and feet. In less time than it takes to tell, he opened his eyes. He spoke to us in his own tongue, then seeing that we did not understand, he struggled to his feet, stretched his arms above his head, stamped his feet and in five minutes or so had almost recovered his strength. One of the sailors near to him was so tired he could hardly pull his oar. The Japanese bustled over, pushed him from his seat, took the oar and worked like a hero until we were finally picked up. I saw Mr Lowe watching him in open-mouthed surprise. After this rescue, all my memories are hazy until the *Carpathia* arrived at dawn. She stopped maybe four miles away from us, and the task of rowing over to her was one of the hardest things that our poor frozen men, and women too had had to face. Many women helped at the oars, and one by one the boats crawled over the ocean to the side of the waiting liner. They let

down rope ladders to us, but the women were so weak that it was a marvel that some of them did not lose their hold and drop back into the water. When it came to saving the babies and young children, the difficulty was even greater, as no-one was strong enough to risk carrying a living burden. One of the mail clerks on the *Carpathia* solved the problem. He let down empty United States mail bags. The little ones were tumbled in, the bags locked and so they were hauled up to safety. We all stood at last upon the deck of the *Carpathia*. More than six hundred and seventy of us, and the tragedy of the scene that followed is too deep for words. There was scarcely anyone who had not been separated from husband, child or friend. Was the last one among the handful saved? We could only rush frantically from group to group, searching the haggard faces, crying out names, and endless questions. No survivor knows better than I the bitter cruelty of disappointment and despair. I had a husband to search for, a husband whom in the greatness of my faith, I had believed would be found in one of the boats. He was not there.

And it is with these words that I can best end my story of the Titanic. There are hundreds of others who can tell and have already told of that sad journey on the *Carpathia* to New York. Friends in America have been good to me and I intend to follow out our original plan. I shall go to Idaho and make a home in the New World of the West. For a while I thought of returning to England, but I can never face the sea again and besides that I must take my little Marjorie to the place where her father would have taken us both. That is all I care about: to do what he would have had me do.

Charlotte Collyer (American Semi Monthly Magazine, May 1912)

Charlotte and Marjorie did eventually return to Bishopstoke where she remarried. Not long afterwards, she died of consumption.

In St. Mary's Church, Bishopstoke, there is a commemorative plaque on an umbrella stand which simply reads 'Sacred to the memory of Harvey Collyer who fell asleep in the deep April 15th 1912. Age 31 years.

★ DISASTER

"All hands on deck"

"I was born in Bolton Road Portsmouth on the nineteenth of November 1893 and I joined the Olympic in 1911 on her maiden voyage and ... after five voyages we were in collision with the Hawke in the Solent so we put back again. Then I did about five voyages and I was transferred, selected I might say ... to be conceited ... selected to go to the Titanic. They were picking out the best of the crew ... pat my back a minute ... best of the crew to go to the Titanic. Well anyway ... we sailed on the 10th April on the Titanic until the ... Sunday evening. Everything went all smooth and quiet and at about half past eleven or twenty past eleven I was in a bunk sleeping, the night watchman came down and said 'All hands on deck, get your lifebelts on'. We thought it was an emergency ... boat drill. We weren't very pleased with it ... so anyway we eventually went up on deck and stood by our boats. We were all allotted certain boats to go to and mine was number thirteen, by the way ... well we just stood around waiting for orders. Dancing around on the deck and the musicians were on board playing different tunes on deck and ... eventually they got orders to get all the women and children up to their lifeboats. I don't know what the time was, but it was getting on. Anyway we got them all up. Well, as many as we could, and got them into the boats. We got away from that and ... got all the boats away ... excepting the last boat, which was a collapsible boat, secured to the top of the wireless room and lashed down with different lashings. And a crowd of them up there unlashing it. Someone shouted out 'Anyone got a pocket knife?' I said, 'Yes, I have, here you are' and passed my pocket knife up. And I think that was the last lashing to the upturned lifeboat."

"Well, by that time, the ship was getting well down ... and all our lifeboats were away excepting this one. I was wandering around ... and ... I went up near the bridge ... I stood ... looked from the port side over to the starboard side, I could see the water coming up the bridge like that ... so I thought ... it's time to leave. ... well I was standing up to my knees in water then and I jumped up onto the rail and ... dived into the water. I climbed up to the davits ... the tap rail by the davits on the ship, then the water's round my knees, ... so I jumped into it. I had nowhere to swim to but I just had to get away from the suction, as I feared the suction would thus take me down. Well, I swam away and, by sheer good luck, I came across a lifebuoy, one of the big round lifebuoys with another man clinging to it. I looked around and I said to this fella 'We're too near for suction, she'll suck us down.' I turned and swam away again, no objective, just swam away. This other fella ... well he never answered, he may have been a foreigner I didn't known who he was but I think he apparently followed me ... and eventually I came across some roll and in the distance, in the darkness, I could see something flash. So I swam to that and it was the upturned lifeboat with the crowd out there. It was the lifeboat out there that they'd tried to cut adrift. So I climbed on that and the other fella apparently followed me and he tried to climb on too but he was too exhausted to get fully on there. I managed to sit up on the keel of the lifeboat, but he just laid across there. He eventually died of exposure."

"Well we sat there, about twenty of us, right through the night. Nothing to do just living in hopes ... well someone started to curse and swear further down on the ship but someone said 'this is no time for swearing, it's time to say your prayers'. Which we did. So we all said our prayers there ... the Lord's Prayer ... But I said to this fella, sitting with his back to me, I said 'I'm tired I'm going to sleep'. He said 'For God's sake, son, don't go to sleep'. Course I didn't: had I gone to sleep I'd never of woke up again, it being so cold. Anyway we sat there through

RMS *Titanic* on maiden voyage.

Peter Boyd-Smith, Cobwebs

the night well, come towards the dawn ... ... well, a ship came into sight. 'Here's a ship', I said, 'there's two'. It turned out that one was the ship and the other was the iceberg ... alongside of each other. It was the Carpathia came up to take us off. Well, our own lifeboats by that time were able to see, (the ones that were afloat proper), able to see any survivors around and

came and took us off, there were twenty of us on the two different boats. And they took us to the Carpathia. That was the first time I ever tasted coffee in my life. When they hauled me aboard the Carpathia they gave me something hot to drink ... I used to hate coffee ... but I didn't care what it was then just something to warm me up. Which I did, they took me

down to the sick bay in the hospital and there I stopped ... for a while."

Sidney Daniels (City Heritage Oral History)

Sidney Daniels (on the right) on board *Olympic*.

The Ocean Ferry/Southampton City Heritage Collections

A Personal Narrative by an Eye-witness Joseph Scarrott, A.B., of the *Titanic* Who described the iceberg for The Sphere

---

"The night of April 14, 1912, will never be forgotten. It was a beautiful starlight night, no wind, and the sea was as calm as a lake, but the air was very cold."

"Everybody was in good spirits and everything throughout the ship was going smoothly. All of a sudden she crashed into an iceberg, which shook the giant liner from stem to stern. The shock of the collision was not so great as one would expect considering the size of the iceberg and the speed the ship was going, which was about 22 knots an hour."

"I was underneath the forecastle enjoying a smoke at the time. It happened about twenty minutes to twelve o'clock. The shaking of the ship seemed as though the engines had suddenly been reversed to full speed astern. Those of the crew who were asleep in their bunks turned out, and we all rushed on deck to see what was the matter."

When Realisation Came

"We found the ship had struck an iceberg as there was a large quantity of ice and snow on the starboard side of the fore deck. We did not think it very serious so went below again cursing the iceberg for disturbing us. We had no sooner got below when the boatswain called all hands on deck to uncover and turn all the boats out ready for lowering. We did not think then there was anything serious. The general idea of the crew was that we were going to get the boats ready in case of emergency, and the sooner we got the job done the quicker we should get below again."

"The port side boats were got ready first and then the starboard ones. As the work proceeded passengers were coming on deck with lifebelts on. Then we realised the situation. Every man went to his station. There was no panic, everybody was cool, and when the boats were ready the usual order was given, 'Women and children first.' That order was carried out without any class distinction whatever. In some cases we had to force women into the boats as they would not leave their husbands."

The Origin of the Revolver Shots

"The men stood back to allow the women to pass, except in one or two cases where men tried to rush, but they were very soon stopped. This occurred at the boat I was in charge of No. 14. About half-a-dozen foreigners tried to jump in before I had my complement of women and children, but I drove them back with the boat's tiller. Shortly afterwards the fifth officer, Mr. Lowe, came and took charge of the boat. I told him what had happened. He drew his revolver and fired two shots between the boat and ship's side into the water as a warning to any further attempts of that sort. When our boat was lowered we had fifty-four women, four children, one sailor, one window-cleaner, two firemen, three stewards, and one officer; total, sixty-six souls."

"When the boat was in the water we rowed clear of the ship. We then saw four other boats well clear and fairly well filled with women and children. We went to them and found none of them had an officer in charge. So the fifth officer took charge of the lot, ordering them to keep with him."

Joseph Scarrott, A.B. of the *Titanic*.

The Sphere/Southampton City Heritage Collections

BOAT DECK

DARK
EARTHY
PATCH

STARBOARD
LIGHT

STARBOARD
SHELTER
ON BRIDGE

PROMENADE
DECK

LOOSE ICE

ICE ON
WELL DECK

How the Stern Sank

"The ship sank shortly afterwards, I should say about 2.20 a.m. on the 15th, which would be two hours and forty minutes after she struck. The sight of that grand ship going down will never be forgotten. She slowly went down bow first with a slight list to starboard until the water reached the bridge, then she went quicker. When the third funnel had nearly disappeared I heard four explosions, which I took to be the bursting of the boilers. The ship was right up on end then. Suddenly she broke in two between the third and fourth funnel. The after part of the ship came down on the water in its normal position

Artist's impression of iceberg.

The Sphere/Southampton City Heritage Collections

143

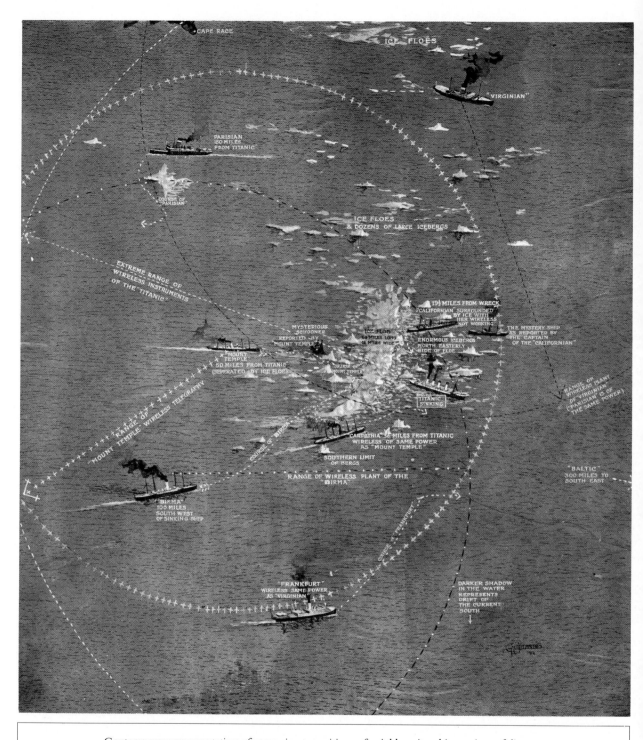

Contemporary representation of approximate positions of neighbouring ships at time of disaster.

G.H. Davis for The Sphere/Southampton City Heritage Collections

and seemed as if it was going to remain afloat, but it only remained a minute or two and then sank. The lights were burning right up till she broke in two. The cries from the poor souls struggling in the water sounded terrible in the stillness of the night. It seemed to go through you like a knife. Our officer then ordered all the boats under his charge to row towards where the ship went down to see if we could pick up anybody. Some of our boats picked up a few. I cannot say how many. After that we tied all our boats together so as to form a large object on the water which would be seen quicker than a single boat by a passing vessel. We divided the passengers of our boat amongst the other four, and then taking one man from each boat so as to make a crew we rowed away amongst the wreckage as we heard cries for help coming from that direction. When we got to it the sight we saw was awful. We were amongst hundreds of dead bodies floating in lifebelts. We could only see four alive. The first one we picked up was a male passenger. He died shortly after we got him in the boat. After a hard struggle we managed to get the other three."

Giving Way to Tears

"One of these we saw kneeling as if in prayer upon what appeared to be a part of a staircase. He was only about twenty yards away from us but it took us half-an-hour to push our boat through the wreckage and bodies to get to him; even then we could not get very close so we put out an oar for him to get hold of and so pulled him to the boat."

"All the bodies we saw seemed as if they had perished with the cold as their limbs were all cramped up. As we left that awful scene we gave way to tears. It was enough to break the stoutest heart. Just then we sighted the lights of a steamer, which proved to be the steamship *Carpathia* of the Cunard line. What a relief that was."

"We then made sail and went back to our other boats. By this time day was just beginning to dawn. We then saw we were surrounded with icebergs and field ice. Some of the fields of ice were from sixteen to twenty miles long. On our way back we saw one of our collapsible boats waterlogged; there were about eighteen persons on it, so we went and took them off. We left two dead bodies on it, and we were told two others had died and had fallen off."

A Joyful Arrival

"All our boats then proceeded towards the *Carpathia*. She had stopped right over where our ship had gone down. She had got our wireless message for assistance. When we got alongside we were got aboard as soon as possible. We found some survivors had already been picked up. Everything was in readiness for us dry clothes, blankets, beds, hot coffee, spirits, etc; everything to comfort us. The last of the survivors were got aboard about 8.30 a.m. The dead bodies that were in some of the boats were taken aboard and after identification were given a proper burial. They were two male passengers, one fireman, and one able seaman. We steamed about in the vicinity for a few hours in the hope of finding some more survivors, but did not find any. During that time wives were inquiring for husbands, sisters for brothers, and children for their parents, but many a sad face told the result."

A Tribute to America

"The *Carpathia* was bound from New York to Gibraltar, but the captain decided to return to New York with us. We arrived there about nine p.m. on Thursday, the 18th. We had good weather during the trip, but it was a sad journey. A list of the survivors was taken as soon as we had left the scene of the disaster. On arrival at New York everything possible was ready for our immediate assistance – clothing, money, medical aid, and good accommodation, in fact, I think it would have been impossible for the people of America to have treated us better. Before closing this narrative I must say that the passengers when they were in the boats, especially the women, were brave and assisted the handling of the boats a great deal. Thank God the weather was fine or I do not think there would have been one soul left to tell the tale."

(Signed) J. Scarrott (A.B.)
(City Heritage Collections)

Harold Bride – wireless operator.

The Daily News/Southampton City Heritage Collections

Graphic Story by the Wireless Operator

New York, Friday 5.15 a.m.

The following thrilling statement was dictated today by Mr. Bride, the assistant Marconi operator on board the *Titanic*, to the New York Times representative, in the presence of Mr. Marconi, who is now staying in New York:

"I joined the *Titanic* at Belfast. I was born in Nunhead, London, S.E., twenty-two years ago, and joined the Marconi staff last July. I first worked on the *Haverford*, and then on the *Lusitania*, and was transferred to the *Titanic* at Belfast. I didn't have much to do aboard the *Titanic*, except to relieve Phillips, the senior operator, from midnight until some time in the morning, when he finished sleeping."

"There were three rooms in the wireless cabin. One was a sleeping room, one a dynamo room, and one an operating room. I took off my clothes and went to sleep in the bed. Then I was conscious of waking

Captain Smith and his dog.

Southampton City Heritage Collections

up and hearing Phillips sending to Cape Race. I read what he was sending. It was only routine matter. I remembered how tired he was, and got out of bed without my clothes on to relieve him. I didn't even feel the shock. I hardly knew it had happened until after the captain had come to us. There was no jolt whatever."

The Help Signal, "C.Q.D."

"I was standing by Phillips, telling him to go to bed, when the captain put his head in the cabin, 'We've struck an iceberg,' the captain said, 'and I'm having an inspection made to tell what it has done for us. You had better get ready to send out a call for assistance, but don't send it until I tell you.' The captain went away, and in ten minutes, I should estimate, he came back. We could hear terrible confusion outside, but not the least thing to indicate any trouble. The wireless was working perfectly. 'Send a call for assistance', ordered the captain, barely putting his head in the door. 'What call should I send?' Phillips asked. 'The regulation international call for help, just that.' Then the captain was gone."

"Phillips began to send 'C.Q.D.' He flashed away at it, and we joked while he did so. All of us made light of the disaster. We joked that way while we flashed the signals for about five minutes. Then the captain came back. 'What are you sending?' he asked. 'C.Q.D.,' Phillips replied."

Joking About the Collision

"The humour of the situation appealed to me, and I cut in with a little remark that made us all laugh, including the captain. Send 'S.O.S.,' I said, 'it's the new call, and it may be your last chance to send it.' Phillips, with a laugh, changed the signal to 'S.O.S.' The captain told us we had been struck amidships, or just aft of amidships. It was ten minutes, Phillips told me, after he noticed the iceberg, but the slight jolt was the only signal to us that a collision had occurred. We thought we were a good distance away. We said lots of funny things to each other in the next few minutes. We picked up the first steamship *Frankfurt*; gave her our position, and said we had struck an iceberg, and needed assistance. The *Frankfurt* operator went away to tell his captain. He came back, and we told him we were sinking by the head, and that we could observe a distinct list forward."

"The *Carpathia* answered our signal, and we told her our position, and said we were sinking by the head. The operator went to tell the captain, and in five minutes returned, and told us the *Carpathia* was putting about and heading for us."

Scene on the Deck

"Our captain had left us at this time, and Phillips told me to run and tell him what the *Carpathia* had answered. I did so, and I went through an awful mass of people to his cabin. The decks were full of scrambling men and women."

"I came back and heard Phillips giving the *Carpathia* further directions. Phillips told me to put on my clothes. Until that moment I forgot I wasn't dressed. I went to my cabin and dressed. I brought an overcoat to Phillips, and as it was very cold I slipped the overcoat upon him while he worked."

"Every few minutes Phillips would send me to the captain with little messages. They were merely telling how the *Carpathia* was coming our way, and giving her speed.

Heroic Telegraphist

"I noticed as I came back from one trip that they were putting off the women and children in lifeboats, and that the list forward was increasing. Phillips told me the wireless was growing weaker. The captain came and told us our engine rooms were taking water, and that the dynamos might not last much longer. We sent that word to the *Carpathia*."

Artist's impression of sinking.

G.H. Davis for The Sphere/Southampton City Heritage Collections

"I went out on deck and looked around. The water was pretty close up to the boat deck. There was a great scramble aft, and how poor Phillips worked through it I don't know. He was a brave man. I learned to love him that night, and I suddenly felt for him a great reverence to see him standing there sticking to his work while everybody else was raging about. I will never live to forget the work Phillips did for the last awful fifteen minutes."

"Phillips clung on, sending and sending. He clung on for about ten minutes, or maybe fifteen minutes, after the captain released him. The water was then coming into our cabin."

"From aft came the tunes of the ship's band, playing the ragtime tune, 'Autumn.' Phillips ran aft, and that was the last I ever saw of him alive."

"I went to the place where I had seen the collapsible boat on the boat deck, and to my surprise I saw the boat, and the men still trying to push it off. I guess there wasn't a sailor in the crowd. They couldn't do it. I went up to them, and was just lending a hand when a large wave came awash of the deck. The big wave carried the boat off. I had hold of an oar-lock and I went off with it. The next I knew I was in the boat. But that wasn't all; I was in the boat, and the boat was upside down, and I was under it. I remember realising I was wet through, and that whatever happened I must breathe, for I was under water. I knew I had to fight for it, and I did. How I got out from under the boat I don't know, but I felt a breath of air at last. There were men all around me – hundreds of them. The sea was dotted with them, all depending on their lifebelts."

Last Glimpse of the *Titanic*

"I felt I simply had to get away from the ship. She was a beautiful sight then. Smoke and sparks were rushing out of her funnels. There must have been an explosion, but we heard none. We only saw a big stream of sparks. The ship was gradually turning on her nose – just like a duck does that goes down for a dive. I had only one thing on my mind – to get away from the suction."

"The band was still playing. I guess all the band went down. They were heroes. They were still playing 'Autumn.' Then I swam with all my might. I suppose I was 150ft away when the *Titanic*, on her nose, with her afterquarter sticking straight up in the air, began to settle slowly. When at last the waves washed over her rudder there wasn't the least bit of suction I could feel. She must have kept going down just as flowing as she had been."

"I felt after a little while like sinking. I was very cold. I saw a boat of some kind near me, and put all my strength into an effort to swim to it. It was hard work, and I was all alone when a hand reached out

Wireless Telegraph Room.

Illustrated London News

from the boat and pulled me aboard. It was our same collapsible boat and the same crowd was on it. There was just room for me to roll on the edge. I lay there not caring what happened. Somebody sat on my legs. They were wedged in between the slats, and were being wrenched. I hadn't the heart left to ask the man to move. There was a terrible sight all around; men swimming and sinking everywhere."

"I saw some lights off in the distance, and knew a steamship was coming to our aid. I didn't care what happened. I just lay and gasped when I could, and felt the pain in my feet. I feel it still. At last the *Carpathia* was alongside, and the people were being taken up a rope ladder. Our boat drew near, and one by one the men were taken off of it. One man was dead. I passed him, and went to a ladder, although my feet pained me terribly."

"The dead man was Phillips. He died on the raft from exposure and cold. I guess he had been all in from work before the wreck came. He stood his ground until the crisis passed and then collapsed. But I hardly thought of that then; I didn't think much about anything. I tried the rope ladder. My feet pained me terribly, but I got to the top, and felt hands reaching out to me. The next I know a woman was leaning over me in a cabin, and I felt

The *Titanic*'s Band – all were lost.
"I don't like jazz music as a rule but I think it helped us all that night." Charles Lightoller

Southampton City Heritage Collections

her hand waving in my hair and rubbing my face. I felt somebody at my feet, and felt the warmth of liquor. Somebody got me under the arms, and then I was carried down below to the hospital. That was early in the day. I guess I lay in hospital until near night, when they told me the *Carpathia*'s wireless man was acting 'queer', and would I help?"

"After that I never was out of the wireless room, so I don't know what happened to the passengers."

Harold Bride (Wireless Operator)
(City Heritage Collections)

Second Officer Lightoller recorded:

"The time we struck was 2.20am (sic) April 14th, of tragic memory, and it was about ten minutes later that the Fourth Officer, Boxall, opened my door and, seeing me awake, quietly said, 'We've hit an iceberg.'

I replied, 'I know you've hit something.' He then said: 'The water is up to F Deck in the Mail Room.'

That was quite sufficient. Not another word passed. He went out, closing the door, whilst I slipped into some clothes as quickly as possible, and went out on deck....

...The ship had been running under a big head of steam, therefore the instant the engines were stopped the steam started roaring off at all eight exhausts, kicking up a row that would have dwarfed the row of a thousand railway engines thundering through a culvert.

All the seamen came tumbling up on the boat deck in response to the order 'All hands on deck' just following the instinct that told them that it was here they would be required. It was an utter impossibility to convey an order by word of mouth; speech was useless, but a tap on the shoulder and an indication with the hand, dark though it was, was quite sufficient to set the men about the different jobs, clearing away the boat covers, hauling tight the falls and coiling them down on deck, clear and ready for lowering.

The passengers by this time were beginning to flock up on the boat deck, with anxious faces, the appalling din only adding to their anxiety in a situation already terrifying enough in all conscience. In fact it was a marvel how they ever managed to keep their heads at all. All one could do was to give them a cheery smile of encouragement, and hope that the infernal roar would soon stop. My boats were all along the port side, and by the time I had got my Watch well employed, stripping the covers and coiling down, it became obvious to me that the ship was settling. So far she had remained perfectly upright, which was apt to give a false sense of security. Soon the Bosun's Mate came to me and indicated with a wave of his hand that the job I had set him of clearing away was pretty well completed. I nodded, and indicated by a motion of my hand for him to swing out....

...Having got the boats swung out, I made for the Captain, and happened to meet him near by on the boat deck. Drawing him into a corner, and, cupping both my hands over my mouth and his ear, I yelled at the top of my voice, 'Hadn't we better get the women and children into the boats, sir?' He heard me, and nodded reply. One of my reasons for suggesting getting the boats afloat was, that I could see a steamer's steaming lights a couple of miles away on our port bow. If I could get the women and children into the boats, they would be perfectly safe in that smooth sea until this ship picked them up; if the necessity arose. My idea was that I would lower the boats with a few people in each and when safely in the water fill them up from the gangway doors on the lower decks, and transfer them to the other ship.

Although boats and falls were all brand new, it is a risky business at the best of times to attempt to lower a boat between seventy and eighty feet at night time, filled with people who are not 'boatwise'. It is, unfortunately, the rule rather than the exception for some mishap to occur in lowering boats loaded with people who, through no fault of their own, lack this boat sense. In addition, the strain is almost too much to expect of boats and falls under ordinary conditions.

However, having got Captain Smith's sanction, I indicated to the Bosun's Mate, and we lowered down the first boat level with the boat deck, and, just at this time, thank heaven, the frightful din of escaping steam suddenly stopped, and there was a death-like silence a thousand times more exaggerated, fore and aft the ship. It was almost startling to hear one's own voice again after the appalling din of the last half hour or so.

I got just on forty people into No. 4 boat, and gave the order to 'lower away', and for the boat to 'go to the gangway door' with the idea of filling each boat as it became afloat, to its full capacity. At the same time I told the Bosun's Mate to take six hands and open the port lower-deck gangway door, which was abreast of No. 2 hatch. He took his men and proceeded to carry out the order, but neither he or the men were ever seen again. One can only suppose that they gave their lives endeavouring to carry out this order, probably they were trapped in the alley-way by a rush of water, for by this time the fo'csle head was within about ten feet of the water. Yet I still had hope that we should save her....

...On the *Titanic*, passengers naturally kept coming up and asking, did I consider the situation serious. In all cases I tried to cheer them up, by telling them 'No', but that it was a matter of precaution to get the boats in the water, ready for any emergency. That in any case they were perfectly safe, as there was a ship not more than a few miles away, and I pointed out the lights on the port bow which they could see as well as I could.

At this time we were firing rocket distress signals, which explode with a loud report a couple of hundred feet in the air. Every minute or two one of these went up, bursting overhead with a cascade of stars.

'Why were we firing these signals, if there was no

Captain Smith on the starboard side of the bridge.

Southampton City Heritage Collections

danger?' was the question, to which I replied that we were trying to call the attention of the ship nearby, as we could not get her with wireless. That ship was the *Californian*. Here again we were to see exemplified, what has become almost proverbial at sea, that in cases of disaster, one ship, the first on the scene, will be in a position to rescue, and yet, through some circumstance or combination of circumstances, fails to make that rescue.

The distress signals we fired were seen by the Officer of the Watch on board the *Californian*, also by several members of her crew. Even the flashes from our Morse lamp were seen but finally judged to be 'Just the masthead light flickering.' Though at one time the thought evidently did arise that we were trying to call them....

...The Bosun's Mate and six of the Watch having been lost to me, the work had become very heavy and still heavier as I detailed two of the remaining Watch to go away with each boat as it was lowered. The practise was, to lower each boat until the gunwale was level with the boat deck, then, standing with one foot on the deck and one in the boat, the women just held out their right hand, the wrist of which I grabbed with my right hand, hooking my left arm underneath their arm, and so practically lifted them over the gap between the boat's gunwale and the ship's side, into the boat.

Between one boat being lowered away and the next boat being prepared, I usually nipped along to have a look down the very long emergency staircase leading direct from the boat deck down to 'C' deck. Actually, built as a short cut for the crew, it served my purpose now to gauge the speed with which the water was rising, and how high it had got. By now the fore deck was below the surface. That cold, green water, crawling its ghostly way up that staircase, was a sight that stamped itself indelibly on my memory. Step by step, it made its way up, covering the electric lights, one after the other, which, for a time, shone under the surface with a horribly weird effect.

Still, it served a very good purpose, and enabled me to form an accurate judgement as to how far she had gone, and how quickly she was going down. Dynamos were still running, and deck lights on, which, though dim, helped considerably with the work; more than could be said of one very good lady who achieved fame by waving an electric light and successfully blinding us as we worked on the boats. It puzzled me until I found she had it installed in the head of her walking stick! I am afraid she was rather disappointed on finding out that her precious light was not a bit appreciated.... ...It was about this time that the Chief Officer came over from the starboard side and asked, did I know where the firearms were?...

...I told the Chief Officer, 'Yes, I know where they are. Come along and I'll get them for you,' and into the First Officer's cabin we went – the Chief, Murdoch, the Captain and myself – where I hauled them out, still in all their pristine newness and grease.

I was going out when the Chief shoved one of the revolvers into my hands, with a handful of ammunition, and said, 'Here you are, you may need it.' On the impulse, I just slipped it into my pocket, along with the cartridges, and returned to the boats. The whole incident had not taken three minutes, though it seemed barely worth that precious time.

As I returned along the deck, I passed Mr. and Mrs. Strauss leaning up against the deck house, chatting quite cheerily. I stopped and asked Mrs. Strauss, 'Can I take you along to the boats?' She replied, 'I think I'll stay here for the present.' Mr. Strauss, calling her by her Christian name said, smilingly, 'Why don't you go along with him dear?' She just smiled, and said, 'No, not yet.' I left them, and they went down together. To another couple, evidently from the Western States, that I found sitting on a fan casing I asked the girl, 'Won't you let me put you in one of the boats?' She replied with a frank smile, 'Not on your life. We started together, and if need be, we'll finish together.' It was typical of the spirit throughout....

...Hurrying back to the two remaining lifeboats still hanging in their davits, I met the Purser, Assistant Purser, and the Senior and Junior Surgeons – the latter a noted wag – even in the face of tragedy, couldn't resist his last mild joke, 'Hello, Lights, are you warm?' The idea of anyone being warm in that temperature was a joke in itself, and I suppose it struck him as odd to meet me wearing a sweater, no coat or overcoat. I had long since discarded my greatcoat, even in pants and sweater over pyjamas alone I was in a bath of perspiration. There was only time to pass a few words, then they all shook hands and said 'Goodbye.' Frankly, I didn't feel at all like 'Goodbye,' although I knew we shouldn't have the ship under us much longer....

...About this time I met all the engineers, as they came trooping up from below. Most of them I knew individually, and had been shipmates with them on different ships of the Line. They had all loyally stuck to their guns, long after they could be of any material assistance. Much earlier on the engine-room telegraphs had been 'Rung off – ' the last ring made on board ships at sea, it releases engineers and stokers from duty....

...There was little opportunity to say more than a word or two to the engineers. Up to that time they had known little of what was going on, and it was surely a bleak and hopeless spectacle that met their eyes. Empty falls hanging loosely from every davit head, and not a solitary hope for any of them.

In point of fact, they were lost to a man, not one single survivor out of the whole thirty-five...

...I stood partly in the boat, owing to the difficulty of getting the womenfolk over a high bulwark rail just there. As we were ready for lowering the Chief came over to my side of the deck and, seeing me in the boat and no seaman available said, 'You go with her, Lightoller.'

Praises be, I had just sufficient sense to say, 'Not damn likely,' and jump back on board; not with any idea of self-imposed martyrdom – far from it – it was just pure impulse of the moment, and an impulse for which I was to thank my lucky stars a thousand times over, in the days to come. I had taken my chance and gone down with the rest, consequently I didn't have to take any old back-chat from anyone....

...With one other seaman I started to cast adrift the one remaining Englehardt on top of the officers' quarters. We cut and threw off the lashings, jumped round to the inboard side ready to pick up the gunwale together and throw her bodily down on to the boat deck. The seaman working with me called: 'All ready, sir,' and I recognized Hemmings' voice – the chap I had ordered away long before, and who returned on board to tend the falls, and in whose place I sent Major Peuchen.

'Hello, is that you, Hemming?'
'Yes, sir.'
'Why haven't you gone?' I asked.

Artist's impression of the lowering of the lifeboats by John Duncan.

The Sphere/Southampton City Heritage Collections

'Oh, plenty of time yet, sir,' he replied cheerily. Apparently the chap had loyally stuck by me all through, though it had been too dark to recognize him. Stout fellow. Later, he slid down one of the falls, swam for it and was saved.

We had just time to tip the boat over, and let her drop into the water that was now above the boat deck, in the hope that some few would be able to scramble on to her as she floated off. Hemming and I then, as every single boat was now away from the port side, went over to the starboard side, to see if there was anything further to be done there. But all the boats on this side had also been got away, though there were still crowds of people on the deck.

Just then the ship took a slight but definite plunge – probably a bulkhead went – and the sea came rolling up in a wave, over the steel-fronted bridge, along the deck below us, washing the people back in a dreadful huddled mass. Those that didn't disappear under the water right away, instinctively started to clamber up that part of the deck still out of water, and work their way towards the stern, which was rising steadily out of the water as the bow went down. A few of the more agile leapt up on top of the officers' quarters where Hemming and I were at the moment. It was a sight that doesn't bear dwelling on – to stand there, above the wheelhouse, and on our quarters, watching the frantic struggles to climb up the sloping deck, utterly unable to even hold out a helping hand.

I knew, only too well, the utter futility of following that driving instinct of self-preservation and struggling up towards the stern. It would only be postponing the plunge, and prolonging the agony – even lessening one's already slim chances, by becoming one of a crowd. It came home to me very clearly how fatal it would be to get amongst those hundreds and hundreds of people who would shortly be struggling for their lives in that deadly cold water. There was only one thing to do, and I might just as well do it and get it over, so, turning to the fore part of the bridge, I took a header. Striking the water, was like a thousand knives being driven into one's body, and, for a few moments, I completely lost grip of myself – and no wonder for I was perspiring freely, whilst the temperature of the water was 28 degrees, or 4 degrees below freezing.

Ahead of me the lookout cage on the foremast was visible just above the water – in normal times it would be a hundred feet above. I struck out blindly for this, but only for a short while, till I got hold of myself again and realized the futility of seeking safety on anything connected with the ship. I then turned to starboard, away from the ship altogether.

For a time I wondered what was making it so difficult for me to keep my head above the water. Time and again I went under, until it dawned on me that it was

the great Webley revolver, still in my pocket, that was dragging me down. I soon sent that on its downward journey.

The water was now pouring down the stokeholds, by way of the fiddley gratings abaft the bridge, and round the forward funnel.

On the boat deck, above our quarters, on the fore part of the forward funnel, was a huge rectangular air shaft and ventilator, with an opening about twenty by fifteen feet. On this opening was a light wire grating to prevent rubbish being drawn down or anything else being thrown down. This shaft led direct to No. 3 stokehold, and was therefore a sheer drop of close on hundred feet, right to the bottom of the ship.

I suddenly found myself drawn, by the sudden rush of the surface water now pouring down this shaft, and held flat and firmly up against this wire netting with the additional full and clear knowledge of what would happen if this light wire carried away. The pressure of the water just glued me there whilst the ship sank slowly below the surface.

Although I struggled and kicked for all I was worth, it was impossible to get away, for as fast as I pushed myself off I was irresistibly dragged back, every instant expecting the wire to go, and to find myself shot down into the bowels of the ship.

Apart from that, I was drowning, and a matter of another couple of minutes would have seen me through. I was still struggling and fighting when suddenly a terrific blast of hot air came up the shaft, and blew me right away from the air shaft and up to the surface.

The water was now swirling round, and the ship sinking rapidly, when once again I was caught and sucked down by an inrush of water, this time adhering to one of the fiddley gratings. Just how I got clear of that, I don't know, as I was rather losing interest in things, but I eventually came to the surface once again, this time alongside that last Englehardt boat which Hemming and I had launched from on top of the officers' quarters on the opposite side – for I was now on the starboard side, near the forward funnel.

There were many around in the water by this time, some swimming, others (mostly men, thank God), definitely drowning – an utter nightmare of both sight and sound. In the circumstances I made no effort to get on top of the upturned boat, but, for some reason, was content to remain floating alongside, just hanging on to a small piece of rope.

The bow of the ship was now rapidly going down and the stern rising higher and higher out of the water, piling the people into helpless heaps around the steep decks, and by the score into the icy water. Had the boats been around many might have been saved, but of them, at this time there was no sign. Organized help, or even individual help, was quite impossible. All one could do

Sidney Sedunary, Third Class Steward, lost.

Southampton City Heritage Collections

Jack (John) Stewart, First Class Steward in the Verandah Café. The keys of the café were in his pocket when he was rescued.

Private Collection

was just wait on events, and try and forget the icy cold grip of the water.

The terrific strain of bringing the after-end of that huge hull clear out of the water, caused the expansion joint abaft No. 1 funnel to open up. (These expansion joints were found necessary in big ships to allow the ship to 'work' in a seaway.) The fact that the two wire stays to this funnel, on the after-part, led over and abaft the expansion joint, threw on them an extraordinary strain, eventually carrying away the port wire guy, to be followed almost immediately by the starboard one. Instantly the port one parted, the funnel started to fall, but the fact that the starboard one held a moment or two longer, gave this huge structure a pull over to that side of the ship, causing it to fall, with its scores of tons, right amongst the struggling mass of humanity already in the water. It struck the water between the Englehardt and the ship, actually missing me by inches.

Amongst the many historic and, what in less tragic circumstances would have been humorous – questions, asked by Senator Smith at the Washington Enquiry was, 'Did it hurt anyone?'

One effect of the funnel crashing down on the sea, was to pick up the Englehardt, in the wash so created, and fling it well clear of the sinking ship.

When I again recognized my surroundings, we were full fifty yards clear of the ship. The piece of rope was still in my hand, with old friend Englehardt upturned and attached to the other end, with several men by now standing on it. I also scrambled up, after spending longer than I like to remember in that icy water. Lights on board the Titanic were still burning, and a wonderful spectacle she made, standing out black and massive against the starlit sky; myriads of lights still gleaming through the portholes, from that part of the decks still above water.

The fore part, and up to the second funnel was by this time completely submerged, and as we watched this terribly awe-inspiring sight, suddenly all lights went out and the huge bulk was left in black darkness, but clearly silhouetted against the bright sky. Then, the next moment, the massive boilers left their beds and went thundering down with a hollow rumbling roar, through the bulkheads, carrying everything with them that stood in their way. This unparalleled tragedy that was being enacted before our very eyes, now rapidly approached its finale, as the huge ship slowly but surely reared herself on end and brought rudder and propellers clear of the water, till, at last, she assumed an absolute perpendicular position. In this amazing attitude she remained for the space of half a minute. Then with impressive majesty and ever-increasing momentum, she silently took her last tragic dive to seek a final resting place in the unfathomable depths of the cold gray (sic) Atlantic.

Almost like a benediction everyone round me on the upturned boat breathed the two words, 'She's gone.'

Fortunately, the scene that followed was shrouded in darkness. Less fortunately, the calm still silence carried every sound with startling distinctness. To enter into a description of those heartrending, never-to-be-forgotten sounds would serve no useful purpose. I never allowed my thoughts to dwell on them, and there are some that would be alive and well today had they just determined to erase from their minds all memory of those ghastly moments, or at least until time had somewhat dimmed the memory of that awful tragedy."

Second Officer Lightoller (Titanic and Other Ships. 1935)

Just before his death (reported in the "Echo") 80 year old Jack Podesta, of Curzon Court, Lordswood, Southampton, fireman in the doomed liner, completed his graphic account of the White Star liner's first and last voyage.

He recalled that everything went well until the Saturday when one of the firemen was taken ill in the stoke-hold.

"He could not tell us what was the matter, he just lost all energy and strength. We got him to his bunk."
"On this very same morning, my chum and I had just gone across firing our boilers and we were standing against a water-tight door – just talking – when all of a sudden, on looking through the forward end on her starboard side, we saw about six or maybe seven rats running towards us. They passed by our feet; in fact we both kicked out at them and they ran aft somewhere."
"They must have come from the bow end, about where the crash came later. We did not take much notice at the time because we see rats on most ships, but I think it is true that they can smell danger."
"Well now came Sunday morning watch and we did our hours; everything was going well all day. The evening watch came and down we went again. In this four hour watch, we were getting towards the ice – little did we think we were so close."

"We came off at 8 pm and went to the galley for our supper. Some of us passed remarks about the persisting cold. My mate and I put on our 'go ashore' coats and went to the mess room, which was up a flight of stairs, just inside of the whale deck. We finished our meal and coming from the mess room to our living quarters, we heard a man in the crows-nest shout 'Ice ahead, sir.' "
"Nutbean (Fireman) and I went on deck and looked around but saw nothing. It was a lovely calm night but pitch black."

Jack Podesta and his friend went back below decks and stayed up talking for an hour or more before turning in.

"We laid in our bunks for about five minutes – several times the man in the crows-next shouted 'Ice ahead, sir' – nothing was done from the bridge to slow down or alter course. So, the crash came – it sounded like tearing a strip off a piece of calico – nothing more, only a quiver. It did not even wake up those who were in a good sleep."
"The few of us who were awake, went out of our room to the spiral ladder of No. 1 hatch. We saw some men running up from the 12 to 4 room which was on the starboard side (about where the ship struck the iceberg). They must have been flooded out as we could hear water rushing into the forward hold."
Going back to our room, we began shaking one or two men up from their bunks (one in particular named Gus Stanbrook (Fireman)). I said, 'Come on Gus, get a lifebelt and go to your boat, she's sinking.' He began laughing and simply lay back again, thinking it was a joke."
"She must have torn her bottom at least a quarter of her length. After shaking up some of our watch-mates, we went on deck and saw about ten tons of ice on the starboard whale deck."

"Upon returning to our room again, we began shaking the men up with no avail. Blann (Fireman) came down from the deck shouting 'Look what I found on deck.' In his hands he had a lump of ice. Then the bo'sun came to our door (his name was Nichols) and shouted 'Get your lifebelts and man your boats.' I knew this was going to happen."
"He was very pale and his lips were in a twitter. He had several ABs with him. I heard he was on his way to the fore-peak to get a gangplank as they thought the Olympic was going to reach us."

Jack Podesta and Nutbean followed the bo'sun's orders, but found the boat they were allotted was already full and they were ordered to help lower it.

Left alone, Nutbean started to walk towards the bridge, while Mr Podesta groped around looking for something to make a raft. Nutbean discovered another lifeboat under the bridge and the Chief Officer, Mr Murdoch, told them to jump.

"There were about three able seamen in the boat and we

Weary survivors draw alongside rescue ship *Carpathia*.

Southampton City Heritage Collections

two firemen – the rest were passengers, including women and children, 72 in all. So we took hold of the rope falls and lowered ourselves into the water. Murdoch shouted over the side, 'Keep handy, in case you have to come back.' He must have thought her water-tight doors were going to keep her afloat."

"I should imagine we were about five or six hundred yards away from the ship, watching her settling down - she was going down at the head all the time. But there was once when she seemed to hang in the same place for a long time, so naturally we thought the water-tight doors would hold her."

"Then all of a sudden, she swerved and her bow went under, her stern rose up in the air. Out went her lights and the rumbling noise was terrible. It must have been her boilers and engines as well as her bulkheads, all giving way. Then she disappeared altogether. This was followed by the groans and screams of the poor souls in the water."

"Soon, it was all silent. I think the ship was about two hours sinking and we were drifting in the boats until dawn. We could see small black objects - bodies and ice floating around, and later we saw some more lifeboats a good distance away. They were burning some papers."

After they were picked up Jack Podesta saw two other firemen who had been picked up off a raft, shivering terribly with cold.

"My mate and I gave them blankets and rubbed their legs to start up their circulation. Their names were John Connor and Wally Hurst."

Jack Podesta (Echo - 27th May 1968)- Fireman

"It was 1 o'clock in the morning and I was in my cabin asleep when one of the head stewards came in and woke me up. He told me if I wanted to see anyone else alive I would have to get up because the ship was sinking. I got up and put a few, a few bits of clothes on and went up to the working alleyway. I went from there to the bow of the ship and when I got up to the bow of the ship the water and the ice was coming over the gunnels. I stood there for a little while and said a prayer. I left there and made my way up to the promenade deck where I saw three ladies arm in arm walking up and down. I said to them, I says, 'You come along with me, I said, the ships sinking and we'll go up and see if there's any lifeboats left'. She said, 'We're, alright Steward, the ship can't sink, we don't want to go down in one of those little boats'. I left them and went up to the boat deck and I saw one lifeboat left in the corner. I started taking the canvas off when a sailor come and help me and we got the boat slung out, an Officer come along and asked me if I could row. I said 'Yes, sir'. He said 'Get in the boat, he says, and take the bow oar'. We were filled up with ladies, with women and children, their husbands had to remain behind, it was very sad, broken hearted."

"We were lowered down to the water and we got away about, five, ten minutes when the ships bow was under the water and the propellers was up in the air. And after another ten minutes we heard a sound as the engines fell off the blocks and then she just slid down under the water. And then we heard the screams and we heard the screams for a little while and it all faded away. It was very calm but bitter cold. We rowed about all night, 'til I got picked up in the Carpathia about half past eight in the morning".

Arthur Lewis, Steward (Echo - 9th December 1972)

"The bump threw us off our feet. We were told to stay at our posts. No one seemed excited and it never occurred to anyone that the ship would sink..... We knew she had hit an iceberg and the situation took a more serious turn when we were ordered to draw the fires in the boilers."

"Then there was a shout: 'Every man for himself.' I was working only in a vest and short pants, but I dashed up to the boat deck, where there were crowds of passengers milling about near the life-boats being lowered..... I helped where I could and got away myself among those in the last lifeboat. There were 70 of us, all passengers except myself and an AB....We watched the Titanic go down and as she sank bow first, saw people falling and jumping into the icy water."

"I was the only one in the boat who was half-naked and a woman passenger, the wealthy Mrs J J Astor, ripped her big fur muff down the middle to wrap round me. That saved my life, for it was four and a half hours in the bitter cold before we were picked up by the liner Carpathia."

James Crimmins – Fireman (Echo 16th February 1956) – printed after his death.

(Mr Crimmins' brother-in-law, Stoker Tommy Kerr, went down with the *Titanic*.)

"It was a beautiful night," (he said, screwing up his eyes for a moment,) *"there wasn't a ripple on the water. When I saw what lay before us I phoned the bridge and said: 'We're in danger here – iceberg right ahead!' "*

"I was ordered into number six life-boat by Mr. Lightoller, the second officer... there were about 40 of us altogether. There were only 16 boats and two small rafts to serve two thousand people. We got into the boat at one o'clock in the morning, and were told to 'pull for that light.' We were picked up by the Carpathia three hours later. She took two hours and forty minutes to sink. And that's an awful long time."

Fred Fleet – Lookout (Echo – 19th June 1967)
(At the time of this interview Fleet was an Echo paperseller)

White Star crew swing out a lifeboat during practice.
Southampton City Heritage Collections

He (Walter Williams) begins his story by recalling that in 1911 attention was drawn to the fact that there were not sufficient boats for all the passengers on the *Olympic*. The Board of Trade replied that as the *Olympic* was unsinkable 16 life-boats were *"quite adequate."*

Mr Williams was on board when the *Olympic* was in collision with another vessel (the *Hawke*) off the Brambles and had to be towed back to Southampton and then to Belfast.

When the *Titanic* struck an iceberg a wag remarked to Mr Williams: *"We've only hit an iceberg. It's another job for Belfast."* The joker went down with the vessel.

When Mr Williams joined the *Titanic* as a second class steward at Southampton he remembers that some paint on the lockers was still wet. He told me he was surprised that there was no boat drill before they left Southampton and no boat drill on the first Sunday at sea as was normal custom.

When the *Titanic* struck, as we all know, the danger of the situation was not at first apparent to the passengers. Eventually Mr Williams made a jump for a boat, No. 13, as it was being lowered and landed safely among other seamen. *"There was plenty of room; many of the ship's boats were far from full."* he says. As they watched the *Titanic* go down, suddenly all the lights went out as the ship dipped beneath the waves.

"During the night we were passed by what looked like a sailing ship. As we got closer we realised it was a small iceberg."
Mr Walter Williams – Second Class Steward (died February 1972) (Echo – 10th May 1962)

"He worked downstairs in the engine room I think more than anything and my grandfather must have worked in the engine room too because when they hit the Titanic dad was asleep in his bunk and my grandfather threw a lump of ice on his bunk and said 'Wake up Wally we've hit an iceberg'. He went down in the engine room and they never saw him again. But my father was saved."
Rosina Broadbere (City Heritage Oral History) (Daughter of Wally Hurst and grandaughter of C.J. Hurst, both Firemen)

The Postal Clerks' Devotion

One of the brave acts that up to now (article written in 1912) has been missed in the various stories given by survivors is that of the postal clerks who were on the *Titanic*. There were five of them, three Americans and two Englishmen. The last were Jago Smith and Edward Williamson. When it was deemed impossible for the ship to remain afloat these five clerks, pressing stewards into their service, laboured earnestly to get their more precious mail

The sole occupants of the controversial Emergency Boat 1 which had a capacity of forty. Requesting the photograph aboard *Carpathia* are Lady Duff Gordon and her husband Sir Cosmo.

Southampton City Heritage Collections

sacks on deck ready for transhipment. By hard work they managed to get practically all the sacks containing registered letters, some 250 or more in number, on the deck, and every one of the five had descended to the mail room for further loads when the ship sank and all were lost while striving to do their duty.

(City Heritage Collections)

Press Association Foreign Special

There were sixteen boats in the forlorn procession which entered on the terrible hours of rowing, drifting, and suspense. Women wept for their lost husbands and sons, and sailors sobbed for the ship which had been their pride. Men choked back their tears and sought to comfort the widowed. Perhaps they said, other boats might have put off in the other direction towards the East. They strove, though none too sure of it themselves, to convince the women of the certainty that a rescue ship would soon appear.

Dawn brought no ship, but not long after 5 a.m. the *Carpathia*, far out of her path and making eighteen knots instead of her wonted fifteen, showed a single red and black stack.

In the joy of the moment the heaviest griefs were forgotten. Soon afterwards Captain Rostron and Chief Steward Hughes were welcoming the children and bedraggled arrivals over the *Carpathia*'s side. The silence of the *Carpathia*'s engines, the piercing cold, and clamour of many voices in the companion ways caused me to dress hurriedly and to awaken my wife. It was 5.40 on Monday morning. Our stewardess, meeting me outside, pointed to a wailing host in the back of the dining room and said, *'From the Titanic. She is at the bottom of the ocean.'*

At the ship's side a moment later I saw the last of a line of boats discharge their loads. I saw women, some with cheap shawls about their heads, some in the costliest fur cloaks, ascending the ship's side. Such joy as the first sight of our ship may have given them had disappeared from their faces.

There were tears and signs of faltering as the women were helped up the ladders or hoisted aboard in swings for lack of room in which to put them. The *Titanic*'s boats after unloading were set adrift. To our north the broad ice field, the length of hundreds of *Carpathia*'s, stretched around us, and on either side rose sharp glistening peaks. One black berg seen about 10 a.m. was said to be that which sunk the *Titanic*.

Few of the men of the *Carpathia*'s passenger list slept in bed on any of the nights that followed. They lay on chairs, on the deck, on the dining tables, or floors.

Press Association Reporter Foreign Special.
(City Heritage Collections)

163

E. Rees.
3rd Officer.

G.H. Barnish
4th Officer.

H.J. Dean
1st Officer.

"Daily Mirror" Copyright London.

J.W. Hankinson
Ch. Officer.

James Gordon Bissel
2nd Officer.

A. H. Rostron.

Autographed photograph of *Carpathia*'s officers given to Fourth Officer Boxhall.

Ford Collection

Five Women Save Pet Dogs

Five women survivors saved their pet dogs, and another has saved a little pig which she regarded as her mascot.

(City Heritage Collections)

I Wanted To Go Back

'There were thirty-five ladies and three men, two of whom were stewards and one sailor in my boat, which was number eight. The captain ordered me to go aboard and row for a light which we saw in the distance, put the passengers in safety, and return as soon as possible to the *Titanic*. I found out that I could not reach this strange light, and it was then that I saw the *Titanic* had sunk, and I wanted to go back and save some of those struggling in the water. Then we lost sight of the strange light and everyone began to cry. I said "We have seven more days to live. We have plenty of everything in the boat." We were picked up by the *Carpathia* after eight hours. On board the *Carpathia*, the lady at the tiller asked for my address at Southampton and I said I should be at the Sailors Home.'

A.B. Thomas Jones, (on receiving a letter from first class passenger Gladys Cherry, cousin of Lady Rothes, saying 'I shall always remember your words, "Ladies, if any of us are saved, remember I wanted to go back. I would rather drown with them than leave them." ')

(Southern Daily Echo, 25th May 1912)

An Ocean Graveyard; Floating Corpses; Mother and her Baby

**From our own correspondent.
New York, Wednesday.**

More than 100 of the *Titanic*'s victims were seen floating on the water by the steamship *Bremen*,

Overcoated passengers on a transatlantic liner watching the ice floe.

The Sphere

which arrived today from Bremen, when, on April 20, the German liner passed over the spot where the *Titanic* went down.

Mrs. Johanna Stunke, a first cabin passenger on the *Bremen*, gave a vivid story of the scene from the liner's rail.

"It was between four and five o'clock on Saturday," she said, "when our ship sighted off the bow to the starboard an iceberg. We had been told by some of the officers that the *Bremen* was going to pass within a few miles of the position given by the *Titanic* when she sank, so when the cry went up that ice was sighted we all rushed to the starboard rail. It was a beautiful afternoon, and the sun glistening on the big iceberg was a wonderful picture, but as we drew nearer and could make out small dots floating around in the sea a feeling of awe and sadness crept over every one, and the ship proceeded in absolute silence. We passed within a hundred feet of the southern most drift of the wreckage, and looking down over the rail we distinctly saw a number of bodies so clearly that we could make out what they were wearing, and whether they were men or women."

Carpathia arrives with survivors in New York.

Deathless Story of the *Titanic*

Several days after the disaster lifeboat and crew of *Oceanic* attending to drifting collapsible lifeboat A and bodies from the *Titanic*.

Private Collection

"We saw one woman in her nightdress with a baby clasped closely to her breast. Several of the women passengers screamed, and left the rail in a fainting condition."

"There was another woman, fully dressed, with her arms tight around the body of a shaggy dog that looked like a St. Bernard. The bodies of three men in a group, all clinging to one steamer chair floated close by, and just beyond them were a dozen bodies of men, all in life-preservers, clinging together as though in the last desperate struggle for life. Those were the only bodies we passed near enough to distinguish, but we could see the white life-preservers of many more dotting the sea all the way to the iceberg."

"The officers told us that was probably the berg hit by the *Titanic*, and that the bodies and ice had drifted along together, but only a few miles south of their original position where the collision occurred. The scene moved everyone on board to the point of tears, even the officers making no secret of their emotion."

(City Heritage Collections)

★ WAITING FOR NEWS

"A great hush descended on the town"

Families congregate outside the White Star offices in Southampton.

Southampton City Heritage Collections

some authentic news from the White Star offices, but her enquiries, like those of hundreds of other friends and relatives of persons who were aboard the vessel, were of no avail.'

(An Oxford Newspaper)

As Reginald Loveless, a Junior Clerk in the White Star Line Office, arrived at the office in Canute Road he found it packed with people waiting for news.

There had been initial disbelief at the posting at 11 am in the window of the Southampton Times, of a brief transcript of the news that *Titanic* was *'probably sinking'* then word spread like wildfire. At first it was rumoured that all her complement had been rescued.

'The next morning the cheering news was contradicted with a bluntness which accentuated more tragically than can be described the blow the previous day. In Southampton Tuesday was a day of gloom, such as was never before experienced in living memory. The name Titanic was on everybody's lips.'

Arthur Paintin's wife 'only married in November last....who has been visiting Oxford, journeyed hurriedly to Southampton on Wednesday in the hope of gaining

At the House and Home pub in Northam, where the night before sailing day members of *Titanic*'s crew had packed in and there was banter about what they would bring back from New York for pretty young barmaid, Alice Brown, *'A few days later came the news she'd gone. We were so upset.'*

The Borough flag was at half mast over the Bargate. In St Mary's Parish the Rev. Arthur Cuming had by him a list of 61 'cases' in the parish arising out of the disaster......the majority were young men who had been wholly or partially supporting their parents. The disaster had intensified the distress which had been felt most acutely in the poorest districts (after the coal strike and consequent lack of employment many of the St Mary's men sailed on *Titanic* after having been out of work for weeks).

'My father, the Reverend J.L. Beaumont James was a curate in St Luke's parish and amongst his first tasks in his new

post was to visit the bereaved families, and in some cases to carry the news for the first time.'

Tom James

On 17th April the first survivors lists were posted outside the Canute Road offices. Crowds kept night vigils but *'No further names yet'* was all the company could say for some while. *'The signals are rather weak'*, said Phillip Curry.

"My next most vivid recollection in College Street was the sinking of the Titanic and..... I don't know if it was before that or just after that it was the heaviest downfall of snow in Southampton. It come down and all we had heaps of snow everywhere and it disappeared quickly. But, however, of course there was no radio or television, or anything like that, naturally. People were running round the street 'the Titanic sunk' panic, panic stations everywhere. Women running out and going down to the Shipping Office, you know, down near the dock gates there and the Titanic, they can't sink the Titanic because everybody talked about the Titanic, it was the unsinkable ship. She had double bottom tanks and all this sort of thing and water-tight doors, it was impossible for her to sink. And even as young as I was it impressed me because there wasn't a family in the whole of that area that never had anybody associated with that ship. Fathers and sons on board, grandsons and all this sort of thing, to be on the great Titanic, you see. And well there were all shipping community, shipping and dock working community and, as I say, everybody run down there, all of us. It was real panic, I can see it now, I can visualise them. The women running out, you know, in their aprons they were busy doing their household chores and forget everything and all run down to the Shipping Office. That was the only place you could get any news you see. Well....they did this and of course child-like I, you know me and the other, I think I went down with my grandmother then. However, everybody, everybody was in distress. They didn't know, you see, then they spent, oh, hours and hours and hours down there. And then later on they, they had a few names of who had been saved and.....it took a long time for it to come through, you know".

Stephen Townsend (City Heritage Oral History)

15 April 1912

A great many girls are absent this afternoon owing to the sad news regarding the Titanic. Fathers and brothers are on the

vessel; and some of the little ones have been in tears all afternoon.

(Northam Girls' School logs)

'The gloom which hangs over Southampton is intensified daily and the agonizing scenes at the docks could move the hardest hearts to compassion.'

(Daily Mirror 1912)

" 'What are we waiting for Mummy? Why are we waiting such a long time.'

'We are waiting for news of father, dear.' "

Overhead Canute Road (Daily Mail 18 April 1912.)

"My father and I were members of the crew of the Olympic, the sister ship of the Titanic. "I still remember the feeling of shock when I heard the Echo boys shouting in the streets: 'Titanic hits iceberg.' I was given a penny to go out and buy the Echo."

W.H. Hirst (Echo 14th August 1986)

"I was serving in the manager's department at the time and we were engaged in dealing with relatives' enquiries," said Mr Loveless. "Most of the staff in other departments were called in and we spent a complete week at the office, sleeping at night on the hard floor."

Relatives leaving White Star offices in London.

Southampton City Heritage Collections

1912.
NOT TO BE TAKEN AWAY 447

Apr. 4th. School closed at noon to day for Easter Vacation.

Apr. 15th. School reopened to day.

Apr. 15th. A great many girls are absent this afternoon owing to the sad news regarding the "Titanic". Fathers & brothers are on the vessel; & some of the little ones in school have been in tears all the afternoon.

Apr. 17th. I feel I must record the sad aspect in school to day owing to the "Titanic" disaster. So many of the crew belonged to Northam & it is pathetic to witness the childrens' grief; & in some cases faith & hope of better news — The attendance is suffering —

Northam Girls' School logs written by headmistress Miss Annie Hopkins.

Southampton Archive Services

Crowds of anxious relatives outside the White Star offices in Canute Road, Southampton waiting for news.

Southampton City Heritage Collections

They recalled that Miss Dolly Curry, daughter of the late Mr Phillip E Curry, then White Star manager at Southampton, served coffee to the waiting crowds, which stretched from St Lawrence Road to Albert Road.

Reginald Loveless and Eric Butcher on their retiring from Cunard (Echo 2/01/1959)

"Mr. Curry went through the same test. Office hours were swept away. Several times this week he has watched the sunrise from the windows of his office, having scarcely moved from the businesslike apartment in which stands his orderly writing table, his complicated telephone service and little else. To him have come, in never ceasing streams, members of staff working no less strenuously. ... The White Star staff have been subjected to the severest test of character – one and all, from the dignified chief to the humblest office boy and have passed in the honours class."

(Echo 20th April 1912)

"Yes, and we used to go down the dock gate with a friend, a friend in Ascupart Street, her father was on there. And her father got lost but we used to go...they put the names up ... outside the dock gates...who was rescued and that. Yeah, I remember ever so plain. This girl at school... ...she used to come and say 'Coming down the dock gate?' me and my sister used to go down the dock gate to see if her father's name was up there. Several girls at school, that had fathers on there... brothers or some relation."

Elsie Whitfield (City Heritage Oral History)

Crowds waiting for News of "Titanic" Survivors.

The scene round the fateful board in Canute Road.

Southampton Pictorial

"Mrs May across the way lost her husband and oldest son (Fireman and Firemen's Mess Man). The son was married a year ago and his wife had a baby six weeks ago. Mrs Allen around the corner lost her husband, George (Scullion). And the young girl there in black, the one on this side, is Mrs Barnes. She lost her brother (Fireman). The woman going into the shop is Mrs Gosling. She lost a son (Trimmer). And Mrs Preston of Princes Street, a widow, she lost her son too (Trimmer)."

Wife of *Olympic* crew member. (Daily Mirror 18th April 1912)

"Yes, its true....husband and son have gone and left eleven of us. It was the first time that Arthur and his father had been at sea together and it wouldn't have happened if Arthur hadn't been out of work because of the coal strike. He tried to get a job ashore but failed and he had his wife and baby to keep. So he signed on aboard the Titanic as a fireman. His father shouldn't have been on the Titanic but a bad leg kept him from going on his own ship, the Britannia. Now they're gone and there are eleven of us. The eldest boy, nineteen, makes a few shillings a week by odd jobs. My own youngest baby is six months old."

Mrs May (Daily Mail 18th April 1912)

Mrs Saunders of 29 Albert Road mourns the loss of a son who had been a *'good boy'* to her. He had followed the sea for some years, transferred from *Adriatic* to the *Olympic*. Lately he had been unwell and dropped

From the Southampton Pictorial

Outside White Star offices, Canute Road, the only remaining hope for the watchers was the alteration of names wrongly posted in the confusion.

Southampton City Heritage Collections

out of the *Olympic*. When he recovered he was transferred to the *Titanic*. Mrs Saunders said she had suffered terribly from anxiety.

"I have bought two or three papers a day in the hope of seeing his name among the saved, but it seems that I shall never see him again."
(D.E.S. Saunders, Saloon Steward, was lost.)
Mrs Saunders (Southampton Times 20th April 1912)

"...my first memories...I think...the first memory that stands out, I think, was the sinking of the Titanic. And the reason that this was so outstanding is that the town, things were not so noisy in those days as they are now, but the town went absolutely quiet. A great hush descended on the town because, I don't think that there was hardly a single street in Southampton who hadn't lost somebody on that ship and it was, as you know, supposed to be unsinkable and it was a very great shock.

I remember, in those days, there wasn't much in the way of assistance for widows and orphans and I can quite clearly remember going to a concert, probably a bit later in the same year that it was sunk, which was in aid of the widows and orphans. The admission was tuppence and I can distinctly remember the 'turns' that went on those days. Because, in those days, these little concerts and charities and one thing and another were quite a feature of life and that is where we got our entertainment from, being no television or wireless or anything like that."
Charles Morgan (City Heritage Oral History)

"Old Northam, where I lived, was plunged in mourning. Nearly every house in Northam had lost a son or husband, its true and every blind was drawn in Northam".
(City Heritage Oral History)

"What a good job they missed their ship! I have thanked God for it ever since."

Q: 'How did they miss the boat?'

"I can't tell you exactly, but they left home in good time. Somehow or other my boys did not seem very keen on going in the ship. ......The engineer called to them to get on board, but for some reason or other they didn't go."
Mrs Slade (Southampton Times 20th April 1912)

"As regards the Titanic, I was born in 1915, so I have
no personal memories, but I am sure the sinking of that ship
must have made a great impression on my parents because as a
small child they talked about it. I remember very well my mother
saying how, .. on the morning.., of the disaster she was
spring-cleaning in our front bedroom and heard a commotion so
she went downstairs to see what it was and it was Echo boys,
running round the streets shouting out 'Disaster at sea, Titanic
sunk' and there was a special edition of the Echo. My
father worked in the Docks, he was in charge of the Pay Office
of the Mechanical Engineers Department of the Southern
Railway and he said on several occasions how, not only the
town was in complete mourning over the disaster, but in the
Docks every single man wore a black armband for some days
afterwards."

Dora Caton (City Heritage Oral History)

Palace Theatre

SOUTHAMPTON.

SOUVENIR PROGRAM
OF GRAND
BENEFIT MATINEE

WEDNESDAY, MAY 8th, 1912, at 2.30.

THE

PALACE THEATRE

SOUTHAMPTON, LTD.

Managing Director . . .	**Mr. Frank Macnaghten**
Resident Manager	**Mr. Will Murray**
Assistant Manager	**Mr. Fred Mason**

Special
Benefit Matinee

*Under the distinguished patronage of
His Worship the Mayor and Mayoress,
Aldermen and Councillors, and other
Influential Ladies and Gentlemen*

**IN AID OF THE MAYOR'S
"TITANIC" RELIEF
FUND**

Hon. Acting Managers .	{	MR. HARRY YARDLEY, Hippodrome
	{	MR. ARTHUR WESTON, Grand Theatre
Hon. Musical Directors . . .	{	MR. JAMES SOUTHWORTH
	{	MR. JOHN W. WILDE
Hon. Stage Managers . . .	{	MR. FRANK MASTERS
	{	MR. WILLIAM FRITTINGHAM

**GRAND
AUGMENTED
PROGRAM**

On ...
Wednesday, May 8
at 2.80 p.m.

"Well, on the Monday morning when I went to work at
Toogoods, a local seed factory, we was all sat having our
breakfast, you know, having something to eat and a cup of tea
and the news came through that the Titanic had sunk and we all
went down to the Dock Gate and it was a terrible gloomy
morning. Everything was cast, overcast and it was proper gloomy
and we went down to the Dock Gate and they had all the
names posted up, and I didn't know Jack Podesta's mother was
there, they were all there, there was crowds of people at the
time".

Mrs Podesta (Echo)

"This happened on the Sunday night. I got up the next
morning to answer the door to the insurance man and he said to
me what an awful thing had happened. I said 'What's that?'
So he said the Titanic's gone down with all hands. I said, don't
say that, I said, my hubby's aboard. And he said, 'Oh,' he
said, 'I wouldn't have told you that for all the world'. And
when he was gone I went indoors it upset me very much and this
was a baby, this young man here, he was a baby and I said to
him his daddy was on the biggest ship in the world".

Left to right: Rose Major (wife of William Major, fireman who survived) with her daughter Rose Major and relative Ellen Ocleford. Outside 4 Oriental Terrace, Southampton.

Private Collection

"...I went to see my sister 'coz I was worried about it and she said, oh, she said, I haven't heard anything, but she said, we shall know all about it, she said, when Will comes in. That was her husband. She said, he has gone to the Docks. And I sat there waiting and I could see when he came in there was trouble and he said that, he said he knew there was some trouble about, but he didn't like to say anything. So he said I'll go out, and get a paper and find out what's gone wrong. And he came back and he said its all right, Vi, they're sailing to Halifax under their own steam. So I thought to myself, well, they must be alright if they're sailing to Halifax under their own steam. And then later on in the day, the paper came out to say the ship had gone down with 1,500 lives lost".

"However, it went on all day and all night. I couldn't sleep or rest, of course. And then the next morning I got up and I went to the Docks and was written up on the board all the hands that was saved and I looked down and his name wasn't there and it went on all the week like that till the Friday. I never knew till the Friday that he was saved. And then I had a telegram from the office to tell me he was saved. My brother

This is probably Millbank Street, Northam, 1912, in the heart of Southampton Dockland.

Southampton City Heritage Oral History

A Northam Street (Mrs Harder, left, in flat cap, who was well known in Northam and had a brother-in-law on the *Titanic* who survived).

Southampton City Heritage Collections

came up from the Docks to tell me everything was all right. What was his initials. I said 'AER Lewis'. He said 'Thank God he's saved' he said. And I said, course with the excitement after the weekend, you know, it was terrible".
Mrs Lewis (Echo)

"In after life, when I got to work, I used to bump into them and 4 or 5 of the chaps that I went to school with were in the same trade as myself, in the shipbuilding line. And there were 2 fellows they were brothers, Willie and Reggie Doling, their father kept the Immigrants' Home. Now the Immigrants' Home was a home that used to accommodate the people that were coming from Middle Europe as immigrants to go to find a new life in America. Accommodation was very poor, they used to go to sleep on concrete floors with just the coats they came in. They always looked grubby and poor and normally the men had huge beards, I think there was a very big proportion of Jews among them, because they were mostly the people that were exported (sic) from Europe, even in those days. And I used to go down below...they were sleeping in the basement usually and I used to go down below with the Doling brothers and stand looking at them and...of course...as a boy I didn't know what to think about it. But in after years it was taken over by the British American Tobacco factory and then beyond that as a Labour Exchange. And although the building is still there I don't know what's happened to it."

"I think the Dolings were the agents between...the liaison between the Americans and the European faction. And, another thing that I remember well, Mrs Doling went away on the Titanic and when the Titanic was sunk she was one of the fortunate ones to get into a lifeboat and come home again."

(Do you remember her coming home?)

"...I don't remember...I do remember the feeling of the boys how pleased that...they were worried at the time...and with a lot of us other boys we used to go down to number 7, what was number 7 Dock Gate in those days and look at the list of people saved and uncles, fathers and quite a lot of relations of the boys that I went to school with were lost. And, of course, there was great grief in the school at the time...but when Mrs Doling was saved...she appeared on the list and I remember the brothers were...how overjoyed they were."
Albert Gibbs (City Heritage Oral History)

"At the lads club meeting at Mission Hall, Queen Street, on Saturday night, the proceedings took the form of a memorial service... ...the 'dead march' in 'Saul' was played by Mr. R. Doling."
(Echo 23rd April 1912)

Five *Titanic* orphans and the House Matron at the Southampton Seamen's 'At Home'.

Southampton Pictorial

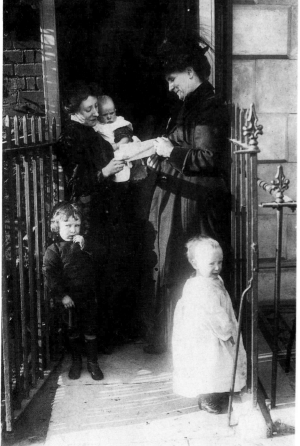

"Well, I didn't want to be a teacher. My mother was, my grandmother was and I think my great-grandmother was and I didn't want to be. In St Mary's, one time the school was called Crabniton then I think they changed the name to Grove Street School and my grandmother was a headmistress there. I remember the story my mother told. She was visiting my grandmother and they went into this one class and grandmother said 'Stand up any child who has a relative on the Titanic' and the whole class stood up. And one little mite said 'Oh, there's no need to worry, Miss, the Olympic is rushing to her aid'. I thought that's the trust of a child isn't it, you know".

Dorothy Cross (City Heritage Oral History)

Mrs Rosina Hurst of Chapel Road with her children George William (in her arms) Walter Charles (in dark clothes) and Henry Edward, discussing with her aunt the news of her husband *Titanic* fireman Walter Hurst who was saved and her father William Hurst who was lost.

Southampton City Heritage Collections

176

17 April 1912

I feel I must record the sad aspect in school today owing to the Titanic disaster. So many of the crew belonged to Northam and it is pathetic to witness the children's grief; and in some cases faith and hope of better news. The attendance is suffering.

(Northam Girls' School logs)

> **Southampton's Grief**
> **The Home of the Crew**
> **Streets of Mourners**

From our special correspondent.
Southampton, Tuesday.

Flags were flying at half-mast here today and women were weeping for the men who went down with the *Titanic*. The crew of the *Titanic* was composed almost entirely of Southampton men, and whole streets are in mourning. When the liner was manned for her first voyage there was an eager rush for berths, and the cream of Southampton seafaring men sailed with Captain Smith. Yesterday the first half-pay notes were distributed to the wives and dependants of the crew. Today women were weeping over the wages of death.

In Northam and Shirley, where nearly every able-bodied man follows the sea for a living, there are many stricken homes. Every house in Russel (sic) Street contains a sorrowing family, and in Northam Road and the adjoining streets the shadow of dreadful suspense looms over the modest brick cottages. Homely little cottages they are, with wallflowers in the windows. Peering through the open doorways one caught glimpses of pictures of ships and quaint knick-knacks from foreign ports. At the street corners stood groups of men wearing the garb of the sea, and all the sorrow of the sea shone in their eyes. They talked of the *Titanic* as sailors talk. They feared to talk of the men who sailed in her. With the women it was different.

They talked little of the ship but much of the crew, and they talked tragedy in simple homely phrases

"She lives nigh me in Union Street, and she has three little children. He was a fireman and a good man at his work." "A poor old man in Cable Street, they say he has four sons on board; and there's Saunders, the shipwright, over the way, he is grieving about his two sons." "In McNaughton Street there is a girl going mad. She has only been married a month. Her husband signed on as a steward."

One of many of the memorial cards issued after the disaster.

Southampton City Heritage Collections

Rose Major, wife of Fireman William Major who was saved.

Private Collection

Sorrowing Inquirers

Outside the White Star Line offices in Canute Road an ever-changing crowd waited anxiously for – hoping and yet dreading to read – the promised list of survivors. There were two young women with babies in their arms, babies who laughed and crowed in the sunlight, while their mothers stared wildly with eyes that had known no sleep through the night. There were old women, some crying quietly, others seeking to comfort: sobbing daughters. And there were men, who bit firmly on their pipes and avoided the eyes. Occasionally a man or a woman would push through the crowd and ask to see a list of the crew or the passengers. Then would enter men and women begging for news. But the clerks could only shake their heads as they nervously fingered the long list.

"It is the suspense that hurts," said an elderly woman whose eyes were dim behind her spectacles. *"If we could only know something – anything."*

So it was with the crowd in Canute Road and with the women in the little brick cottages beyond the

bridge. They were waiting for voices from the silent deep.

Later in the afternoon hope died out and suspense gave way to despair. The waiting crowds thinned and silent men and moaning women sought their homes over the bridge. In the humble homes of Southampton there is scarcely a family that has not lost a relative or a friend. Children returning from school appreciated something of the tragedy, and woeful little faces were turned to the darkened fatherless homes. Six firemen who had signed on arrived on the quayside last Wednesday in time to see the last gangway removed, and are now congratulating themselves on having missed the boat.

**Loss of the *Titanic*
The Brave Crew
Help for the Widows
Distribution Today**

From Our Special Correspondent.
Southampton, Thursday

The wives and children of the *Titanic's* heroes expect to know the worst tomorrow morning. Most of them believe that their breadwinners are gone. I have said the distress is very great. Why? it will be asked. The answer is easy and convincing. Nearly one half of the rank and file of the dead crew are victims of the coal strike. A large proportion of the men on the *Titanic's* glorious roll would have been sailing in other ships if their vessels had not been laid up through a shortage of coal. To these men and their families the disaster is a coal strike tragedy; but it is small comfort to the bereaved to be told that if their beloved ones had not been lost, others would.

The men of some of the liners laid up in Southampton Docks for want of bunker coal were out of work for four or five weeks before the *Titanic's* crew signed on. Some of them had made many voyages in the ships from which they were discharged, and the *Titanic* was able to have the pick of the seamen and firemen in the port. She had a fine and as efficient a crew as ever sailed in a British merchant ship, so at least an authority tells me, but as the majority had been idle for some time they left very little money behind them. This is why destitution has so swiftly overtaken those who know only too well that their fears of widowhood are correct. In the Town Ward an alderman, who, like his father, has performed civic duties for many years told me that the condition of some families in the ward he represented is extremely pitiable. Today he had inquired into the wants of twelve mothers, who between them have nearly sixty children. One of them, the wife of a steward, had seven young children, and was absolutely penniless. Another had six youngsters and was expecting another – there will be a large number of posthumous children of men who observed the *"Women and children first"* rule on the *Titanic* – and she had not one farthing. The money on advance notes had all gone in rent and discharging debts. Most of the women were wives of firemen and trimmers and the good alderman's words of comfort and hope fell on deaf ears.

"There may be 100 of the crew saved," say they; *"but not a fireman or a trimmer will be among them."* They, poor forlorn creatures, know the story.

All day long the White Star offices in Canute Road have been thronged by anxious relatives of men who sailed in the *Titanic*. There was little murmuring at the absence of news. The long-drawn-out agony was having its effect on the crowd of women whose pale, solemn faces spoke of the pain at their hearts. Their stoicism was wonderful. One could not help remarking they were worthy mates for the humble, chivalrous sailormen who had so nobly done their duty. There was no hysterical sobbing, and very little talking; the women just waited silently, watching the wide blackboard on which, sooner or later, they were to learn the fate of good husbands, fathers, and sons. Their vigil was painfully prolonged. From daybreak till dusk not a word of hope appeared, save the announcement that the Marconi Company thought they had got into touch with the *Carpathia*, and any news which reached the wireless station in Nova Scotia would be transmitted direct to Southampton. All the women had put on a *"bit of black."* some of them waited all day, others came and went, and a few, as if afraid that their overstrung nerves would get the better of their determination to wait till they got home before the tears flowed, sent a child to read the bulletins, while they remained round a corner, nervously picking at their aprons.

(City Heritage Collections)

Miss Annie Hopkins, headmistress of Northam School presenting Amy Wiltshire with a doll which had been subscribed for by the children of Fourth Avenue Girls' School, Manor Park, London. It was to be given to the youngest orphan in the school whose father went down on the *Titanic*.

Southampton Pictorial, May 1912.

Toll of the "Titanic."

Northam School children who lost a relative in the *Titanic* disaster.

Southampton Pictorial

The Homes of the Crew
Southampton's Widows and Orphans

From our special correspondent.
Southampton, Friday

This morning the thirst for news that has tortured Southampton for three days was at last assuaged. At seven o'clock a clerk came out of the White Star offices down by the docks, and placed on the huge blackboard outside the list of the saved among the crew. At that time there was no one about except the women who have waited there in the street almost without moving none of them certainly have slept since Tuesday night. As the names appeared, printed in big blue letters, a dreadful gasp of apprehension was heard, and the women pressed up close, eager and yet hardly daring to read. Some sent a friend less vitally concerned to read the list for them. And then when it was at last realised that hope must be abandoned there were scenes of pitiful

sorrow which must be imagined, not described. As the day wore on a sort of dreary relief became the prevalent mood. At any rate the worst was known and there was an end to the racking uncertainty of the last few days. It was even better than was hoped. Yesterday no one here thought that 200 of the crew would be found still alive. A fireman's wife, in the night vigil, was heard saying

"Oh, I'll never see him again. They'd never let any of the firemen get in the boats; they're too deep down."

But over 70 firemen are on the list. Nothing can soften the terrible blow which the disaster has dealt in Southampton, but there is at least this meagre consolation. All through this shining day the townsfolk have been flocking to read the lists.

Although it was announced that this was the complete roll of the saved, some women would not give up hope. You saw them standing in the dusty road under the fierce sun patiently watching the board. *"Perhaps they'll find they've forgotten one or two,"* said a young mother. Among the women were groups of sailors discussing the fate of their mates. They would tell one another, *"It's no use looking for Jack, he was on the death-watch, poor bloke."*

A Crowning Torture

But even yet there is a wretched loophole of uncertainty. About a score of the names as they are posted up have no initials, and as in some cases there

180

are two or three men of the same name on the board their relatives do not know which of them is bereaved. This is a cruel infliction from which one feels they ought to have been spared. The townsfolk are very bitter about it. It is freely said that there has been far too much reticence and delay in publishing the names and that full and accurate lists should have been sent before anything else. On the top of everything – three days' sleepless misery for these poor folks, while in London the first class lists were published two days ago – comes this crowning torture of the initials.

The agony of the disaster is concentrated in Southampton. The town is as if widowed. I got my first impression of what it means when I saw from the railway carriage as the train neared the station old Union Jacks at half-mast in the dingy back gardens of the sailors' quarter. Flags hang at half-mast over all the public buildings, the pillars of the Guildhall are draped in crepe, and nearly every man and woman you meet is wearing black.

Two-thirds of the crew of the *Titanic* were Southampton men, and I am told that today there are probably 500 homes robbed of the chief breadwinner. In one school in Northam (where many firemen and trimmers live) there are 125 children who have lost their fathers. I spent a long time this afternoon in the network of Northam – stretches of mean, stucco cottages, and here and there a balcony or a decorated door reminiscent of better days. There was no spectacular grief. It was curious to see the children playing just as gaily as usual on the sunny pavement. Many of them had been orphaned. In each of these streets there are at least three or four bereaved houses. The women gathered in groups talking quietly. I heard one of them say – she was fatalistically cleaning her step at the time –

"It's no use going to look at any lists. He's gone, right enough. I'll have to try for a bit of the Mayor's money."
The coal strike had already brought many of these families to destitution. Down in Bridge Road the Seamen's Friendly Society have opened a depot for giving out bread, milk, and meat. The room is always besieged. The Mayor (an old pilot) is doing his best at the Guildhall. He has been distributing money to the women most urgently in need. One woman has lost eight relatives – her husband, two brothers, a son, and four cousins. The Mayor told me that one woman who had received relief, afterwards, finding her husband's name among the saved, brought the money back as a sort of thanks offering. Most of the women rely entirely upon the half pay they receive every Monday.

I find that there is a wholesome anger mixed with the people's sorrow. They are angry about the lifeboats; they are angry because they think there has been unnecessary delay in giving out the names, and because news has been withheld; but the greatest indignation is roused by what one sailor described to me today as *"a dirty lie."* He meant the story in some of today papers to the effect that Captain Smith shot himself on the bridge. This is the point that touches Southampton nearest, and the people seem to feel it as a sort of stain on their honour; for everyone here knew Captain Smith and speaks admiringly of him. The window of a local newspaper has put out the big placard: *"The final scene. Captain Smith remained at his post on the bridge and went down with the ship. There was no panic"* (this last in immense letters).

Seamen stand round and spell it out to their comrades. *"I should think so,"* said one. *"Shot himself! That wasn't Smith's way. I know what I'd do to the feller that put that in"* (here he spat).
(City Heritage Collections)

May 18 1912
The acute distress among the people is daily becoming more evident. 24 free meals given today and the shoeless and hungry children are many.
Northam Girls' School logs

> ## White Star and Cunard
> ## Reciprocal Generosity

The White Star Line announce that they recently requested the Cunard Company to permit them to present a hundred guineas to Captain Rostron, fifty guineas each to Surgeon McGee, Purser Brown, and Chief Steward Hughes, and one month's pay to all other members of the *Carpathia*'s crew as a slight token of gratitude for the services rendered on the occasion of the loss of the *Titanic*. This the Cunard Company have acceded to.

(City Heritage Collections)

BRITISH SEAFARERS' UNION MEETING

A special meeting of members was held at the Southern District Schools on Monday April 22 1912.
The chair was taken by the President who called upon the assistant secretary to read the minutes of the last meeting which were passed as read. The financial statement for the preceding week was also passed.
In opening the meeting the President stated that it was the first time that they had met since the terrible disaster which had overtaken the *Titanic* he regretted that he had to report the loss of a large number of the members of the union but while we were mourning for their loss it

This is thought to be Mayor Henry Bowyer and a colleague.

Southampton City Heritage Collections

was the duty of all members to increase their demands for better manning of ships and better accommodation for the crew.

He also moved that a note of sympathy be passed to the relatives of the members of (who) had lost their lives. Taken Standing.

The matter of the lifeboat and manning was next raised after discussion the following resolution was moved seconded and carried unanimously.

This meeting strongly condemns the neglect of the board of trade in not making the necessary regulations for the provisions of sufficient and satisfactory accommodation to safeguard the lives of crew and passengers on board ship and also the efficient manning of same. It also demands that immediate steps be taken to deal with the matter in a thorough manner and prevent the possibility of such terrible disasters in the future. It was also decided that the President and Secretary interview the White Star Line to negotiate for the increase of seamen in the *Olympic*.

It was also reported that the survivors of the *Titanic* were due to arrive at Plymouth about the following Sunday and it was decided that the President and Secretary be empowered to go and meet them.

After a spirited address by Mrs Palmer the meeting closed.

T Lewis. 7/5/12.

R.M.T. Union Records (University of Warwick)

A message from Captain Smith's wife was posted outside the White Star offices.

'To my poor fellow sufferers - my heart overflows with grief for you all and is laden with sorrow that you are weighed down with this terrible burden that has been thrust upon us. May God be with us and comfort us all. Yours in sympathy, Eleanor Smith.'
(City Heritage Collections)

The War Cry, April 27, 1912

The General Manager of the White Star Company received 'The War Cry' representative very considerately, and expressed his thanks to The Army for its offer of assistance, and his appreciation of the efforts which were being made locally in conjunction with the relief fund inaugurated by the Mayor (Councillor H. Bowyer, R.N.R.), who it is interesting here to note, holds a chief pilot's certificate, and whose brother was the local pilot to the ill-fated liner.

Captain Huggins and Lieutenant Craig, the Southampton Slum Officers, whom 'The War Cry' correspondent interviewed, have been visiting hundreds of homes of late in the very district where the death-roll is highest. They had just come from Northam, the district referred to, and were full of most pathetic stories.

Double Tragedy

Adjutant Gwyn, of the Divisional Headquarters, visited a home where a double tragedy had occurred, the father had gone down with the doomed liner, and the mother and her newly-born infant had died, leaving behind her six little children.

At every turn, where possible, our Officers are succouring the grief-stricken. *'It was heart-breaking'*, says Adjutant Otter, *'to see how quickly the handkerchief came out the moment Mrs Otter spoke a word to any of the women who were waiting for news. I felt quite helpless in face of such sorrow.'*

The work of ministering to the sufferers is women's work. This is true, whether it be Adjutants Clark, Groome, and Marsh, and Lieutenant Mills, the Officers of Battenberg Home for Women and Girls, who supply hundreds of quarts of soup or milk to the needy, or the Slum Officers, who deliver many gallons of milk to nursing mothers and children, and take gifts of tea, bread, sugar, rice, and other provender to the homes where the grim spectre of want has long been seen, and where the shadow of death has now fallen.

The law of *'women and children first'* cuts both ways, and this is specially true in Southampton at this time of trial, for it is upon the heads of the defenceless women and innocent children that the blow has fallen first and fallen with crushing weight.

At Army's Home

At The Army's Home for Working-men, Captain Haynes, the Officer in charge, says that a number of the *Titanic*'s crew were in residence there, and some of them were present at the services which are held in connexion with the Home. The district where the Home is situated is right in the heart of the area where a large percentage of the crew lived. In Bond Street, York Street, Millbank Street, Princes Street, Clarence Street, and many another, numbers of bread-winners are missing.

Everything is being done by our comrades to help to minimize suffering on the part of the women and children. Brigadier Glover, the Divisional Commander, has requested the Officers at Southampton, Freemantle, St. Denys, Woolston, and other Corps, whose districts are affected, to pay special attention to *Titanic* cases, and to report all cases of distress to him. Many affecting stories were related to 'The War Cry' representative; perhaps one of the most moving was that of a woman whose husband and son it was thought had both been drawn down to death by the sinking liner. The weeping woman showed the Slum Officer two little texts, the gift of her husband just as he departed. They only cost a few pence, but pence were very valuable just then. *'He gave them to me just as he took his farewell'*, she sobbed. The words on the card were: *'Seek ye the Lord'* and *'God is good'*. While the woman was speaking the assurance official came in to see about the policies of her husband and son. It was then that she realized the terrible significance of her double bereavement. It is at such moments as these that our Officers are seen at their best, and one can well understand how that grief-stricken mother made articulate what many a broken-hearted wife has felt during these distressing days when she cried, *'O Captain, I'm so glad to have you with me in this time of trouble.'* (We are glad to say that news has since been received that the husband is among those saved. – Ed.)

(War Cry)

> ### THE *OLYMPIC* RETURNS TO SOUTHAMPTON
> ### "ON BOARD THE *OLYMPIC*"

After receiving the *Titanic*'s distress messages her sister ship sought to come to her rescue and take off her passengers. Emergency preparations were made to receive them as fireman and trimmers down

"TITANIC" DISASTER.
IMPORTANT NOTICE TO CUSTOMERS.
We beg to tender our deepest sympathy to every one who has lost those near and dear to them in this terrible catastrophe. Many of our customers are unfortunately amongst those lost. Under our Free Gift Scheme they who are entitled to a free conveyance of the Furniture, irrespective of the amount owing. Claims should be sent in as soon as ever possible to

F. BAKER & SONS, 55 to 59, Northam Rd., NEAR SIX DIALS,
HOUSE FURNISHERS. SOUTHAMPTON.

below were training every nerve to drive the ship..... the message then leaked out that the *Titanic* had sunk. All the survivors.. were housed in the *Carpathia*.... it was all over and nothing more could be done... the feelings of all of us on board at this crisis can be better imagined than described. The whole catastrophe was so sudden so appalling and tragic that not one of us could realise what had happened. There was nothing for us to do but steam to Southampton. A subscription was at once started on board for a 'TITANIC FUND' and if I remember correctly resulted in a collection of nearly £2000.

On arrival we found everyone in a state of dismay the White Star Line Office there (as in London and Liverpool) being besieged by heart broken relatives clamouring for the latest list of those "missing" in the disaster.

Dr J C H Beaumont of the *Olympic*
(From 'Ships and People' 1927.)

16 April 1912

The Chairman, H. Bowyer referred to loss of WSS Titanic: Adjourn meeting as a mark of sympathy.

20 April 1912

Vote of sympathy to Councillor Ede upon the loss of his son in the Titanic disaster. (G.B. Ede was a steward)
(Minutes of Southampton Harbour Board)

> ### *Titanic*'s Second Officer

Mr C.H. Lightoller, the second officer on the ill-fated *Titanic*, who is reported among the survivors, lives at Netley Abbey, and yesterday one of our representatives called on his wife at their residence at Hound, to convey congratulations on Mr Lightoller's providential escape.

Mrs Lightoller, who has two little boys, had just returned from Southampton where she had been visiting the wives of other officers less fortunate than herself, and said how terribly anxious she had been, but how thankful she felt now that she was assured of his safety.

Mrs Lightoller said that she had endeavoured to see the Mayor of Southampton to ask what she might do to help in collecting at Netley, as she thought she ought to do everything in her power now she herself had been relieved from anxiety. In conclusion Mrs Lightoller said she had been beseiged with telegrams of inquiry and congratulations, and wished to thank those who had sent, for she could not possibly reply to so many.

(Echo 18th April 1912)

This postcard was sent by a Southampton resident to a friend.

To Miss L. Finkleton, 'Beresford', Genoa Avenue, Putney.
Dear L,
Thanks for nice Easter card. I bought this card for your album to *fill up. Went to town yesterday. Dizzie with me. She sends her love. Quite excitement here. Gardener's wife relative lost on the ship. Awful sad. Saw her going out from dining last Wednesday.*
Hope you are quite well.
Love Bid.
(Peter Boyd-Smith, Cobwebs)

Posted Southampton April 19 1912

To Miss M Smith, Freshwater Bay Hotel, Freshwater, Isle of Wight.
Staff
Dear Mill
I hope you will be able to manage what I ask you. Mill don't you think this is dreadful hope (W) will get home safe.
Love Lill.
***Titanic* memorial postcard**
(Private Collection)

Crowds outside White Star Line offices in London.

Southampton City Heritage Collections

★ COLOUR SECTION

"Honour and Glory"

S.S. *New York* at sea. Painted by A. Jacobsen, 1909.

Southampton City Heritage Collections

RMS *Adriatic* being met by a paddle steamer with mayoral welcoming party, 1907. Painted by George Washington Sandell.

Southampton City Heritage Collections

VIEW OF "OLYMPIC'S" BOTTOM (June, 1910).

in the ship. Each engine crank shaft weighs 118 tons, bedplate 195 tons; each column 21 tons, and the heaviest cylinder, with liner, 50 tons;

wing propeller 38 tons. The weight of the casting for the turbine cylinder is 163 tons, and of the propeller, which is of solid bronze, 22 tons. The anchors are 19 feet in length and over 15 tons in weight, and each link of their chains weighs several hundredweight. Twelve horses were required to drag one of the anchors to the Naval Exhibition at Olympia, where it is now being displayed.

The foregoing particulars apply of course to the "TITANIC" as well, and this steamer should take the water a few months after the launch of her sister ship "OLYMPIC." It is anticipated that the latter will make her maiden voyage to New York about July, 1911; and as far as it is possible to do so, these two wonderful vessels are designed to be unsinkable.

"OLYMPIC" AND "TITANIC." (August, 1910).

WHITE STAR LINE.

R.M.S. "OLYMPIC" AND "TITANIC," EACH 45,000 TONS,
AS THEY WILL APPEAR WHEN COMPLETED.

THE White Star steamers "OLYMPIC" and "TITANIC," now in course of construction at Belfast for the Company's Mail and Passenger service between Southampton, Cherbourg, Queenstown, and New York, will each be approximately 45,000 tons, and thus immeasurably the largest vessels in the world. As it is intended to launch the "OLYMPIC" on October 20th and the "TITANIC" some few months later, the accompanying views illustrating the progress of work

BIRD'S EYE VIEW FROM GANTRY (April, 1909).

Above: White Star Line advertising leaflet.
Left: Surgeons Instrument List book made for suppliers of *Titanic*.
Below: White Star Line sugar shaker of the type used on *Olympic* and *Titanic*.

All Private Collections

Royal Crown Derby plate from the à la carte restaurant of *Titanic*, given to a stewardess on the *Olympic*. Many years later the plate was given to Southampton Maritime Museum.

Southampton City Heritage Collections

Watercolour by Esther Patterson of *Titanic* Third Officer Herbert Pitman in White Star Line uniform.

Southampton City Heritage Collections

'The Approach of the New World' (New York Harbour). Painted by Norman Wilkinson for the *Olympic*.

Southampton City Heritage Collections on permanent loan from Rio Tinto Zinc

Honour and Glory Crowning Time, carved by Charles Wilson for the *Olympic*. Presently on display in Southampton Maritime Museum.

Southampton City Heritage Collections

Titanic by Walter Dane Bryer, 1912. The son of a master baker in Northam, he was an electrician and a keen artist.

Southampton City Heritage Collections

Titanic passing Calshot Castle under a leaden sky. Painted by George Washington Sandell.

Southampton City Heritage Collections

Top left: Unused 'oilette' postcard.   Top right: Titanic in
White Star Dock, painted by G. Fraser.   Bottom right:
Second class breakfast menu on which dining room steward
Edward Hendy wrote a hurried note to his wife.
All Southampton City Heritage Collections

Bottom left: Souvenir badge bought by Arthur Shore, barber
on Olympic.
Private Collection

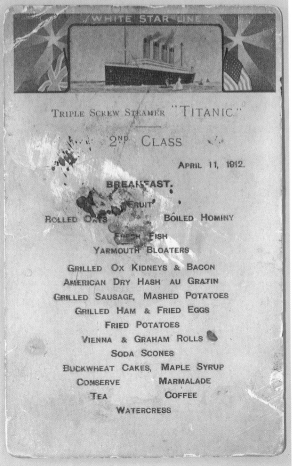

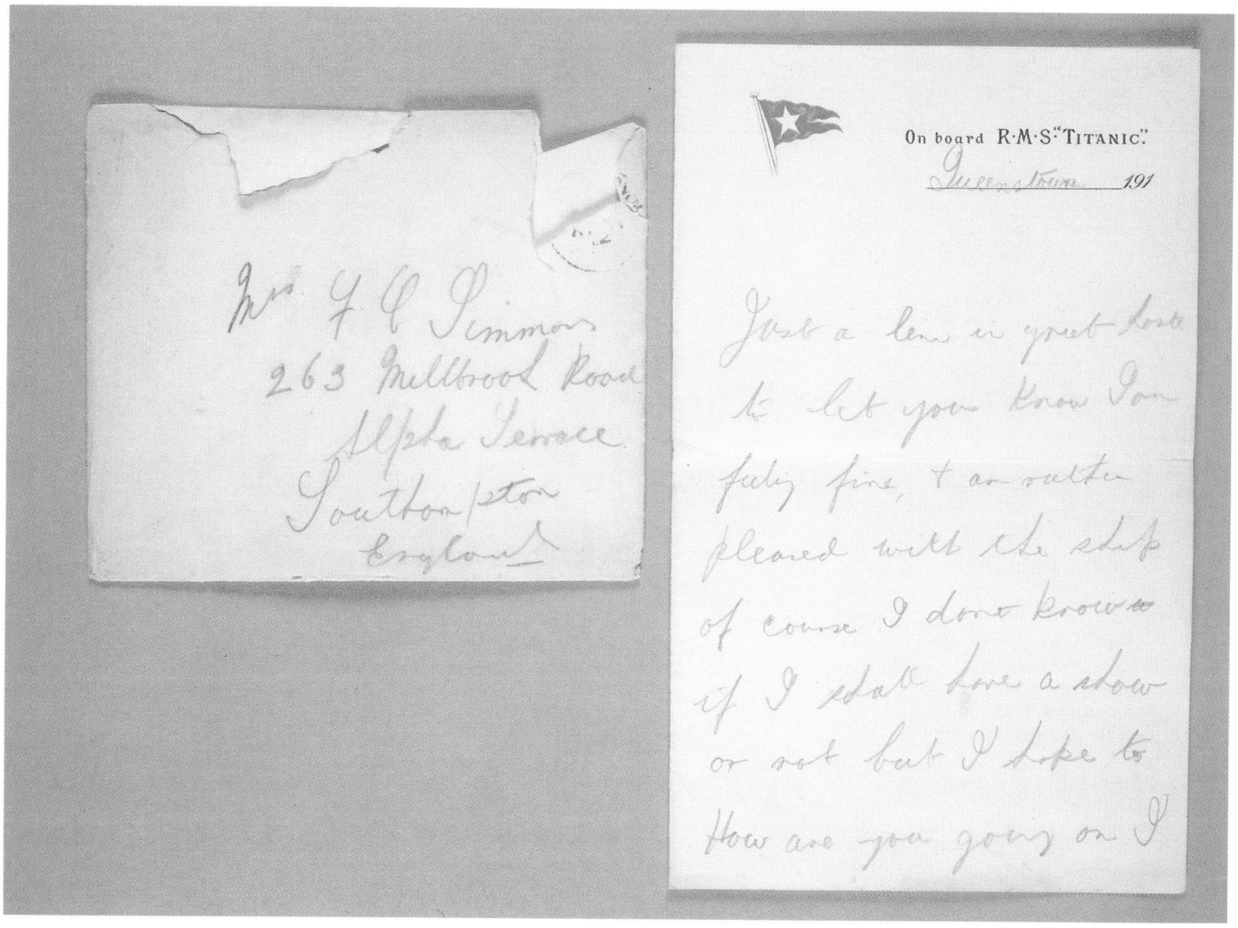

Mrs F C Simmons
263 Millbrook Road
Alpha Terrace
Southampton
England

On board R.M.S. "Titanic".
Queenstown   191

Just a line in great haste
to let you know I am
fairly fine, & am rather
pleased with the ship
of course I dont know
if I shall have a show
or not but I hope to
How are you going on I

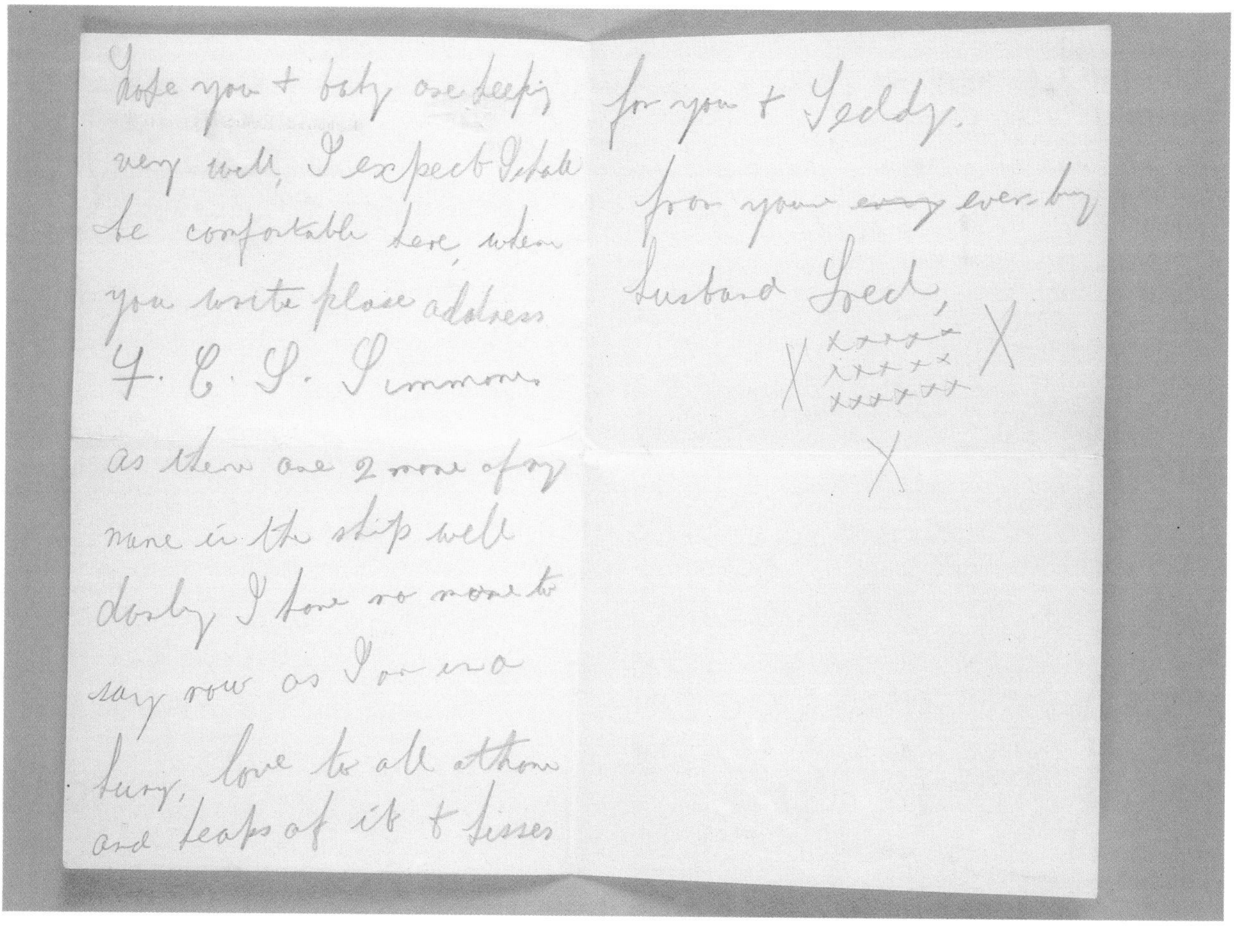

hope you & baby are keeping
very well, I expect I shall
be comfortable here, when
you write please address
F. C. S. Simmons
as there are 2 more of my
name in the ship well
dearly I have no more to
say now as I am in a
hurry, love to all at home
and heaps of it & kisses

for you & Teddy.
from your ever ever, loving
husband Fred,
X x x x x x   X
   x x x x x x
   x x x x x x
      X

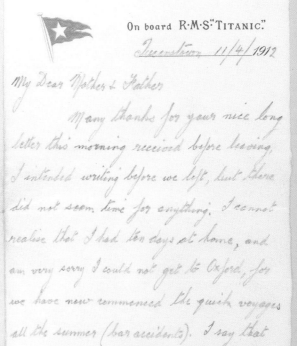

I wonder if I shall see Nellie before she leaves home, I think you had better bring her down to Southampton for a day or two while we are there, for I don't see any chance of getting away. Do you think she has enough money to go on with? If not, let her have some from Elsie's account, for no doubt she wants a lot of extra things. Alice was very pleased with book and I told her to return it when she has finished. Now I think I must say Au Revoir once again with Best love to all from

Your loving Son

Arthur

On board R.M.S. "TITANIC."

Queenstown 11/4/1912

My Dear Mother & Father

Many thanks for your nice long letter this morning received before leaving, I intended writing before we left, but there did not seem time for anything. I cannot realise that I had ten days at home, and am very sorry I could not get to Oxford, for we have now commenced the quick voyages all the summer (bar accidents). I say that because the Olympic's bad luck seems to have followed us, for as we came out of

---

Opposite page: Envelope and letter written on *Titanic* by saloon steward F.C. Simmons to his wife from Queenstown.
Above: Part of letter sent by Arthur Paintin (Captain Smith's tiger) to his parents.
Below: Rebate ticket from the first class dining saloon for passengers who took meals in the à la carte restaurant.

All Private Collections

WHITE STAR LINE.   No.

R.M.S. "TITANIC"

Voyage No. _____   191

Name of Passenger _____

No. of Ticket _____   No. of Persons _____

Received from the Purser the sum of £_____

rebate for taking meals in the Restaurant.

Passenger's Signature _____

Pocket watch found on the body of Steward Sidney Sedunary. Note the time.

Southampton City Heritage Collections

Spare waistcoat left at home by Saloon Steward F.C. Simmons who was lost.

Private Collection

Plymouth Harbour, 1996, by Rodney Norman Wilkinson, who extensively researched his father's estate in order to identify the 1910 Plymouth Harbour painting (see page 36). Working from meticulous details, in his father's style, he has recreated the painting which hung in the *Titanic's* First Class Smoking Room.

Rodney Norman Wilkinson Collection

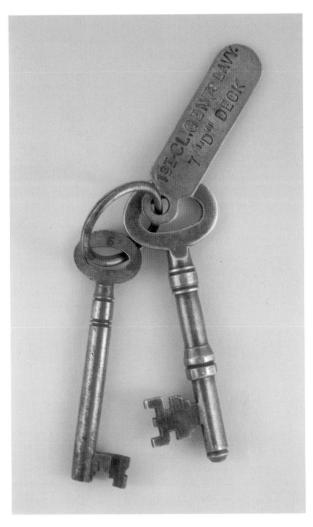

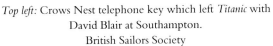

Top left: Crows Nest telephone key which left *Titanic* with David Blair at Southampton.
British Sailors Society

Top right: Keys to D Deck, 1st Class gent's lavatory, found on the body of Steward William Cox, from Shirley.

Bottom left: Verandah Café keys used and saved by survivor Steward John Stewart.
Both Private Collections

Bottom right: Wages account for Sidney Daniels. Note the crew's pay stopped when the ship sank.
Southampton City Heritage Collections

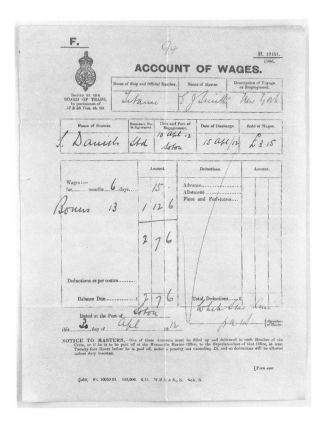

1. Testament presented to Greaser Frederick Scott by the Sailors Mission after the disaster. 2. Photograph of Fourth Officer Joseph Boxhall, taken in Hong Kong by Clifton & Co. 3. Blanket given to Greaser Frederick Scott in the lifeboat by a fellow survivor. 4. *Titanic* locker keys found on the body of Saloon Steward Robert Bristow.

Southampton City Heritage Collections

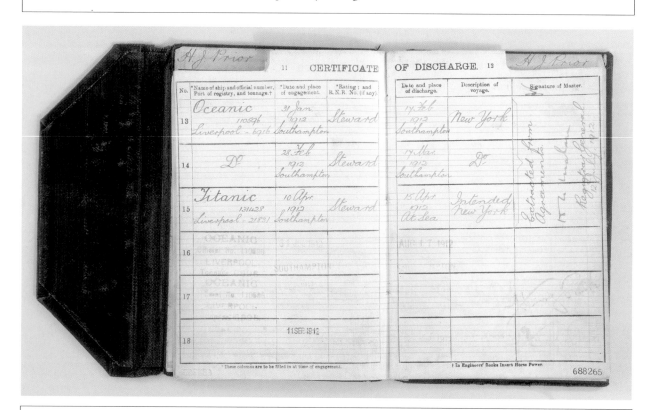

Entry for *Titanic's* voyage in Steward H.J. Prior's Discharge Book.

Private Collection

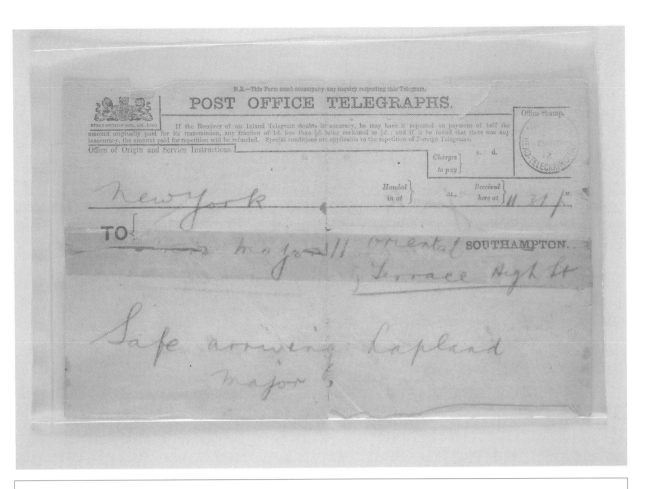

Titanic Fireman William Major sent this telegram (similar to many sent by surviving crew) to his home announcing his safety and imminent arrival home on S.S. *Lapland.*

Private Collection

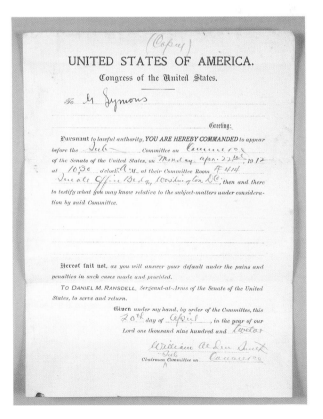

Right: Copy of the Congress of the United States Command to George Symons to testify to the Senate on 20th April 1912.

Above: Members Pass to the Visitors Gallery of the United States House of Representatives, issued to George Symons by Congressman William Cary, 23rd April 1912.

Both Private Collection

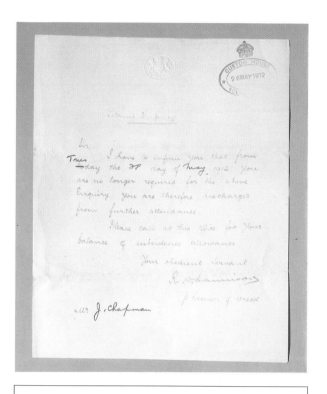

Top left: The Receiver of Wrecks releases crew member Joe Chapman from the British Enquiry.
Top right: Surviving crew member Joe Chapman, post disaster.
Both Southampton City Heritage Collections
Below: Letter from Sir Cosmo Duff Gordon to George Symons after their interrogation at the British Enquiry.
Private Collection

MARYCULTER HOUSE.
BY ABERDEEN.

Sunday 25th

I was very glad to hear from you Symons. Many thanks for your letter – I think the whole of the Inquiry showed how entirely unable Lord Mersey was to appreciate

what the circumstances really were – what are you doing now. Have you gone back to sea, or have you become a landman for a time? Lady Duff Gordon is I'm glad to say none the worse for her experience either by land or sea
Yrs truly Cosmo Duff Gordon

Top left: Charity record entitled 'Be British' which was produced after the disaster.

Southampton City Heritage Collections

Top right: Commemorative sheet music issued in aid of the *Titanic* Relief Fund.

Private Collection

Right: Cheque book for payments to dependants of the *Titanic* Relief Fund during 1917 (1st October to 26th November).

Southampton City Heritage Collections

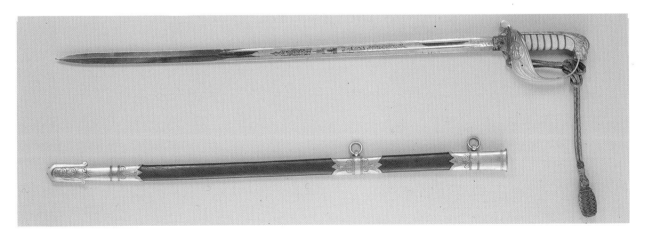

This Royal Naval Reserve Dress Sword belonged to Captain Smith and was presented to Southampton's new Tudor House Museum on the first anniversary of the *Titanic* disaster, 15th April 1913, by his widow and daughter.

Southampton City Heritage Collections

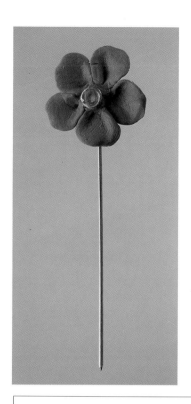

Above left: Titanic memorial pin (with modern petals) bought from a Southampton street vendor in 1912 by Errol McGaw.
Above right: One of two memorial plaques to *Titanic* crew members associated with St. Augustine's Church, Northam.
Private Collection and Southampton City Heritage Collections

Casket presented to Colonel Edward Bance at the end of his third mayoralty. Casket features the *Olympic*.

Mayor's Parlour, Civic Centre, Southampton.

★ U.S. ENQUIRY

"Safe. S.S. Lapland. Sid."

"**T**hey had a roll call but they missed me, I was never on the survivors' list ... still never was ... I'm still missing ... Yeah, my father had a letter from the Company saying that I was missing. But unfortunately, prior to that, when we got to New York we were transferred to the Lapland (another ship), the crew this is, and ... the express people in New York gave us all permission to send our cablegrams to our parents and let them know we were all alive. So fortunately my father got the cablegram before he got the letter from the Company ... so you know ... all I signed was 'Safe. SS Lapland. Sid'. Well it was rather brief to him, he didn't know SS Lapland, he was looking on the map for Lapland thinking a fishing boat had come along and picked us up. Anyway he knew that I was safe and that was the main thing. And a couple of days afterwards he got the letter from the Company saying that I was missing. Of course, that confused him again."

Sidney Daniels (City Heritage Oral History)

HOMECOMING

Monday 15th April: From the moment the *Titanic* sinks the crew are unemployed and will receive no payment.

Thursday 18th April: *Carpathia* arrives at Pier 54 in New York besieged by press and spectators. After the passengers had departed the surviving crew were loaded onto the tender *George Starr* and taken to Pier 61 where they embarked the Red Star Line *Lapland*.

Friday 19th April: Some of the crew attend a memorial service at the Institute of the Seaman's Friends Society. United States Enquiry begins. It will end on 25th May.

Saturday 20th April: Federal subpoenas to appear at the United States Enquiry into the disaster are served on crew members. *Lapland* leaves New York with the other crew members bound for Plymouth. A tug pursues *Lapland* bringing back five more of the crew.

Tuesday 23rd April: Lookout Frederick Fleet and Quartermaster Hichens give their evidence at the United States Enquiry.

Monday 29th April: After an uneventful crossing the *Lapland* arrives at Plymouth. The protesting crew members are detained in the dock's third class waiting room as depositions are taken. An open air memorial service is held on the Marlands at Southampton attended by tens of thousands of people. At 6pm some 85 seamen and firemen leave Plymouth on a special train for Southampton. Hundreds gather at West Station and the Terminus Station Southampton to meet the returning crew.

Tuesday 30th April: Eighty six stewards and stewardesses return by train to Southampton again met by crowds at the town's stations.

Monday 6th May: *Celtic* arrives in Liverpool with some of the crew detained for the US Enquiry including lookouts Frederick Fleet and Reginald Lee and quartermaster Robert Hichens.

Saturday 11th May: *Adriatic* arrives in Liverpool with Officers Charles Lightoller, Herbert Pitman, Harold Lowe and Joseph Boxhall, Chairman Bruce Ismay and passengers the Dean family.

Saturday 18th May: *Baltic* arrives in Liverpool with wireless operator Harold Bride.

THE US ENQUIRY

While Southampton waited, the US Senate in Washington immediately appointed a sub committee to investigate the disaster, under Senator William Alden Smith. He would call 82 witnesses, and 53 of these were British, mostly the crew. The first days hearings began in the Waldorf Astoria Hotel in New York on 19 April with J.B. Ismay. On 20 April 29 *Titanic* crew were subpoenaed before they could leave for Plymouth on IMM Co's *Lapland* with the rest of the crew. After the *Lapland* left a further 5 crew were called back and a tug went after *Lapland* and brought them back. More crew were interrogated at the US Enquiry in New York and Washington than at the subsequent British Investigation, which produced a broader and more detailed report of what the crew thought, remembered, felt, or chose to say. Most of the crew in Washington gave Southampton addresses. They did not all enjoy the experience, notably Fred Fleet, and the officers who were questioned most closely. Some of them enjoyed the stay in Washington, they received a limited hotel allowance and witness fee, were shown the sights, attended various church services, and a few appeared in performances at the Imperial Theatre, recounting their experience, for which they received the proceeds from the first show. They were mostly allowed to leave on 29 April on the *Adriatic*, sailing for Liverpool.

"I remember an old lady about 70 who was sitting there. She wanted my belt as a souvenir and I let her have it. In return, she gave me a dollar. After that, we got our voyage pay - single men got £3 and married £5, out of the Union funds."

Jack Podesta (Echo)

As one of the principal witnesses, Fred Fleet had to spend eight days in Washington giving evidence. At that time a new branch of Woolworth's had been opened in New York.

Titanic crew members outside the 'Institute of the Seaman's Friend', 507 West Street, New York. They have been given new clothes and attended a memorial service there.

Southampton City Heritage Collections

'The Americans put Titanic survivors behind the counters and told them to pocket the money they took. I didn't get a cent out of that caper ... I was too busy going from the hotel to the court of enquiry to give my evidence.'

Fred Fleet (Echo)

The following crew members were interrogated at the United States enquiry:

Andrews, C.E., assistant steward, 145 Millbrook Road, Southampton

Archer, Ernest, seaman, 59 Porchester Road, Southampton

Barrett, Frederick, leading fireman, Southampton

Brice, W., seaman, 11 Lower Canal Walk, Southampton

Bride, H.S., telegrapher, London, England

Bright, A.J. quartermaster, 105 Firgrove Road, Southampton

Buley, E.J., seaman, 10 Cliff Road, Woolston, Southampton

Burke, W., saloon steward, 57 Bridge Road, Southampton

Clench, F., seaman, 10 The Flats, Chantry Road, Southampton

Collins, J., assistant cook, 65 Ballycarry, Belfast

Crawford, A., bedroom steward, 22 Cranbury Avenue, Southampton

Crowe, G.F., steward, 89 Milton Road, Southampton

Cunningham, A., bedroom steward, 60 Charlton Road, Southampton

Evans, F.O., seaman, 14 Bond Street, Southampton

Etches, H.S., bedroom steward, 23a Gordon Avenue, Southampton

Fleet, F., lookout (sailor), 9 Norman Road, Southampton

Haines, Albert, boatswain's mate, 52 Groves Street, Southampton

Hardy, J., steward, Oakleigh, Holyrood Avenue, Highfield, Southampton

Hemming, Samuel S., lamp trimmer, 31 Kingsley Road, Southampton

Hitchens, Robert, quartermaster, 43 James Street, Southampton

Hogg, G.A., lookout (sailor), 44 High Street, Southampton

Jones, Thomas, seaman, 68 Wesfield, Liverpool, and Sailors Home, Southampton

Moore, G., seaman, 51 Graham Road, Southampton

Olliver, A., quartermaster, 38 Anderson Road, Southampton

Osman, F., seaman, 43 High Street, Itchen, Southampton

Perkis, W.A., quartermaster, Victoria Road, Bitterne, Southampton

Pitman, H.J., third officer, Castle Carry (sic), Somerset, Southampton (sic)

Ray, F.D., saloon steward, Palmer Park Avenue, Reading

Rowe, G.T., quartermaster, 63 Henry Street, Gosport

Symons, G., lookout (sailor), 55 Franchise Street, Weymouth

Taylor, W.H., fireman, 2 Broad Street, Southampton

Ward, W., saloon steward, 107 Millbrook Road, Southampton

Wheelton, E., saloon steward, Norwood House, Shirley, Southampton

Widgery, J., (baths), 25 Rokeby Avenue, Redland, Bristol

Address: REV. HENRY LUBECK, LL. D.
Rector Zion and St. Timothy's Church, New York City

Relief Offering in Behalf of Bereaved Families of the Crew

Anthem by Choir

Prayers and Benediction

De Profundis (To be sung kneeling)

Out of the deep have I called unto thee, O Lord: Lord, hear my voice.
O let thine ears consider well: the voice of my complaint.
If thou, Lord, wilt be extreme to mark what is done amiss: O Lord, who may abide it?
For there is mercy with thee: therefore shalt thou be feared.
I look for the Lord; my soul doth wait for him: in his word is my trust.
My soul fleeth unto the Lord; before the morning watch, I say, before the morning watch.
O Israel, trust in the Lord, for with the Lord there is mercy: and with him is plenteous redemption.
And he shall redeem Israel: from all his sins.
Glory be to the Father, and to the Son, and to the Holy Ghost;
As it was in the beginning, is now, and ever shall be: world without end. Amen!

Hymn 679

There is a blessed home
Beyond this land of woe,
Where trials never come,
Nor tears of sorrow flow;
Where faith is lost in sight,
And patient hope is crowned,
And everlasting light

Oh, joy all joys beyond,
To see the Lamb Who died,
And count each sacred wound
In hands, and feet, and side!
To give to Him the praise
Of every triumph won,
And sing through endless days

Look up, ye saints of God!
Nor fear to tread below
The path your Saviour trod
Of daily toil and woe!
Wait but a little while
In uncomplaining love!
His own most gracious smile
Shall welcome you above.

"Father, in Thy gracious keeping
Leave we now Thy servants sleeping."

Memorial Service
for Crew and Passengers Lost at Sea from S. S. Titanic

Church of the Holy Comforter
(SEAMEN'S CHURCH INSTITUTE)
341 West Street
New York

Sunday Evening, April 21st, 1912

REV. ARCHIBALD R. MANSFIELD
Superintendent

REV. CHAS. B. CARPENTER
Chaplain

MUSIC BY ST. ANDREW'S CHOIR
RICHMOND, STATEN ISLAND

MR. ROBT. GRANT WALKER, ORGANIST AND CHOIRMASTER

The cover and inside pages of a memorial service brochure for crew and passengers at the Seaman's Church Institute, New York, April 21st 1912.

Memorial Service

Hymn 674

Peace, perfect peace, in this dark world of sin?
The blood of Jesus whispers peace within.

Peace, perfect peace, by thronging duties pressed?
To do the will of Jesus, this is rest.

Peace, perfect peace, with sorrows surging round?
On Jesus' bosom naught but calm is found.

Peace, perfect peace, with loved ones far away?
In Jesus' keeping we are safe and they.

Peace, perfect peace, our future all unknown?
Jesus, we know, and he is on the throne.

Peace, perfect peace, death shadowing us and ours?
Jesus has vanquished death and all its powers.

It is enough: earth's struggles soon shall cease,
And Jesus call us to heaven's perfect peace.

Sentences

Psalm

God is our hope and strength: a very present help in trouble.
Therefore will we not fear, though the earth be moved: and though the hills be carried into the midst of the sea;
Though the waters thereof rage and swell: and though the mountains shake at the tempest of the same.
The rivers of the flood thereof shall make glad the city of God: the holy place of the tabernacle of the Most Highest.
God is in the midst of her, therefore shall she not be removed: God shall help her, and that right early.
Be still then, and know that I am God: I will be exalted among the heathen, and I will be exalted in the earth.
The Lord of hosts is with us: the God of Jacob is our refuge.
Yea, like as a father pitieth his own children: even so is the Lord merciful unto them that fear him.
For he knoweth whereof we are made: he remembereth that we are but dust.
The days of man are but as grass: for he flourisheth as a flower of the field.
For as soon as the wind goeth over it, it is gone: and the place thereof shall know it no more.
But the merciful goodness of the Lord endureth for ever and ever upon them that fear him: and his righteousness upon children's children;
Even upon such as keep his covenant: and think upon his commandments to do them.
Glory be to the Father, and to the Son, and to the Holy Ghost;
As it was in the beginning, is now, and ever shall be: world without end. Amen!

Apostles' Creed

Lord's Prayer

Prayers

Hymn 335

Jesu, lover of my soul,
Let me to Thy bosom fly,
While the nearer waters roll,
While the tempest still is high:
Hide me, O my Saviour, hide,
Till the storm of life be past;
Safe into the haven guide,
Oh, receive my soul at last!

Other refuge have I none,
Hangs my helpless soul on Thee;
Leave, ah! leave me not alone,
Still support and comfort me:
All my trust on Thee is stayed;
All my help from Thee I bring;
Cover my defenseless head
With the shadow of Thy wing.

Plenteous grace with Thee is found,
Grace to cleanse from every sin;
Let the healing streams abound,
Make and keep me pure within:
Thou of life the fountain art,
Freely let me take of Thee:
Spring Thou up within my heart,
Rise to all eternity.

Lesson: I. Cor. XV.—v.20

Gallia.—Chas. Gounod

Solitary lieth the city, she that was full of people! How is she widowed! She that was great among the nations; Princess among the provinces, how is she put under Tribute! Sorely she weepeth in darkness, her tears are in her cheeks: — And no one offereth consolation, yea all her friends have betrayed her, they are become her enemies, Zion's ways do languish, none come to her solemn feasts: all her gates are desolate: her priests sigh; yea, her virgins are afflicted, and she is in bitterness. Is it nothing to all ye that pass by? Behold and see if there be any sorrow like unto my sorrow. Now behold, O Lord, look Thou on my affliction: see the foe hath magnified himself. Now behold, O Lord, look Thou on my affliction. Jerusalem! O turn thee to the Lord thy God, O turn thee unto thy God.

Address: THE RT. REV. CHAS. SUMNER BURCH, D. D.
Bishop Suffragan of New York

Hymn 306

Eternal Father! strong to save,
Whose arm hath bound the restless wave,
Who bidd'st the mighty ocean deep
Its own appointed limits keep;
Oh, hear us when we cry to Thee
For those in peril on sea!

O Christ! Whose voice the waters heard
And hushed their raging at Thy word,
Who walked'st on the foaming deep,
And calm amidst its rage didst sleep;
Oh, hear us when we cry to Thee
For those in peril on the sea!

Most Holy Spirit! Who didst brood
Upon the chaos dark and rude,
And bid its angry tumult cease,
And give, for wild confusion, peace;
Oh, hear us when we cry to Thee
For those in peril on the sea!

O Trinity of love and power!
Our brethren shield in danger's hour;
From rock and tempest, fire and foe,
Protect them wheresoe'er they go;
Thus evermore shall rise to Thee
Glad hymns of praise from land and sea!

TESTIMONY OF GEORGE MOORE

(Testimony taken separately before Senator Newlands on behalf of the subcommittee.)

The witness was sworn by Senator Newlands.

Senator NEWLANDS. *"State your age and residence?"*

Mr MOORE. *"Fifty-one years old; Graham Road, Southampton."*

Senator NEWLANDS. *"What is your occupation?"*

Mr. MOORE. *"Able seaman, sir."*

Mr. MOORE. *"We joined the ship on Wednesday morning, the 10th of April, and had boat drill and proceeded at 12 o'clock. We called at Cherbourg and Queenstown."*

"On a Sunday it came in rather cold, Sunday afternoon. Sunday night about a quarter to 12 I was on the watch below and turned in, and there was suddenly a noise like a cable running out, like a ship dropping anchor. There was not any shock at all. About 10 minutes to 12 the boatswain came and piped all hands on the boat deck, and started to get out boats."

Senator NEWLANDS. *"How many were there of them, about 40?"*

Mr. MOORE. *"No; 13 in one watch and 12 in the other. Then there was a man who used to work in the alleyway, and there were promenade daymen, saloon daymen, and second-class daymen."*

Mr. MOORE. *"When there is an order, "Boat stations", everyone goes to boat stations – firemen, stewards, and all are called. There is a list showing where each man is to go. Every man in the ship has a fire station and a boat station. But in a case of emergency, where there is a man overboard or anything like that, it is only the watch on deck, the boat's crew, that is called."*

Mr. MOORE. *"When we started lowering the boats all I saw was first-class ladies and gentlemen all lined up with their life belts on and coming out of the saloon. I could not say what was on the after part of the ship at all. There was a lot of space between the boats."*

Senator NEWLANDS. *"Where were the steerage passengers, do you think?*

Mr. MOORE. *"I could not answer that. I should say that*

they were making for the boat deck as well.

Senator NEWLANDS. *"You knew that there were not enough boats to accommodate the entire crew and the passenger list?"*

Mr. MOORE. *"I knew there were only 20 boats, and I knew*

(copy)

UNITED STATES OF AMERICA.

Congress of the United States.

To G. Moore

Greeting:

Pursuant to *lawful authority*, **YOU ARE HEREBY COMMANDED** *to appear before the* Sub *Committee on* Commerce *of the Senate of the United States, on* Monday, April 22, 1912 *at* 10:30 *o'clock* a.M., *at their Committee Room* # 414 Senate Office Bldg. Washington, A.C. *, then and there to testify what you may know relative to the subject-matters under consideration by said Committee.*

Hereof fail not, *as you will answer your default under the pains and penalties in such cases made and provided.*

TO DANIEL M. RANSDELL, *Sergeant-at-Arms of the Senate of the United States, to serve and return.*

Given *under my hand, by order of the Committee, this* 20 *day of* April *, in the year of our Lord one thousand nine hundred and* twelve

Wm Alden Smith
Chairman Committee on Commerce

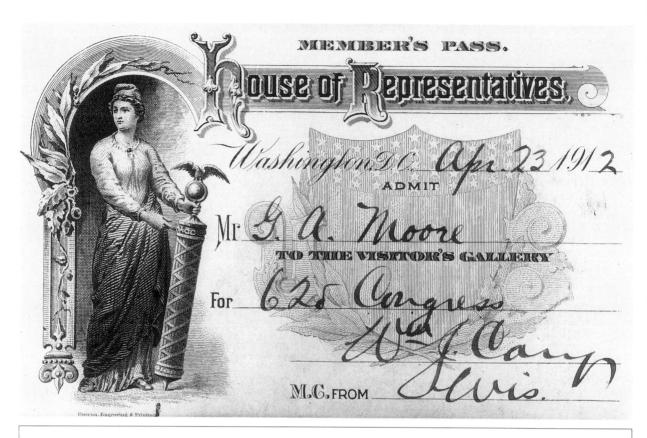

Members pass to admit George Moore to Visitors Gallery, House of Representatives, Washington.

Southampton City Heritage Collections

they would not carry all the people."

Senator NEWLANDS. *"How many did you estimate a boat ought to carry?"*

Mr. MOORE. *"Fifty or sixty in a boat."*

Senator NEWLANDS. *"And 50 in a boat would make 1,000, and 60 in a boat would make 1,200?"*

Mr. MOORE. *"Yes, sir."*

Senator NEWLANDS. *"So all the crew knew that the boats were not sufficient to carry all the passengers and crew off?"*

Mr. MOORE. *"I suppose they did, sir."*

Senator NEWLANDS. *"But they regarded the ship as unsinkable?"*

Mr. MOORE. *"Yes, sir."*

Senator NEWLANDS. *"Who was the officer in charge on the starboard side, where you loaded these boats?"*

Mr. MOORE. *"Mr. Murdock (sic) was one. He was the only one I recognized."*

Senator NEWLANDS. *"Did you take any passengers on your boat in the water?"*

Mr. MOORE. *"No, sir."*

Senator NEWLANDS. *"How far were you from the ship when it sank?"*

Mr. MOORE. *"I should say just over a quarter of a mile, sir."*

Senator NEWLANDS. *"You heard the cries of the people in the water, did you not?"*

Mr. MOORE. *"Yes, sir; everybody heard that, sir."*

Senator NEWLANDS. *"What was the appearance of the ship at that point of time?"*

Mr. MOORE. *"I saw the forward part of her go down, and it appeared to me as if she broke in half, and then the after part went. I can remember two explosions."*

Senator NEWLANDS. *"Did your boat make any effort to go back?"*

Mr. MOORE. *"No, sir."*

Senator NEWLANDS. *"Why not?"*

Mr. MOORE. *"All the people in the boat wanted to get clear of the ship. They did not want to go near her. They kept urging me to keep away; to pull away from her. In fact, they wanted to get farther away."*

Senator NEWLANDS. *"Did you make any effort to go back to the ship?"*

Mr. MOORE. *"No, sir."*

Senator NEWLANDS. *"Why did you not go back and attempt to rescue some of the people who were sinking?"*

Mr. MOORE. *"Well, sir, we were about a quarter of a mile away, and the cries did not last long. I do not think anybody could live much more than 10 minutes in that cold water. If we had gone back, we would only have had the boat swamped."*

Senator NEWLANDS. *"Do you think it would have been swamped?"*

Mr. MOORE. *"Yes; if there were any alive. Five or six pulling on that boat's gunwales would no doubt have capsized the boat."*

LOOK-OUT'S TESTIMONY

The next witness was Frederick Fleet, aged 25, a weather-tanned sailor, who was on the look-out at the time of the collision. He seemed dazed as he entered the witness-box, and did not at first comprehend the drift of Senator Smith's questions. Once he replied somewhat testily. When asked how high was the crow's nest from the sea dock, he said: *"I'm no hand at guessing."*

As Fleet, a tall thin man, with blue eyes, became accustomed to the novelty of being examined, his mind became clearer, and he answered more readily. Senator Smith, regarding Fleet as a vital witness, in a good-natured, patient fashion, encouraged him to tell his story frankly. Witness's chief failing was a rather limited vocabulary. Often he did not reply at all, except to say, *"I don't know,"* or *"I don't remember,"* and often he simply nodded his head. Fleet, with a man named Lee, were two of the six look-outs employed on the *Titanic* at five guineas a

Frederick Fleet, Lookout.

Private Collection

Titanic crew members outside the Capitol in Washington D.C.

Southampton City Heritage Collections

month. Fleet and Lee were on duty at the time of the collision. Their routine was two hours' look-out and four hours off. They faced the Atlantic voyage in the crow's-nest without protection as regards the forward position, but canvas enclosed them on three sides. On the night of the collision Fleet and Lee took their places in the crow's-nest at ten p.m., relieving Simonds (sic) and Jewell. Both the latter said, as they came from the crow's-nest, *"Keep a sharp look-out for small ice."* Fleet replied, *"All right."* Lee said the same.

Senator SMITH: *"Now, did you keep a sharp look-out all the time?"* FLEET: *"Yes, and just about seven bells I reported that I saw a dark mass right ahead. I reported to the bridge by telephone from the crow's-nest, and also sounded a warning by striking the gong three times."*

Senator SMITH: *"How long before the accident did you report the ice?"* FLEET: *"I don't know."*

Senator SMITH: *"Was it an hour, half an hour, twenty minutes, ten minutes?"* FLEET: *"I can't say."*

Size of the Iceberg

Senator SMITH: *"Can you tell us how high was this dark mass of ice?"* FLEET: *"No."*

Senator SMITH: *"Come now; was it as high as a house, or as this table where you are seated?"*

Fleet reflected, and replied that when he first saw the ice it seemed about no higher than the table, but at close quarters it might have been just about 100ft above the water.

Senator SMITH: *"When you reported ice ahead to the*

bridge, did you get a prompt reply?" FLEET: *"Yes, sir; they understood the question."*

In further replies, the witness said that when the berg was alongside it was a little higher than the forecastle head.

Senator SMITH: *"Do you know whether the ship was stopped after you gave the telephone warning?"* FLEET: *"She didn't stop, sir, until we had passed the berg. We struck the berg on the starboard bow, just before the foremast. There was scarcely any jar, and I thought and said we had had a narrow shave. In the crow's-nest the collision didn't disturb our balance in the least. A little ice fell on deck, not much, and as far as I knew nobody was hurt by the falling ice."*

Both Lee and the other look-out men in the *Titanic* all survived the collision.

No Glasses Supplied

There was something in the nature of a painful sensation amongst the landsmen in court when Fleet, replying to Senator Smith's question, said: *"We were not supplied with glasses aboard the Titanic, and we relied upon our own eyesight."*

Senator SMITH: *"On the White Star's Oceanic did you have glasses?"* FLEET: *"Yes."*

Senator SMITH: *"What sort?"* FLEET: *"Rather poor."*

Senator SMITH: *"Did you ask for glasses for the Titanic?"* FLEET: *"We asked at Southampton for a glass, and they said there were none for us."*

Senator SMITH: *"Whom did you ask?"*

George Moore, George Symons and other crew witnesses with Senator Cary in Washington, April 1912.

Southampton City Heritage Collections

FLEET: *"Lightoller."*

Witness, who mumbled a great deal, was here understood to say that the look-outs had glasses from Belfast to Southampton, but not from Southampton.

Senator SMITH (speaking very slowly): *"Now supposing you had been supplied with glasses such as you had aboard the Oceanic, and such as you had from Belfast to Southampton, could you have seen this black object ahead at a greater distance than you did?"*

Fleet reflected a moment, and replied: *"We could have seen it a bit sooner."*

Senator SMITH: *"How much sooner?"* FLEET: *"Time enough to get away."* (Sensation.)

Senator SMITH: *"Did you discuss this matter of no glasses with your mates?"* FLEET: *"We certainly did."*

Senator SMITH: *"Did you express surprise or regret?"* FLEET: *"We did both."*

Senator SMITH: *"Did the officers on the bridge use glasses?"* FLEET: *"Yes."*

The remainder of Fleet's evidence related to the launching of the boats. In his boat there were thirty occupants – one first class passenger, two steerage, two of the crew, including himself, and all the rest women. Witness did not see the *Titanic* sink, because his boat pulled well away to the open sea to escape the danger of being sucked down with the vessel.

The inquiry adjourned for lunch at 2.30, and assembled an hour later.

(City Heritage Collections)

TESTIMONY OF G SYMONS

(Testimony taken before Senator Perkins on behalf of the subcommittee.)

Mr Symons was sworn by Senator Perkins.

Senator PERKINS. *"Where is your home port?"*

Mr SYMONS *"Weymouth."*

Senator PERKINS. *"Weymouth England?"*

Mr SYMONS *"Yes, sir."*

Senator PERKINS. *"Were you a sailor on the steamer Titanic that went down?"*

Mr SYMONS. *"Yes sir."*

Senator PERKINS. *"How long have you followed the sea?"*

Mr SYMONS. *"Eight and a half years."*

Senator PERKINS. *"As a sailor man?"*

Mr SYMONS. *"Yes, sir."*

Senator PERKINS. *"Tell me, in a general way, what happened when the ship went down, and when she was stuck?"*

Mr SYMONS. *"I was on the watch below at the time. I was asleep at the time the Titanic was struck."*

George Moore, George Symons and other crew witnesses with Senator Cary in Washington, April 1912.

Southampton City Heritage Collections

Senator PERKINS. *"It was your watch hour below?"*

Mr SYMONS. *"Yes sir. I came on deck and I saw the ice, and then I dressed myself and waited."*

Senator PERKINS. *"Which watch were you in on the ship?"*

Mr SYMONS. *"I was on the lookout on the 8 to ten watch. I came off at 10 o'clock."*

Senator PERKINS. *"Were you one of the six lookout men?"*

Mr SYMONS. *"Yes, sir."*

Mr SYMONS. *"I stayed by the boats. I helped lower no 3. From there I was sent down to no 5."*

Senator PERKINS *"How many were in the boat when she was lowered."*

Mr SYMONS. *"I could not say for certain."*

Senator PERKINS *"Approximately, how many? Were there 10 or 20?"*

Mr SYMONS. *"I should say, roughly, about 40, sir."*

Senator PERKINS. *"There were 40 in the boat when she was swinging in the davits."*

Mr SYMONS. *"Yes, sir; when she was hanging in the davits."*

Senator PERKINS. *"Who handled the falls of the boat?"*

Mr SYMONS. *"I handled the forward fall. I could not say who handled the after fall."*

Mr SYMONS. *"I was sent to no 5, and assisted there. I cleared the fall."*

Senator PERKINS. *"Did you get in her?"*

Mr SYMONS. *"No, sir."*

Senator PERKINS. *"What boat did you go from the ship in?"*

Mr SYMONS. *"No 1"*

Senator PERKINS. *"Who was in command of her?"*

Mr SYMONS *"I was."*

Senator PERKINS. *"How many passengers did you have on her?"*

Mr SYMONS. *"From 14 to 20."*

Senator PERKINS. *"Were they passengers or crew?"*

Mr SYMONS. *"They were passengers. At first they put in seven of the crew. There were seven men ordered in; two seaman and five firemen. They were ordered in by Mr Murdock (sic)."*

Senator PERKINS. *"How many did this boat carry?"*

Mr SYMONS. *"I could not say for certain. It was one of the small accident boats."*

Senator PERKINS. *"After she got into the water, would she take any more?"*

Mr SYMONS. *"She would have taken more."*

Senator PERKINS. *"How many did you have, all told?"*

Mr SYMONS. *"I would not say for certain. It was 14 or 20. Then we were ordered away."*

Senator PERKINS. *"You did not return to the ship again?"*

Mr SYMONS. *"Yes; we came back after the ship was gone, and we saw nothing."*

Senator PERKINS. *"Did you rescue anyone that was in the water?"*

Mr SYMONS. *"No sir, we saw nothing when we came back."*

Senator PERKINS *"Was there any confusion or excitement among the passengers?"*

Mr SYMONS. *"No, sir; nothing whatever. It was just the same as if it was an every day affair."*

Senator PERKINS. *"Was there any rush to get into either of these boats."*

Mr SYMONS. *"No, sir; I never saw it. I never saw any rush whatsoever."*

Senator PERKINS *"Did you hear any cries of people in the water?"*

Mr SYMONS. *"Oh, yes, sir; I heard the cries."*

Mr SYMONS. *"After we rowed around, and picked up with another boat, and both stuck together; one boat with a lot of people."*

Senator PERKINS. *"Did you pass a painter from one boat to another?"*

Mr SYMONS. *"No sir; we went close to her. They did not want any assistance, as the women were pulling. I asked if they wanted any assistance, and they would not take it. They said they could pull through."*

Senator Smith and the *Titanic*
Report of his Committee
The *Californian's* Captain Severe Censure
Senator's Wild Oration
Attacks on all Concerned
Charge Against The White Star

The American Court of Inquiry into the loss of the *Titanic* presented its report to the Senate yesterday. The report states that no one person can be blamed for the disaster, declares that the *Californian* and the *Titanic* saw each other's lights during the tragedy, severely censures the *Californian's* captain and officers, urges that every liner should carry searchlights and enough lifeboats for all, and recommends international revision of the rules of the sea.

Senator Smith in presenting the report made a most remarkable speech, in which he indulged in the wildest flights of sentiment and rhetoric in the intervals of denouncing everybody concerned. Captain Smith, he said, was over-confident and careless. The *Titanic's* surviving officers, he added, ought not to have left the ship so soon.

The crew were undisciplined and untrained, the officers and the crew did not know each other, and the passengers knew neither the one nor the other (which the Senator apparently considers a grave fault). And the White Star Line, the Senator finally alleges, had news of the disaster as early as 2.30 a.m. on Monday, April 15, a few hours only after the wreck.

(City Heritage Collections)

★ HOMECOMING

"The hectic greeting"

On *Lapland*'s arrival at Plymouth with the crew survivors, they were met by White Star directors Harold Sanderson and E.C. Grenfell, Board of Trade representatives, Custom officials, White Star's Plymouth agent and John Bartholomew, their Southampton victualling superintendent. The Board of Trade wished to immediately take down the crew's evidence but they were prevented by Thomas Lewis and Mr Cannon of the British Seafarers' Union, who refused permission to board *Lapland*, hired a small boat and spoke to *Titanic*'s crew through a megaphone.

On the tender *Sir Richard Grenville* the crew refused to speak to the Board of Trade who were forced to invite Lewis & Cannon on board. The crew now gave their accounts, beginning with the stewardesses and they finally landed at midday. To their surprise and annoyance they were detained in the dock's third class waiting room while their waiting families, the press and the general public remained outside a high iron fence while depositions continued. Some of the crew had to stay overnight – bedding, tables and food were provided; and they talked to their friends and family through the windows when they got the chance.

Finally released after 1.30pm when the press swooped, some 85 seamen and firemen left for Southampton on the 6pm train. Travel plans for the stewards and stewardesses, cooks and victualling assistants were cancelled, and they would return to Southampton the next day.

Meanwhile in Southampton an open air service was being held at the Marlands to celebrate the crews homecoming. 50,000 of the general public attended with Territorials, Army and Navy reserve men.

Crowds converged at Southampton West station. Police would only admit relatives and dignitories including Mayor Bowyer and White Star's Philip Curry, to the platform. The crowds broke through as the train arrived and the survivors were welcomed with great emotion, as the crew found their families in the crowd. Others waited in the crowd in vain, or asked for news. Then they made their way home amidst cheers and tears.

The same reception awaited 86 stewards and stewardesses the next day just after 9pm with massive crowds eager to meet them.

Q. And you were in New York for how long?

'...oh, just the day, that's all. They transferred us to the Lapland and brought us back to Plymouth. Then they put us on the train from Plymouth to Southampton, the crew, and so they had the hectic greeting. You could just imagine it, can't you. You can imagine what it was like on the Falkland business? There was everyone there to greet us, it was quite an exciting time.'

DAILY SKETCH.
No. 975—MONDAY, APRIL 29, 1912.   THE PREMIER PICTURE PAPER.   [Registered as a Newspaper.]   ONE HALFPENNY.

FIRST SURVIVORS OF TITANIC TO REACH ENGLAND.

SS *Lapland* arrives off Plymouth.

Daily Sketch/Peter Boyd-Smith, Cobwebs

Q. So the Company did not want to see you before you came home?

"No, no, no well they wrote us afterwards and told us to 'stand by' for any...any...sort of hearing."
"I was never called up, some were taken in to be recorded, I wasn't. That's about all there was to it. I just stopped at home and after a couple of days I went down with quinsy...a reaction had set in then and they put me in bed for a week or so with quinsy. But I got over that, but of course I was on the dole then for about 6 months. Sort of convalescing and on the dole."
Sidney Daniels (City Heritage Oral History)

"And then I joined a ship called the Lapland and I worked my way home to Plymouth. And when we arrived at Plymouth they give us accommodation in the Dock and we were not allowed out. And after that we were sent home by train to Southampton. When we arrived at Southampton, my mother and my wife was there to meet me, which I was delighted to see".
Arthur Lewis (Southern Daily Echo)

'After that we got our voyage pay - single men got £3, and married £5, out of the Union funds.'
Jack Podesta (Echo)

Titanic crew in process of leaving Lapland and being advised, by megaphone from a small boat, by their Union representatives.

Daily Sketch/Peter Boyd-Smith, Cobwebs

**From Our Special Correspondent
Plymouth, Monday Night**

Today the authorities taking the depositions of the *Titanic* survivors performed a complete volte face, and so far from trying to prevent the survivors who did not go on to Southampton last night from enjoying the utmost freedom, or putting any impediments in the way of Press representatives, went out of their way to be bland and courteous. The dock gates were thrown open to everybody. Some sixty-one stewards and twenty stewardesses and restaurant cashiers made their depositions today. Of these the Receiver of Wrecks himself undertook to subpoena about thirty for Lord Mersey's inquiry. It will be in the discretion of the Board of Trade in London to add to the number. The form of the document handed to each witness was as follows:

**In the Court of the Wreck Commissioner for the United Kingdom.
Whereas the Board of Trade has requested me, the undersigned, a Wreck Commissioner for the United Kingdom, to hold a formal inquiry into the circumstances attending the loss of the British steamship *Titanic*, of Belfast, in the North Atlantic Ocean, on or about the 14th day of April, 1912, and the loss of life which thereby ensued or occurred; and whereas it appears to me that you are likely to give material evidence therein, you are herby summoned to appear before my Court, sitting in the Scottish Hall, Buckingham Gate, Westminster, London, S.W., on Friday, 3rd day of May, 1912, at 10.30 in the forenoon, to testify what you know in such matter.
Given under my hand this 29th day of April, 1912.
(Signed) Mersey, Wreck Commissioner for the United Kingdom.**

Following yesterday's procedure, three or four witnesses were examined at one time in a waiting room of the dockyard, and their statements taken down in writing by typists. After the stewards had completed their evidence – and much of it was very much alike – the women who served on the *Titanic*

Survivors arrive at Plymouth by tender from the *Lapland*.

Southampton City Heritage Collections

as stewardesses were brought down to the dock in a brake. These depositions had all been taken by half-past three, and nearly all the survivors had left for their homes half an hour later. The second Southampton detachment, over fifty strong, were taken to their destination by special train.

Mr. P. Keene, of 14, Rigby Road, Southampton, a saloon steward, was one of the *Titanic's* crew who went to his home today. Before he left Plymouth he thus described to me the scene on the sinking vessel, his narrative including one or two points not previously mentioned by survivors.

"Most of us were asleep when the iceberg cut into the Titanic's side. I heard the impact, but the sound was in no way alarming, for it seemed to be nothing worse than a blade falling off a propeller. That, in fact, was what I thought had happened. A number of my fellow-stewards were not conscious of the accident, and they had to be aroused from their sleep. We had great difficulty in calling Butterworth (Saloon Steward), and when we got him out of his berth he said, in a sleepy voice, 'What's up?' He was not saved. Some of the stewards were ordered to the store-room to get provisions for the boats, and these we carried on deck."

Heroic Bedroom Stewards

"We found that the bedroom stewards had formed
themselves into a police force. They ranged themselves opposite each boat and saw to it that the sea rule, 'women and children first', was strictly observed. Others of the bedroom stewards went below and brought up the women and children. Their behaviour was beyond praise, and they went about their duties with a calmness which must have assisted to maintain the splendid discipline, let out with their fists at one or two men who attempted to get into the boats, and you may take it from me they acted as bravely as the heroic engineers."

"The boat I was in was No. 5 on the starboard side. It was the last boat on that side of the ship to leave. The Titanic had then a heavy list to port, and as our boat was lowered away it scraped the side, and we had some trouble to keep it off. When it was in the water about ten minutes were occupied in attempting to release the boat falls, and then somebody cut the ropes. There was no seamen with us, and a fireman took command. After the Titanic sank we hailed several boats, and asked if they had an officer to spare; but we could not get one, and the fireman remained in charge. It was common conversation throughout the voyage that the Titanic was unsinkable, and many people could not be prevailed upon to enter the boats, because they thought there was no real danger of the Titanic foundering. When the ship took a heavy dip forward the passengers began to realise that the position was serious. We left the

214

Titanic crew being kept from the public at Plymouth.

Southampton City Heritage Collections

ship about an hour before the Titanic sank. Afterwards we saw the fore part of the ship break away up to the foremost funnel, and it appeared to us that when the ship had listed heavily to port the engines fell out and crashed through the side. The second funnel broke off, and killed a number of people in its fall."

"Discipline was magnificent until the last boat got away. Even then it remained good, as far as we could tell, until those left on board knew they were prisoners because no more boats remained. They must have realised, a good while before the end came, that all was lost. We rowed the long, heavy oars for some distance, and when we rested we heard a fearful noise on the ship, and it seemed to us that a lot of people were fighting. One of the engineers got horribly jammed when the doors in the bulkheads were closed. His injuries were terrible, and, as there was no chance of releasing him, he implored that he might be shot to be put out of his misery. This, I have been told, was done."

"Yes, I did see lights after the Titanic had gone down, but they were rockets sent up by an officer, who discovered them in a box which had been put on the boat for a case of biscuits."

Asked whether there had been any boat drill on the *Titanic*, the steward replied: *"Not on the voyage."* Before he signed on the *Titanic* he had served on the *Oceanic*, when she was commanded by Captain Haddock, now the *Olympic*'s captain. In the *Oceanic* the watertight doors were closed every day to see if they were in perfect order, and there was boat drill on Sundays. All hands except the firemen, who through their union obtained a special exemption from taking part, had to engage in boat drill. These drills were not carried out on the *Titanic*.

Among the survivors who were sunning themselves at the dockside outside the offices of the Board of Trade this morning was Mr. Prentice, a storekeeper on the *Titanic*. He did not appear to be much the worse for the trying experience he had gone through. In conversation, he said:

"I was in the storekeeper's room when the collision occurred, and did not notice any impact at all. For some time after the order had been given to go on deck none of us anticipated any real danger. I and the other storekeepers chatted on deck and smoked cigarettes. As the forepart of

Crew members interned at Plymouth on their return to England.

Southampton City Heritage Collections

in the boat as the result of exposure. The other fireman went crazy, and kept trying to clamber out of the boat, but I managed to keep him down. He is now recovered."
(City Heritage Collections)

the ship became unseaworthy we got on to the poop, eventually climbing to the extreme end. I heard crowds of passengers singing hymns just before the vessel went down. I hung on by the rail and then let myself drop into the sea. The distance to the water was quite 75ft, and I thought I was never going to get there. When I did come into contact with the water it was like a great knife cutting into me. My limbs and body ached for days afterwards. However, when I came to the surface I was able to strike out. Before leaving the ship I went to the store and got a bottle of brandy, which I put into my pocket, and it caught the eye of the seaman in charge of a lifeboat which was coming to save me. When he dragged me into the boat he took away the bottle of brandy, which I had not made use of, and threw it into the water, with the remark that he would not let anyone have it in the boat. The women in the boat were hysterical, and he was afraid that the brandy, if drunk, might have a worse effect, but it might have been the means of saving life, as we picked up two firemen who had been in the water a long time, and one afterwards died

Mr Ismay And The Women

From Our Special Correspondent
Plymouth, Monday

Today the stewardesses and stewards of the *Titanic* told the stories of their escape. Being more amenable to official control than the trade unionist firemen and sailors, the men had spent the night at the dock station and the women at an hotel, and they were permitted to tell their experience only after making formal depositions of their evidence. Their statements show very clearly how little the imminence of danger was realized until the ship actually began to tilt downwards for the plunge. The first boats left the ship's side half empty because the passengers said they would not leave the *Titanic* to go in a cockleshell, said Mrs. Gould, a first class stewardess on B deck. "Mrs Wallace (sic), the steerage matron, even went back to her cabin after seeing her passengers into their boats and locked herself in, remarking *'I am going to stay where I am safe.'* She was a nervous little woman."

"Mrs. Snape, too, a second cabin stewardess, a woman of twenty one, who had left a baby behind in Southampton, shook hands with her passengers as they got in, but would not go in a boat herself." Among the passengers in Mrs. Gould's section was Mr Bruce Ismay. She saw him on deck when she went up and he put her into a boat. He was wearing an overcoat over pyjamas. "I saw him again in a boat near to ours when we were rowing up to the *Carpathia*", said Mrs. Gould. "He was sitting on the gunwale at the stern of the boat. His face was blue with cold and he sat perfectly still, staring straight in front of him, expressionless like a statue."

Mrs. Maclaren (sic) was another stewardess whom Mr Ismay put in a boat. When Mr Ismay told them to get in the boat they said, "We are not passengers; we are members of the crew." "It doesn't matter," Mr Ismay replied. "You are women, and I wish you to get in."

Mrs. Martin, a tall, graceful woman, who was a first stewardess, told how, when the steward came to call them to get up and put on lifebelts, they thought it was a practical joke.

(Lloyds Weekly News, April 21st 1912. City Heritage Collections)

Proof of evidence given to the Wreck Commissionaire by George Thomas Macdonald Symons of 6 Moreland Road, Southampton states:

I am an AB and have had sea experience of about thirteen or fourteen years. I have for the last fourteen months been lamp trimmer on the Union Castle steamship Braemar Castle. Previous to that I had some work on shore and had been lamp trimmer on the White Star liner Oceanic. I was an AB on board the Titanic at the time of her loss and was one of the men specially selected for lookout. I was on duty on the day of the disaster from 2 to 4 and again from 8 till 10.

Titanic crew being kept from the public at Plymouth.
Southampton City Heritage Collections

Witnesses being summoned to appear before the commission in London.

Southampton City Heritage Collections

Previously to being on the Titanic I had been AB and lookout man on the Oceanic and whilst employed was in the habit of using glasses which were supplied for the lookout men and kept in a canvas pocket in the crows nest. There was a similar pocket for the glasses in the crows nest of the Titanic but there were no glasses there and on my applying to the second officer for them I was told that we should not have any on that voyage but we should have them on the next voyage. From my three years experience of lookout man on the Oceanic I am of the opinion glasses are a great assistance to the men on lookout and although I have very good eyesight having passed special tests from time to time yes I am satisfied that you can pick up object sometimes with the glasses which you cannot see with the naked eye. My practise with regard to the glasses was not merely to use them for examining an object I had already seen or fancied I had seen but to keep sweeping the horizon when I had instructions to look out for light or desire to look out for some particular object.

The night in question the 14th of April 1912 was a dark starlight night with no moon and a very smooth sea

A group of stewards photographed on landing at Plymouth.

Southampton City Heritage Collections

Crew members interned at Plymouth. Notice the formal clothes that were given to them in New York.

Southampton City Heritage Collections

Crew survivors at lunch in their temporary quarters, Plymouth.

Southampton City Heritage Collections

there being apparently no swell or ripple at all the sea being quite glassy. It was the practice to have two men on the lookout in the crows nest and the other man with me was Jewell. It was the 2nd officers watch on the bridge and we received instructions from the bridge by means of telephone. About 9.30 we had an order to keep a sharp lookout for ice as far as I can recollect the exact words were 'keep a sharp lookout for ice and growlers' we had previously noticed that it was very cold and chilly and we had the sensation or feeling that you get when you have had experience of ice that there was ice about and I made the observation to Jewell that we could smell ice about. I remember that although it was a star light night and clear overhead that there was a slight low lying haze on the horizon which some what obstructed the view of the skyline and this to the best of my recollection was so during the time I was on watch. At 10 o'clock Jewell and myself were relieved by Fleet and Lee and we passed on to them the orders which we had received after keeping a sharp lookout for ice and growlers.

(Signed) George Symons

Minutes of the British Seafarer's Union meeting in June 1912 reflect the role played by the Union in the crews return to Britain and the members determination to make sure other ships, particularly *Olympic*, have adequate safety in the future.

This issue came to a head on 24th April when 285 of *Olympic*'s crew refused to sail as they regarded the hastily added collapsible lifeboats as insufficient. Tommy Lewis from the Seafarer's Union went aboard to negotiate but with the ship anchored off Ryde, White Star engaged a non-Union crew from the Sheffield area. This provoked all but three of the seamen left on the ship to leave. P.E. Curry and Captain Haddock of *Olympic* regarded these actions as 'mutiny' and many were charged, but eventually the voyage was abandoned. People such as Dr. Beaumont of *Olympic*, who regarded some elements of the crew as almost sub-human, in his memoirs accused them of cowardice after the *Titanic* disaster. However, it is more probable that Beaumont was irked by the crew daring to challenge their 'betters' and a reflection of the fact that they were no longer willing to follow unquestioningly their employers and officers.

British Seafarers' Union Meeting

A general meeting of members was held at The Southern District Schools on Tuesday May 7th. The chair was taken by the President who called upon the Assist Sec to read the minutes of the last meeting which were passed as read.

The financial settlement for the preceeding week was also read and passed.

The President in opening the meeting gave a brief

Crew members at Plymouth on their return to England.

Southampton City Heritage Collections

outline of the action taken by him to ensure the representation of the Union upon the Court of Inquiry sitting in London to deal with the "*Titanic* Disaster".

He also reported to the meeting that he had accompanied by the Secretary gone to Plymouth to meet the *Titanic* survivors and he was also pleased to say that owing to the action taken by them the men had been allowed to proceed direct to their homes instead of having to stay as laid down by the Board of Trade.

The subject of the strike which had taken place upon the *Olympic* over life-saving equipment was next raised and the President stated though the men had won a great victory yet in future they must bear in mind that they must always consult their Union officials before taking any action.

The recommendation of the Executive Committee that subject to the approval of the Gen Meeting the sum of 10/- be paid to all members of the union who left their work on the RMS *Olympic* was read and after a long discussion a note was taken and there being only a few against the recommendation was declared carried.

The following resolution was moved by G Maskell seconded by H Bailey. That the attention of the Stewards Union be called to the unorganised state of the stewards of the R.M.S. *Olympic* and also of the need to

Titanic survivors steward J. Whitter and stewardess Annie Robinson at Plymouth.

Southampton City Heritage Collections

organise the same to prevent a recurrance of such a contemptible action which occured when the ship was taken away from the Quay.

Carried unanimously.

It was also reported to the meeting that the painters of the docks and yards locally were on strike and all members were warned about doing any of the work usually done by the strikers.

There being no further business the meeting closed.

T Lewis

11/6/12

R.M.T. Union Records (University of Warwick)

Survivor Samuel Rule (left), a bath steward for thirty five years. He was allowed to see his brother under the escort of two police officers.

Southampton City Heritage Collections

Two stewardesses after landing at Plymouth.

Southampton City Heritage Collections

Survivors at Plymouth shows H. Maynard (left) entrée cook. It was claimed that while aboard his lifeboat, shortly after the sinking, Captain Smith swam up to him handing him a baby before swimming away.

Southampton City Heritage Collections

Able seaman Horswill, 44 Derby Road, Southampton. Reunited with his wife and children he is perhaps examining the cheque (one of several) given to the crew in lifeboat number 1 by Sir Cosmo Duff-Gordon, which caused much controversy afterwards.

Southampton City Heritage Collections

Survivors who the Commissionaire had called to give evidence at the British Enquiry. Pictured at Plymouth.

Southampton City Heritage Collections

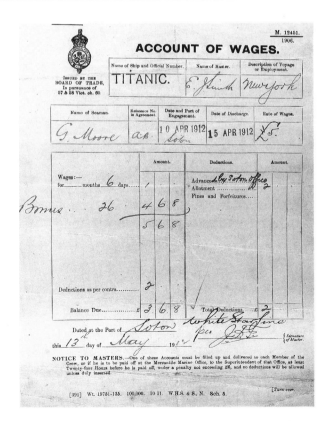

Account of wages which shows George Moore's pay
stopped on April 15th 1912.

Southampton City Heritage Collections

The first of the survivors return to Southampton. Seaman Pascoe reunited with his mother and three brothers.

Southampton City Heritage Collections

Crew arrive at Southampton station on the special train. Monday April 29th. Second from right George 'Scooch' Kemish.

Southampton City Heritage Collections

Brother and sister reunited at Southampton station.

Southampton City Heritage Collections

Crew survivors arriving in Southampton.

Southampton City Heritage Collections

Quartermaster Humphries arrives at Southampton. *"One of the men who has heroism written on his face now."*

Southampton City Heritage Collections

Survivor William Major, fireman (right), telling his mates the story of lowering the last boat to leave the ship which he was in. Outside South Western Hotel, Southampton.

Southampton City Heritage Collections

BRITISH INVESTIGATION

"Hands on the whitewash brush"

Interior of the British Investigation court showing a model of the *Titanic*.

Southampton City Heritage Collections

THE BRITISH INVESTIGATION

The formal British Investigation began on Thursday 2nd May in the Scottish Drill Hall, Buckingham Gate, complete with a twenty foot model of *Titanic*. Proceedings were conducted under the watchful eye and at times exceedingly sharp tongue of Lord Mersey. The commission would meet on twenty eight days of public hearings until Friday 21st June. Friday 3rd May was the first day that witnesses would be called. But before they could be heard the issue of allowing various interests, including Thomas Lewis for the British Seafarers, to be represented was discussed.

'When the sitting opened a renewed attempt was made to persuade Lord Mersey to allow various interests to be represented. On Thursday he peremptorily refused the claims of several sets of interests. On Thursday night there were protests in Parliament. This morning he showed himself much more conciliatory. He withdrew his opposition to the representation of the Seafarers' Union, the Southampton trade union which lost nearly 200 of its members in the *Titanic*, and he also admitted the Imperial Merchant Service Guild, the society that looks after the interests of officers, and the National Union of Stewards.

A score of the rescued crew were there with scarves round their necks and "quiffs" hanging over their foreheads. They are being kept by Government in a sailors' home in Whitechapel, much to their annoyance, it is said.'

(City Heritage Collections)

Most of the early witnesses were the crew, what follows are excerpts from some of their testimonies. The first witness to be called was Archie Jewell, one of the lookouts.

LIST OF
WITNESSES IN THE ORDER IN WHICH THEY APPEARED.

Date.	Name of Witness.	Description.	Numbers of Questions.	Page.
2nd day (3rd May, 1912).	1. ARCHIE JEWELL	Lookout man	1 to 331	16 to 21
	2. JOSEPH SCARROTT	Able seaman	332 to 651	22 to 29
3rd day (7th May).	3. GEORGE WILLIAM BEAUCHAMP	Fireman	652 to 892	31 to 36
	4. ROBERT HITCHINS	Quartermaster	893 to 1385	36 to 46
	5. WILLIAM LUCAS	Able seaman	1386 to 1834	46 to 53
	6. FREDERICK BARRETT	Leading stoker	1834 to 2075	53 to 60
4th day (8th May).	FREDERICK BARRETT (continued)		2076 to 2361	61 to 66
	7. REGINALD ROBINSON LEE	Lookout man	2362 to 2761	66 to 74
	8. JOHN POINGDESTRE	Able seaman	2762 to 3339	74 to 83
	9. JAMES JOHNSON	Night watchman in 1st saloon	3340 to 3508	83 to 86
5th day (9th May).	JAMES JOHNSON (continued)		3509 to 3707	87 to 91
	10. THOMAS PATRICK DILLON	Trimmer	3708 to 3980	91 to 95
	11. THOMAS RANGER	Greaser	3981 to 4181	96 to 99
	12. GEORGE CAVELL	Trimmer	4182 to 4501	99 to 104
	13. ALFRED SHIERS	Fireman	4502 to 4830	104 to 109
	14. CHARLES HENDRICKSON	Leading fireman	4831 to 5274	109 to 116
6th day (10th May).	15. FRANK HERBERT MORRIS	Bathroom steward	5275 to 5505	117 to 121
	16. FREDERICK SCOTT	Greaser	5506 to 5906	121 to 130
	17. CHARLES JOUGHIN	Chief baker	5907 to 6366	130 to 139
	18. SAMUEL JAMES RULE	Bathroom steward	6367 to 6669	139 to 144
7th day (14th May).	19. STANLEY LORD	Master of ss. "Californian"	6670 to 7411	145 to 160
	20. JAMES GIBSON	Apprentice of the ss. "Californian."	7412 to 7802	160 to 166
	21. HERBERT STONE	2nd Officer of the ss. "Californian."	7803 to 8110	166 to 172
8th day (15th May).	22. CHARLES VICTOR GROVES	3rd Officer of the ss. "Californian."	8111 to 8564	172 to 181
	23. GEORGE FREDERICK STEWART	Chief Officer of the ss. "Californian."	5565 to 8918	181 to 187
	CHARLES VICTOR GROVES (recalled)		8919 to 8923	188
	24. CYRIL F. EVANS	Marconi operator on the ss. "Californian."	8924 to 9218	188 to 193
	25. JAMES HENRY MOORE	Master of the ss. "Mount Temple."	9219 to 9415	194 to 197
	26. JOHN DURRANT	Marconi operator on the ss. "Mount Temple."	9416 to 9590	198 to 201
9th day (16th May).	JOHN DURRANT (recalled)		9591 to 9596	202
	SAMUEL RULE (recalled)		9597 to 9832	202 to 207
	27. JOHN EDWARD HART	3rd class steward	9833 to 10325	207 to 216
	28. ALBERT VICTOR PEARCEY	3rd class pantryman	10326 to 10497	216 to 219
	29. EDWARD BROWN	1st class steward	10498 to 10672	219 to 222
	30. CHARLES DONALD MACKAY	Bathroom steward	10673 to 10867	222 to 225
	31. JOSEPH THOMAS WHEAT	Assistant 2nd steward	10868 to 11071	226 to 230
10th day (17th May).	CHARLES HENDRICKSON (recalled)		11072 to 11302	232 to 236
	32. GEORGE SYMONS	Able seaman	11303 to 12007	237 to 252
	33. JAMES TAYLOR	Fireman	12008 to 12304	252 to 257
	34. JAMES CLAYTON BARR	Master of the ss. "Caronia"	12305 to 12318	257
	35. ALBERT EDWARD JAMES HORSWILL	Able seaman	12319 to 12447	258 to 260
	36. Sir COSMO DUFF-GORDON	Passenger	12448 to 12591	260 to 268
11th day (20th May).	Sir COSMO DUFF-GORDON (continued).		12592 to 12868	268 to 271
	37. Lady DUFF-GORDON	Passenger	12869 to 12970	271 to 273
	38. SAMUEL COLLINS	Fireman	12971 to 13053	274 to 275
	39. FREDERICK SHEATH	Trimmer	13054 to 13092	276
	40. ROBERT WILLIAM PUSEY	Fireman	13093 to 13155	276 to 277
	41. Mrs. ELIZABETH LEATHER	1st class stewardess	13156 to 13185	278
	JOSEPH JAMES WHEAT (recalled)		13186 to 13271	278 to 280
	42. Mrs. ANNIE ROBINSON	1st class stewardess	13272 to 13314	280 to 281
	43. WALTER WYNN	Quartermaster	13315 to 13407	281 to 283
	44. CHARLES HERBERT LIGHTOLLER	2nd Officer	13408 to 13796	283 to 292
12th day (21st May).	CHARLES HERBERT LIGHTOLLER (continued).		13797 to 14910	293 to 325
13th day (22nd May).	45. HERBERT JOHN PITMAN	3rd Officer	14911 to 15304	325 to 333
	46. JOSEPH GROVE BOXALL	4th Officer	15305 to 15766	334 to 345
	47. HAROLD GODFREY LOWE	5th Officer	15767 to 16091	345 to 350
	48. GEORGE ELLIOTT TURNBULL	Deputy Manager of the Marconi International Marine Communication Company.	16020 to 16087	351 to 352
14th day (23rd May).	GEORGE ELLIOTT TURNBULL (continued)		16088 to 16284	353 to 361
	49. HAROLD BRIDE	Marconi operator	16285 to 16286	361
	GEORGE ELLIOTT TURNBULL (recalled)		16287 to 16322	361 to 362
	HAROLD BRIDE (recalled)		16323 to 16801	362 to 372
	CHARLES HERBERT LIGHTOLLER (recalled)		16802 to 16906	373 to 376
	JOSEPH GROVE BOXALL (recalled)		16907 to 17017	376 to 378
	HERBERT JOHN PITMAN (recalled)		17018 to 17040	379
	HAROLD GODFREY LOWE (recalled)		17041 to 17052	380

List of some of the ninety-seven witnesses who were called to the British Investigation.

Department of Transport (Marine Accident Investigation Branch)

Archie Jewell, lookout. He was the first witness to be called at the British Investigation. Jewell earned a rare word of thanks from Lord Mersey for his answers to a lengthy series of questions.

Southampton City Heritage Collections

3 May 1912
Archie Jewell, Sworn
Examined by the Solicitor General

Q. *Is your name Archie Jewell?*
A. *Yes.*
Q. *And were you one of the lookouts on the 'Titanic'?*
A. *Yes quite right.*
Q. *On the 'Titanic' did all the able seamen take their turns at the lookout or had you a special set of lookouts.*
A. *Yes six special lookouts.*
Q. *You were one of the six.*
A. *Yes.*
Q. *Now on the night of that Sunday the 14th of April which was your lookout which was your watch?*
A. *From 8 to 10.*
Q. *And where were you, were you in the crows nest or at the forecastle head or where?*
A. *In the crows nest on watch.*
Q. *Was there a second lookout with you in the crows nest?*

A. *Yes there were two, one at a time.*
Q. *There were two of you together in the crows nest.*
A. *Yes.*
Q. *Who was the man who was with you?*
A. *Symons, he is back in New York.*
Q. *And he was saved too?*
A. *Yes…*

On May 6th Mersey had granted the Attorney General more time to prepare questions for the crew. This gave Mersey and his assessors the opportunity to examine the *Titanic's* sistership *Olympic* at Southampton. White Star's Harold Sanderson met most of the party at the West Station and escorted them to the White Star Dock where Southampton company manager P.E. Curry was waiting. On board they inspected the operation of the watertight doors and watched closely as one of the lifeboats was launched.

Proceedings at the investigation resumed on 7th May. Charles Joughin, the Chief Baker, gave his testimony on 10th May.

Extra lifeboats are hurriedly put aboard *Olympic* at Southampton. This action did not prevent her crew from striking over unsatisfactory safety.

Southampton City Heritage Collections

THE THIRD CLASS PASSENGERS

John (sic) Joughin, chief baker, said he was awakened by the collision, and at 12.15 he received the order passed down, *"Provision boats."* He sent up the whole of his staff, thirteen in number, with 40lb. of bread each. Biscuits should have been in the boats already. The witness was assigned to duty at No. 10 boat, on the port side. Everything was orderly. The

C. Mackay and E. Brown (both saloon stewards) who gave evidence before the commissionaire in London on 16th May.

Southampton City Heritage Collections

chief officer was there and many passengers. The chief officer called for the men to be kept back, but there was no need for it, for the men kept back. The discipline was splendid. The stewards formed into line and passed women and children along. When the boat was half full some difficulty was experienced in getting the women to enter the boat. They ran away, saying they were safer where they were. He was sure of that. He saw plenty of third class women passengers.

The Solicitor General: *"So far as you saw, was any difference made between first, second, and third class ladies?"*

Joughin: *" None at all. In ordinary times the boat deck would be used for first class passengers only, but there were no barriers there on this night. There was an emergency door leading from the third class avenue into the second class broad staircase. That door was open on the night of the disaster. The staircase rose through several decks right up to the boat deck."*

The witness knew the door was open because he went through it. He went down to his room for a drink. He saw third class passengers leaving the lower deck by that door, some of the women carrying packages. The witness with other men

brought some women forcibly from the lower decks to the boats and pushed them in.

Two Hours In The Water

The witness, it appeared, according to the list, was supposed to be captain of the boat.

Q. *"Why did you not get in?"*

Joughin *"I was waiting for orders to get into the boat, but there were two sailors and a steward in already, the boat being otherwise full of women and children."*

The witness received no order to get in the boat he supposed it was because there were sufficient in it already, and it left.

Q. *"Where did you go then?"*

Joughin *"Well, I went scouting round, so to speak. I went down to my room and had a drop of liquor, and after speaking to the old doctor I went up again on deck and saw that all the boats had gone. I went down to "B" deck and threw some deck chairs overboard."*

Q. *"Why?"*

Joughin *"Well, I was looking out for something to cling to. I threw about 50 overboard. The list of the ship was increasing on the port side. I went to the deck pantry and heard a noise as if something was buckling and some people running along. I went up on deck again and found people running and clambering on to the poop. The buckling seemed like the cracking of iron. I kept out of the crush of people getting towards the well of the ship. The ship then gave a great lurch and a great crowd of people were thrown in a heap – many hundreds of people. The ship never recovered from the lurch."*

Q. *"What happened to you?"*

Joughin *"I eventually got to the starboard side of the poop on the side of the ship. I clung to the rail on the outside of the ship. I was wondering what next to do, and was changing some things from one pocket to another when she went."*

Q. *"Did you go under water?"*

Joughin *"No, I don't think I went under at all. My head might have been wet."*

Q. *"Are you a good swimmer?"*

Joughin *"Yes."*

Q. *"How long were you before rescued?"*

Joughin *"Until daylight broke, about two hours, when I was rescued by a collapsible. The water was like a pond. I was treading water. I swam to a collapsible boat which was on its side, with Officer Lightoller and from 20 to 25 men clinging to it. They were on the side, holding each other up."*

Pushed From A Boat

Q. *"Was there any room for you?"*

Joughin *"No."*

Q. *"You agree there was no room?"*

Joughin *"Yes."*

Q. *"Did you cling to it?"*

Joughin *"No, I was pushed from it and sort of hung

Lord Mersey, President, and his son Captain Bingham, Secretary at the British Enquiry.

around, and a chap named Maynard (entree cook), who knew me, gave me a hand and helped to hold me up. The edge of my lifebelt rested on the edge of the boat."

Q. *"Was the water cold?"*

Joughin *"Well, I was colder when I got into a lifeboat. I had a lifebelt on. The lifeboat people said they could only take 10 people, and I said to Maynard, "Let go my hand," and I swam to the lifeboat. I was in the water altogether about two and a half hours. The lifeboat was crowded with women."*

Further questioned, the witness said that, although he was *"captain"* of boat No. 10 he had no nautical knowledge and gave way to others. The lifebelt would have supported him without his treading water. They were a patent kind in use on the *Titanic.* Replying to Mr. Harbinson, the witness said the avenue to the emergency door to which he had referred was known by the men as *"Scotland Road Avenue."* He saw one man, a foreigner, with two boys over his shoulder and one in his hands getting up the staircase.

Replying to Mr. Cotter (for the Stewards' Union), the witness said he helped to get two children and their mother and a mother and child to the boats. The former woman tried to jump to the boat, missed her footing, and fell. They tried to drag her by her feet to the "A" deck, but she disappeared, and he did not see her again. Her two children were saved.

Q. *"You say when you got to the collapsible boat you were pushed off?"*

Joughin *"Yes."*

Q. *"Who pushed you off?"*

Joughin *"I don't know."*

Q. *"Did you say anything to them?"*

Joughin *"No."*

The witness said he was all right when he got to the *Carpathia* except that his feet were swollen, and he had to go up the ladder on his knees. Joughin, in answer to the Solicitor General, said the lights on the ship were burning right to the finish. After the luncheon adjournment, Mr. Laing, K.C., intimated on behalf of the White Star Line, that they were willing that any of the gentlemen to whom his Lordship had allowed representation should visit the *Olympic* on Monday next at twelve o'clock.

(City Heritage Collections)

THE MAN IN CHARGE

George Symons, able seaman, was then called (17th May). Replying to the Attorney General, he said he had been a seaman for nine years and had crossed the Atlantic fifty or sixty times. He was look-out on the *Titanic*, and had been engaged similarly on other liners. He was in the crow's nest from 8 to 10 o'clock on the night of the disaster. He had asked Mr. Lightoller if he had any glasses for the look-out men, and he was told there were none. On the night of April 14, about 9.30, he received orders from the bridge to keep a sharp look-out for small ice and bergs till daylight. It was very cold, and he told his mate he could smell ice. When he went on deck after the collision he assisted generally in getting the boats out. Mr. Murdock (sic) was in charge of the starboard side, and there was no difficulty in getting out the boats there. He had never seen things better worked on any ship. The passengers already had their lifebelts on and kept very good order. After lifeboats 3, 5, and 7 had been cleared away, the witness went to No. 1 emergency boat. Two ladies came running out of the foremost end of the top saloon deck towards the boat, and asked if they could get in. Mr. Murdock said, *"Yes, jump in."* Then three gentlemen came running out and they were allowed to jump in. Mr. Murdock looked round for more, and seeing no one but the crew he gave the order *"Lower away."* As they were being lowered, he asked who was in charge, and the witness replied, *"Symons, the look-out."* Mr. Murdoch said, *"Very well, Symons, take charge of that boat, and make all those under you obey you, and make them do what you tell them."* There were twelve people in the boat.

The Attorney General: *"There was plenty of room in your boat for a good many more passengers than you had?"* Symons: *"Yes, but the order was 'Lower away,'*

Notice to release George Moore from the British Enquiry.

Southampton City Heritage Collections

and you had to obey orders."
The President: *"If there was plenty of room in the boat for more people, why was the order given to lower away? Was it because there were no other people about to put in her?"* Symons: *"There were no more people about in sight on the ship when the order was given to lower the boat."* Replying to the Attorney General, the witness said that after No. 3 boat went away he saw a white light, one white light about a point and a half away on the port bow as the *Titanic* was standing. He took it to be the light of a *"cod banksman"* a fishing vessel. The President: *"What time was that?"* Symons: *"About half-past one – about an hour before the Titanic foundered."* The witness said he also saw the light after his boat was launched and got away. The distance the light was away was from five to ten miles.

Why Did Not The Boat Go Back?

The witness went on to say that when he got into the boat, Mr. Murdoch gave him an order to *"Stand a little way off, and come back when called."* After they had pulled away about 200 yards he told the men to lie on their oars. They moved further away when the ship went down in order to keep out of the suction. Symons: *"I heard cries from the Titanic as she disappeared, but I came to the conclusion that it was not safe to go back."*

(City Heritage Collections)

'Men who have important tales to relate.'

Southampton CIty Heritage Collections

Second Officer Lightoller was called on 20th May and was interrogated with more than 1,600 questions. He is regarded as a key witness in countering the criticism of the way the *Titanic*'s navigation had been conducted. He later made this reference to the experience.

'In Washington it was of little consequence, but in London it was very necessary to keep one's hands on the whitewash brush.

Sharp questions that needed careful answers if one was to avoid a pitfall, carefully and subtly dug, leading to a pinning down of blame on to someone's luckless shoulders. How hard Mr. Scanlan and the legal luminary, representing the interests of the Seamen and Firemen, tried to prove there were not enough seamen to launch and man the boats. The same applied to the passengers, and quite truly. But it was inadvisable to admit it then and there, hence the hard-fought verbal duels between us. Mr. Scanlan's conquest of the higher legal spheres of recent years proves he was no mean antagonist to face. His aim was to force the admission that I had not sufficient seamen to give adequate help with the boats, and consequently that the ship was undermanned. How many men did I consider necessary to launch a lifeboat? *A: "What size lifeboat?" Q: "Take one of the Titanic's lifeboats." A: "Well"*, I pointed out, *"it would depend greatly on weather conditions." Q: "Make your own conditions,"* replied my legal opponent impatiently.

I suggested, as an example, we should take the wind as force six Beaufort's scale. *"Yes"*, he agreed. *"Then,"* I added, *"there would be an accompanying sea, of course." "Yes, yes"*, he again agreed, and fell into the trap which Lord Mersey proceeded to spring, by informing Mr. Scanlan that in the circumstances described it would be impossible to launch any boat.

So the legal battle went on. Still, I think we parted very good friends. A washing of dirty linen would help no one. The Board of Trade has passed that ship as in all respects fit for sea, in every sense of the word, with sufficient margin of safety for everyone on board. Now the Board of Trade was holding an enquiry into the loss of that ship – hence the whitewash brush. Personally, I had no desire that blame should be attributed either to the Board of Trade or the White Star Line, though in all conscience it was a difficult task, when handled by some of the cleverest legal minds in England, striving tooth and nail to prove the inadequacy here, the lack there, when one had known, full well, and for many years, the ever-present possibility of just such a disaster. I think in the end the Board of Trade and the White Star Line won.

The very point, namely the utter inadequacy of the lifesaving equipment then prevailing, which Mr. Scanlan and his confrères had been fighting tooth and nail to prove, has since been wholly, frankly, and fully admitted by the stringent rules not governing British ships, 'Going Foreign'. No longer is the Boat-Deck almost wholly set aside as a recreation ground for passengers, with the smallest number of boats relegated to the least possible space. In fact, the pendulum has swung to the other extreme and the margin of safety reached the ridiculous.

Be that as it may, I am never likely to forget that long-drawn out battle of wits, where it seemed that I must hold that unenviable position of whipping boy to the whole lot of them. Pull devil, pull baker, till it looked as if they would pretty well succeed in pulling my hide off completely, each seemed to want his bit. I know when it was all over I felt more like a legal doormat than a Mail Boat Officer. Perhaps the heads of the White Star Line didn't quite realize just what an endless strain it had all been, falling on one man's luckless shoulders, as it needs must, being the sole survivor out of so many departments – fortunately they were broad.

Still, just that word of thanks which was lacking, which when the *Titanic* Enquiry was all over would have been very much appreciated. It must have been a curious psychology that governed the managers of that magnificent Line.

(Charles Lightoller. *Titanic* and Other Ships. 1935)

21st May 1912
Charles Herbert Lightoller
Examined by Mr. Scanlan.

Q. *The question I ask is, how many of a crew would you desire to have?* (In a lifeboat.)
Say four.
Q. *There would be four able seamen?*
Four men generally useful in a boat, with a fair knowledge of boating.
Q. *You think four would be sufficient?*
I would handle any of these lifeboats with four men.
Q. *Would you require four experienced men?*
Not necessarily experienced men – men who have a fair knowledge of boats, who know one end of the oar from another, and know which end of the sail goes up.
Q. *You would not expect to get such men from amongst the stokers, would you?*
Why not?
Q. *Would you?*
Yes.
Q. *You would not require to have these four men ordinary seamen, deckhands?*
No, not at all.
Q. *But they would require to be skilled in the management of lifeboats or boats?*
Not necessarily skilled; they want to be skilled in doing what they are told, and be able to do it.

The Right Hon. A.M. Carlisle, designer of the *Titanic*, at the investigation. He gave evidence on 10th June.

Southampton City Heritage Collections

Q. But in a sudden emergency you would not have time to tell them what to do, just as you had not time to tell the crews you sent from the 'Titanic'?
But you are speaking of riding out at sea now, working a boat in a sea way.
Q. I am speaking of anything a boat's crew would have to do, from the launching of the boat from the boat deck until they get to safety, if they ever get there. I do not wish to detain your Lordship with this.
(The Commissioner) You have indicated your point.
(Mr Scanlan – To The Witness)
Q. It has been suggested in evidence which has been given in this case to my Lord that a crew of nine is desirable and necessary?
Then that would mean five less passengers, would it not?
Q. It would, of course, and on the other hand, Mr Lightoller, it would mean more boats. Do you agree with that?
The necessity of nine men to a boat?
Q. Yes?
Emphatically no.
Q. I understand your point of view. I am reading from what
purports to be the official note of the evidence in America, my Lord. It is the first day, and the first time you were in the witness-box, and it is on page 68 of the copy I have. You were asked, 'Do you know where you were at the hour you turned over the watch to Mr. Murdoch?
(Mr Lightoller) Not now, Sir.
(Senator Smith) Did you know at the time?
(Mr Lightoller) Yes, Sir.
(Senator Smith) Can you give us any idea?
(Mr Lightoller) When I ended the watch I roughly judged we should be getting towards the vicinity of the ice, as reported by that Marconigram I saw somewhere about 11 o'clock.
Do you follow this?
Yes.
(Senator Smith) That you would be in that latitude?
(Mr Lightoller) Longitude.
(Senator Smith) At 11 o'clock?
(Mr Lightoller) Somewhere about eleven, yes.
(Senator Smith) Did you talk with Mr Murdoch about that phase of it when you left the watch?
(Mr Lightoller) About what?

(Senator Smith) *I said, did you talk with Mr Murdoch about the iceberg's situation when you left the watch?*

(Mr Lightoller) *No, Sir.*

(Senator Smith) Did he ask you anything about it?

(Mr Lightoller) *No, Sir.*

(Senator Smith) *What was said between you?*

(Mr Lightoller) *We remarked on the weather, about its being calm, clear. We remarked the distance we could see. We seemed to be able to see a long distance. Everything was clear. We could see the stars setting down on the horizon.*

Q. *From this it appears that when you gave your evidence you were under the impression that you had not told Mr Murdoch about the icebergs and the conclusion you arrived at as to approaching them?*

I may say by the questions that were put to me that those answers you might agree were correct as far as I understood the questions at that time.

Q. *Is it your explanation then that this is incorrect or imcomplete?*

Incomplete, I say, yes.

Q. *And that notwithstanding this evidence, you did tell Mr Murdoch about the icebergs?*

Undoubtedly, yes.

Q. *You will admit, I suppose, that this is misleading, and I suppose, you would like to correct it?*

Yes, I should.

The Solicitor-General: *I think if you look a little earlier, Mr Scanlan, you will find that this gentleman was asked, 'Did you communicate to Mr Murdoch this information that the Captain had given you on the bridge?' And he speaks of having communicated to him about the ice then, I think. 'So that the officer in charge, Mr Murdoch, was fully advised by you that you were in proximity to these icebergs,' and he says: 'I would not call it proximity,' but I think the answers show that he did say that then. I know you want to be fair.*

(Mr Scanlan) *I do, and I hope you will understand that, Mr. Lightoller?*

(The Witness) *Quite right.*

(Mr. Scanlan – To The Witness) *From the evidence you gave to the court yesterday at what distance ahead to you think you yourself in the peculiar conditions which prevailed on this Sunday night could have picked out an iceberg?*

About a mile and a half to two miles.

Q. *Do you mean by the naked eye?*

Yes.

Q. *And with glasses could you discern it at a greater distance?*

Most probably.

(The Commissioner) *I do not follow the answer?*

I meant to convey (it is rather a difficult question to answer) that we do not have the glasses to our eyes all the time, and naturally I should see it with my eyes first. If I happened to be looking directly ahead at the moment an iceberg came in view and I had the glasses to my eyes at that particular moment it is possible I should see it, whereas I should not have seen it quite as soon with my eyes.

Q. *Apparently binoculars are placed in a bag or a box in the crow's nest at times. At the time of the accident it is said there were no binoculars on the 'Titanic' in the crow's nest: is that true?*

That there were none?

Q. *No, is it true that there is a place for them in the crow's nest?*

I believe so.

Q. *Then, presumably, it is intended that they should be there?*

Yes.

Q. *We are told you know they were not there this night?*

Yes.

Q. *And they are there to be used, I suppose?*

Yes.

Q. *When they are being used in the crow's nest are they used in the sense of being always held up by the look-out man to his eyes, or are they merely had recourse to as occasion seems to suggest?*

That is it, your Lordship.

Q. *The man on the look-out is not always standing with the binoculars up to his eyes?*

No, certainly not.

Q. *They are there for use when he thinks it desirable to use them?*

Precisely. You see, if I may point out, binoculars, with regard to lights, are extremely useful; that is to say, there is no doubt you will distinguish a light quicker. If you set a man to look out for a certain light, and he reports a light it is quite a matter for us to ring him up on the telephone and ask, 'What character is that light'? The man may, on a clear night, see the reflection of the light before it comes above the horizon. It may be the loom of the light and you see it sometimes sixty miles away. He may just make sure of it with the glasses, because there is any amount of time – hours; there is no hurry about them on a clear night at all. You make absolutely certain then about the light, and so as to be in that position we ring him up to say exactly what it is: but when it comes to derelict wrecks or icebergs, the man must not hesitate a moment, and on the first suspicion, before he has time to put his hand to the glasses or anything, one, two, or three bells must be immediately struck, and then he can go ahead with his glasses and do what he likes, but he must report first on suspicion.

(Mr. Scanlan – To The Witness) *For the purpose which my Lord has been explaining to you is it not very desirable to have glasses provided for look-out men so that they can use them when necessary?*

It is a matter of opinion for the officer on watch. Some officers may prefer the man to have glasses and another may not; it is not the general opinion.

Q. *I am not talking about the opinion of officers in general, but the particular opinion which you entertain as to the usefulness of glasses?*

Yes – now I can answer you decidedly – certainly I uphold glasses.

Q. *For look-out men? I am glad you do. Do you know now*

that a complaint was made at Southampton by the look-out man that glasses were not provided in the crow's nest.
I know of no complaint.

Q. Do you know there were not glasses in the crow's nest?
I do.

Q. You say there was no complaint made. You mean —
(The Commissioner) No, he does not; he says he knows of no complaint.

(Witness) I meant to convey that impression, that there was no complaint — there was no right to make a complaint.

Q. Do you mean to tell me that if the look-out man goes into the crow's nest and finds that there are no binoculars in the pocket or box or whatever it is, he has no right to come and say so?
Yes, he has the right to come and report, and there the matter ends.

(The Commissioner) I call that complaining.

(Mr. Scanlan – To The Witness) So far as you know it was not reported that there were not glasses?
It was reported.

(The Commissioner) It is only a question of words.

(Mr. Scanlan) That is so.

(The Commissioner) He does not think a report is a complaint.

(Mr. Scanlan) I meant it in the sense of a report taken.

(Witness) There was a report; I am sorry I misunderstood you.

Q. Can you explain to my Lord why, when such a report was made, glasses were not provided for the look-out man on the 'Titanic'?
No, I cannot offer you any explanation.

Q. If it had been a matter in your discretion, would you have provided glasses then?
Had they been on the ship I might have done.

Q. Were there glasses on the ship available for the use of the look-out man?
That I cannot say.

Q. Had you glasses on the bridge?
We had.

Q. How many pairs?
A pair for each senior officer.

Q. How many pairs altogether; you have five or six officers?
A pair for each senior officer and the Commander, and one pair for the bridge, commonly termed pilot glasses.

Q. So that there would be from time to time during the whole course of the voyage a pair of glasses available?
On the bridge.

Q. On the bridge that could have been handed up or given to the look-out man?

(The Commissioner) Mr. Scanlan, I want you to know what is passing in my mind. It appears to me that whether those glasses were there or not made very little, if any, difference, because the man would not have them to his eyes, and when he did sight this thing it was too late to use glasses.

(Mr. Scanlan) My instructions are, my Lord, up to the present that the utility of glasses consists in this: you sight something, and do not know what it is; then you apply the glasses, and you are able to say whether it is an iceberg or a derelict.

(The Commissioner) That is quite right.

(Mr. Scanlan) That seems to be a most important thing, my Lord.

(The Commissioner) What I am pointing out to you is this: here the thing was sighted at a time when lifting up glasses and looking to see what it was would have been of no use whatever; they were right on it.

(Mr. Scanlan) Except this: we do not know but that before the man discerned this object, a speck, or a mast, or something.

(The Commissioner) That is not my view of the evidence; I think the look-out man rang out three bells the moment he saw something ahead.

(Mr. Scanlan) We are in this position yet, that we have not had here the identical man who rang the bells and who shouted 'An iceberg ahead, sir.' So that it must be a surmise. I think I have indicated my point.

(The Commissioner) You are quite right.

(Witness) I should like to point out that when I speak favourably of glasses it is in the case of a man on whom I can rely, but if I have a man in a case like this which Mr. Scanlan speaks of, a derelict or an iceberg, who is to put the glasses to his eyes before he reports, I must utterly condemn glasses. The man must report first and do what he likes afterwards.

(The Commissioner) I believe Mr. Scanlan that is right, it would be quite improper for a man who sees something ahead with his eyes, to wait until he has used glasses before he reports.

(Mr. Scanlan) Surely, my Lord, that would depend on the distance at which the object was seen; if it were seen 10 miles ahead with the ship going as slowly as some of those ships go.

(The Commissioner) We need not contemplate a case of that kind, it was not this case. Here the iceberg was right close to the ship.

(Mr. Scanlan) I shall be prepared at a later stage in the case to offer your Lordship evidence on this point, and it is in that view that I have pressed the matter so far.

(The Commissioner) Quite right.

(Mr. Scanlan – To The Witness) This night you have described as being a particularly bad night for seeing icebergs. Is not that so?
I do not think I mentioned that word 'bad', did I?

(Mr. Scanlan) Can you tell me at what speed the 'Titanic' was going when you left the bridge at 10 o'clock?
About 21½ knots.

Q. What was the indication from which you make that calculation?
I judge from what I remember of the revolutions. I think, as far as I remember, the revolutions were 75, and I think that will give an average of about 21½.

Q. The speed was taken down, I understand, in the log.
Yes, that would be kept in the scrap log.

Q. I do not suggest that you wanted to make a record passage on this occasion, but had not you all in mind the desirability of making a very good first trip, from the speed point of view?

No, I am afraid not, because we know that in the White Star, particularly the first voyages – in fact you may say pretty well for the first 12 months – the ship never attains her full speed.

Q. Were not you on this occasion taking as much speed as you could get out of the 'Titanic'?

Oh, no, not at all; I am under the impression she was under a very reduced speed compared with what she was capable of doing.

Q. What maximum speed do you think you could have attained?

Well, just as a matter of hearsay, or rather, what we estimated roughly, for instance myself, I judged that the ship would eventually do about 24 knots.

Q. Did you say yesterday that you were going at as high a speed as you could in view of the coal you had on board?

Did I say so yesterday?

Q. Yes?

I was not on the stand yesterday.

(The Solicitor-General) Yes, you were.

(Mr. Scanlan) You were being examined yesterday?

Oh, yes; I beg your pardon. Not only with regard to shortage of coal, but I understand several boilers were off.

Q. Do you know any reason for those boilers being off?

Merely that there was no wish for the ship to travel at any great speed.

Q. There was no reason, I take it, why you should not go fast; but, in view of the abnormal conditions and of the fact that you were nearing ice at ten o'clock, was there not a very obvious reason for going slower?

Well, I can only quote you my experience throughout the last 24 years, that I have been crossing the Atlantic most of the time, that I have never seen the speed reduced.

Q. You were asked by my Lord this forenoon how an unfortunate accident like this could have been prevented in what you describe as abnormal circumstances?

Yes.

Q. Is it not quite clear that the most obvious way to avoid it is by slackening speed?

Not necessarily the most obvious.

Q. Well, is it one way?

It is one way. Naturally, if you stop the ship you will not collide with anything.

Q. There was no reason why you might not slacken speed on this voyage, you were not running to any scheduled time?

No.

Q. Am I to understand, even with the knowledge you have had through coming through this 'Titanic' disaster, at the present moment, if you were placed in the same circumstances, you would still bang on at 21½ knots an hour?

I do not say I should bang on at all; I do not approve of the term banging on.

Q. I mean drive ahead?

That looks like carelessness you know; it looks as if we would recklessly bang on and slap her into it regardless of anything. Undoubtedly we should not do that.

Q. What I want to suggest to you is that it was recklessness, utter recklessness, in view of the conditions which you have described as abnormal, and in view of the knowledge you had from various sources that ice was in your immediate vicinity, to proceed at 21½ knots?

Then all I can say is that recklessness applies to practically every commander and every ship crossing the Atlantic Ocean.

Q. I am not disputing that with you, but can you describe it yourself as other than recklessness?

Yes.

Q. Is it careful navigation in your view?

It is ordinary navigation, which embodies careful navigation.

Q. What I want to suggest is that the conditions having been so dangerous, those in charge of the vessel were negligent in proceeding at that rate of speed?

No.

Q. I will pass from that point. Amongst the precautions which it would be proper to adopt, would it not be desirable to station more look-outs, more look-out men on the bows or the stem-head?

Anything which would be conducive to avoiding danger.

Q. Would that be conducive to avoiding danger?

It might be.

Q. I am speaking to you, as a man of great practical experience?

I could not exactly say whether look-outs in the stem head would be. We do not place very much reliance on them; we hope they will keep a very good look-out, but those men in the first place are not regular look-out men, and you have not the same control over them as you have over the look-out men. They have nothing to sacrifice in the way of a good berth, which the look-out man's is.

Q. I think the difference between a regular look-out man and an irregular look-out man – that is, an ordinary A.B. – is 5s. a month?

Five shillings a month in pay and a difference in watches and a difference in work on board the ship.

Q. But there is no passing of an examination to go from one grade to the other?

Yes.

(The Solicitor-General) Is there?

Yes, I should explain to you, it is customary when a ship is in running for all look-out men to have an eye test as well as the Quartermaster's. That does not apply necessarily to A.B.'s.

(Mr. Scanlan) I was going to ask you about the eye test. Is there an eye test of each look-out man in the White Star Line?

Well, as far as possible we maintain the condition of having look-out men who have passed the eye test.

Q. I want to understand. We have had evidence on this point already. We have had the evidence of a man who told us that his sight was not tested, and this was his first voyage in a White Star vessel, the 'Titanic'?

Yes.

Q. How do you explain that?

By her being a new ship, and the difficulty of obtaining a perfectly satisfactory crew at such short notice. You see, you have to have men with you some little time; on the other hand, I can tell you of look-out men who have been on the look-out of the White Star for some considerable time, and who have had eye tests.

Q. *Will you admit, in view of the importance of the duties which look-out men have to perform, that there should be a proper eye test?*

Oh, yes. I think it is quite a reasonable precaution, and is maintained on the White Star, and I may say only the White Star.

Q. *Have you in the White Star any system of drilling and training seamen for manning life-boats.*

Oh, yes.

Q. *Did you train them on the 'Titanic'?*

No, except in Belfast. We put some boats in the water there, I think that was done by the builders though.

Q. *So far as the officers were concerned there was no testing of the men in lifeboat practice?*

Oh, yes, in Southampton as well we put boats in the water and the men were put in.

Q. *How many?*

Probably eight and a quarter-master in each boat.

(Mr. Scanlan) *There is one other point.* (To The Witness) *You have a master's certificate and an extra master's certificate? Yes.*

Q. *Do you know whether or not a Captain of a first-class ship like the 'Titanic' has a great many duties to perform of a social nature apart from his duties on the bridge; I mean looking after the passengers?*

Oh, no. Of course the purser is responsible to him, as everyone in the ship is responsible to him.

Q. *Has not the Captain as a matter of fact to be a great deal away from the bridge?*

Oh, dear no, not at all. He does not need to be away from the bridge at all.

Q. *In practice is not the Captain a good deal away?*

No. Do not misunderstand me. Say it is hazy weather or anything like that, he would never be away from the bridge. You might go from New York to Southampton and the Captain never away down amongst the passengers as far as that goes…

Harold Sanderson (White Star Line) and Captain Haddock (with coat) outside the Court of Enquiry, London.

Southampton City Heritage Collections

Titanic stewardesses photographed in Plymouth. Stewardess Annie Robinson, in middle at back with veil. Violet Jessop, third from left.

Southampton City Heritage Collections

20th May
Mrs Elizabeth Leather, Sworn.
Examined by Mr Scanlan

Q. *"Have you been for a considerable time a stewardess?"*
Leather *"Yes."*
Q. *"Is it the practice on liners to give each stewardess a boat station?"*
Leather *"Yes."*
Q. *"And at some time on the voyage are the stewardesses as well as the other hands called to their stations?"*
Leather *"Only on sailing days; there is then a boat muster."*
Q. *"But you had not that on the Titanic?"*
Leather *"On the sailing day we all mustered in the companion to pass the doctor."*
Q. *"You mean the day you left Southampton?"*
Leather *"Yes."*
Q. *"But were you told then what your boat station was?"*
Leather *"No, we were supposed to look for it ourselves on the list."*

20th May
Mrs Annie Robinson, Sworn
Examined by Mr Raymond Asquith

Q. *"You were a First Class Stewardess on the Titanic, were you not?"*
Robinson *"Yes."*
Q. *"And at the time the ship struck the iceberg I think you were in bed?"*
Robinson *"I was."*
Q. *"What deck were you on?"*
Robinson *"E deck."*
Q. *"When you got to the top of the stairs which lead down to the mail room what did you see?"*
Robinson *"I saw two mail-bags and a man's Gladstone bag, and on looking down the staircase I saw water within six steps of coming on to E deck."*
Q. *"That would mean that it had gone up to the top of the mail room and into the compartment above that?"*
Robinson *"Certainly."*

Q. *"About what time was this?"*
Robinson *"About half an hour after she struck."*
Q. *"After the collision?"*
Robinson *"After the collision about half an hour."*
(Mr Raymond Asquith) *"Did you see the Captain and Mr Andrews about this time?"*
Robinson *"The mail man passed along first and he returned with Mr McElroy and the Captain and they went in the direction of the mail room, but that was before."*
Q. *"It was seeing the Captain and Mr Andrews going to the mail room that made you go there?"*
Robinson *"I followed after they had come back."*
The Commissioner: *"Are we to understand that at this time the mail room was covered with water?"*
Mr Raymond Asquith: *"Yes, and not only the mail room but the storey immediately above it too."*
(To the Witness) *"When you saw the water there I suppose you realised that things were rather serious?"*
Robinson *"I did."*

Q. *"Did you go and look after your ladies?"*
Robinson *"I did."*
Q. *"How many ladies were under your charge?"*
Robinson *"Seven ladies and one maid and a governess."*
Q. *"Did you see other stewardesses doing the same thing, looking after their passengers?"*
Robinson *"The stewardess on my deck was doing exactly the same thing."*
Q. *"Were you told by a steward there to put on your coat and lifebelt?"*
Robinson *"Mr Andrews told me first."*
Q. *"Did Mr Andrews tell you anything else?"*
Robinson *"Yes. Mr Andrews told me to put my lifebelt on after I had been on E deck."*
Q. *"Did he say something to you about blankets?"*
Robinson *"We had already got the blankets and the lifebelts out of the rooms which were unoccupied at the foot of the staircase. Mr Andrews said to me, "put your lifebelt on and walk about and let the passengers see you." I said to him, "It*

Some of the witnesses leaving the court in London. George Moore centre.

Southampton City Heritage Collections

looks rather mean," and he said to me, "Well, if you value your life put your belt on."

Q. "Did you put your belt on and walk about in it?"

Robinson "I did."

Q. "So far as you know were all the ladies on E deck warned by the stewardesses whose business it was to look after them?"

Robinson "Yes, and they were all saved, too."

Q. "You told us you were responsible for seven or eight ladies: were they all saved?"

Robinson "They were."

Q. "Eventually you were put into boat number 11?"

Robinson "Yes."

The Solicitor General: "That is the one the last witness Wheat referred to."

(Mr Raymond Asquith – (to the Witness) "I will not ask you about what happened in the boat, but there is one thing I should have asked you about what happened before: did you see the carpenter?"

Robinson "I did; he was the first man I saw. He came along when I was looking down at the water, and he had the lead line in his hand."

Q. "Had he taken a sounding do you know?"

Robinson "I could not tell you that."

Q. "Did he say anything to you?"

Robinson "No, the man looked absolutely bewildered, distracted. He did not speak."

Q. "You think he looked alarmed?"

Robinson "He certainly was."

Q. "When your boat left the ship was the band still playing?"

Robinson "It was."

Q. "Can you remember at all what time it was when your boat left?"

Robinson "Well, I looked at my watch when the ship went down and it was twenty minutes to two. That was by altered time when we were in the boat, and I do not think we were in the boat more than three-quarters of an hour."

Q. "You left about three-quarters of an hour before the ship went down?"

Captain Clarke and Commander Lyon, two of the assessors at the investigation.

Southampton City Heritage Collections

Robinson *"Yes."*

Examined by Mr Cotter.
Q. *"Have you ever been in a collision before?"*
Robinson *"Yes."*
Q. *"What ship was that? The 'Lake Champlain'?"*
Robinson *"Yes."*
Q. *"Also an iceberg?"*
Robinson *"Yes."*
Q. *"So that you knew exactly what to do on this occasion?"*
Robinson *"Yes."*
Q. *"And you did it?"*
Robinson *"Yes."*

One of the more controversial issues, certainly for the press, during the investigation was the role of the occupants of lifeboat number one. The boat had left with twelve people out of a possible forty, among them Sir Cosmo and Lady Duff-Gordon. The controversy over the boat being nearly empty was compounded by the revelation that Sir Cosmo had gifted the crew members in the lifeboat £5 each to 'replace their lost possessions'. Sir Cosmo denied any suggestion of impropriety.

Sir Cosmo Duff Gordon at the British Enquiry
The Presents to the Crew

Q. *"I must ask you about the money. Did you make any promise to the men in the boat?"*
Duff Gordon – *"Yes, I did. There was a man who sat next to me in the boat in the dark – I did not know who he was – who said, some 20 minutes after the Titanic had sunk, "I suppose you have lost everything, sir?" I replied, "Of course we have." He said: "Well, you will be able to replace it again, but we have lost the whole of our kit, and the Company won't give us any more. We shall get no pay after the time the vessel went down. All they will do will be to send us back to London." I said: "You fellows need not worry about that. I will give you a fiver each to start a new kit." That was all that was said, but on the Carpathia I believe it was Hendrickson who got a list of names for me."*
The Court adjourned until Monday, Sir Cosmo Duff Gordon being still under examination.

(City Heritage Collections)

George Symons, the look-out who was in charge of lifeboat number 1 in which the Duff Gordon's were rescued, later received this letter from Cosmo Duff Gordon.

Mary Culter House, by Aberdeen. Sunday 25th.
I was very glad to hear from you Symons, many thanks for your letter. I think the whole of the inquiry showed how entirely unable Lord Mersey was to appreciate what the circumstances really were. What are you doing now have you gone back to sea or have you become a land man for a time? Lady Duff Gordon is I am glad to say none the worse for her experiences either by land or sea.
Yours truly Cosmo Duff Gordon.
(Private Collection)

While Officers such as Lightoller, publicly at least, tried to be positive about the Investigation, the British Seafarers Union were in no doubt about what they thought.

'The Whitewashing '*Titanic*' Inquiry has cost the nation £20,231. The items of expenditure include the following: Wreck Commissioners' salary, £1,050; assessor's remuneration and expenses, £950; shorthand writing, £622; hire of hall and fitting up as court, £260; stationery and printing, £1,214; Sir Rufus Isaacs, £2,458; Sir J. A. Simon, £2,425; Mr. Aspinall, £2,345; Mr. Rowlatt, £1,249; Mr. R. Asquith, £864; payments for detention of witnesses, £1,908; solicitors, £2,500; plans and models, £564.

It will be seen that the lawyers take between them just on £13,000. Sir Rufus Isaacs is the Liberal Attorney-General and Sir J.A. Simon is Liberal Solicitor-General, and are paid big salaries for these offices; the latter will also be paid huge fees for his services at the recent Telephone Arbitration proceedings. Mr. Rowlatt has been made a Judge and Mr. R. Asquith is a son of the Prime Minister. The ruling classes rob and plunder the people all the time, and the Inquiry has shown that they have no scruples in taking advantage of death and disaster. Who said Sharks?

The charges and expenses of Mr. T. Lewis in connection with his appearance at the Inquiry on behalf of the British Seafarers' Union, was £72 0s 6d., and Mr. Cotter's for the Stewards' Union, £68 2s.'
The British Seafarer (University of Warwick)

Sir Robert Finlay, KC, MP (second left), who led the White Star Line's representation, and Thomas Scanlan (right), representing the National Sailor's and Firemen's Union.

Southampton City Heritage Collections

On 30th July the Mersey Commission presented its findings. The Commission only seemed to see a few individuals as worthy of any blame in the disaster. Captain Smith, who of course was now beyond any mortal hurt, by the fact of *Titanic*'s excessive speed at the time of the collision. They found that Captain Lord and the crew of the Californian may have reached *Titanic* if they had tried. This was the opening shot in a bitter side argument which still rages today. The other critical findings were general, manning arrangements for the lifeboats were insufficient, the need for more lifeboats, and the regret that Lifeboat Number One did not return to pick up more survivors.

J. Bruce Ismay, the chairman and managing director of the White Star Line was exonerated of improper conduct as was Sir Cosmo Duff-Gordon, an occupant of lifeboat number one.

Most astoundingly the Commission managed to deduce that third class passengers were not discriminated against in the saving of life. No third class passengers had been called to the Enquiry but one of only two surviving stewards (John Edward Hart) stationed in third class had testified that the men had been kept below deck as late as 1.15am. It may be a comment on the strict class structures which existed in Britain at the time that neither the third class passengers nor the press saw this as an issue. The fact remains that in a disaster which has become synonomous with the phrase 'women and children first', more children from third class perished than men from the first class.

For the crew who had also suffered so badly, their five minutes of international fame was about to end leaving them to pick up the pieces of their lives again. For many other 'women and children' in Southampton the struggle was just beginning.

RELIEF FUND

"No sympathy and no jeering"

'**D**own below in the world of steam
*In the heat and fiery glow
Worked hundreds of devoted men*
To make the great ship go.

*Yet they had wives and children who
Would never see them more
Thinking them safe on the largest ship
That ever left the shore.*

*In Southampton, good old sea port
Wives made widows, what a list
But so recently together
Husbands now forever missed.'*

From 'The Chief Incidents of the *Titanic* Wreck treated in verse by Edwin Drew'. Formerly belonging to G.H. Husher, a ganger and carpenter who fitted out *Titanic*. (City Heritage Collections)

As we have seen the 'casual' nature of a working life at sea saw White Star's contractual duty to the surviving crew ended when the ship sank. The families of those killed had no claim to compensation and although some of the richer American passengers sued, it would have been virtually impossible for any of the crew's families to seek legal redress. Southampton remained a town in a state of shock. Flags flew at half mast, condolence notices filled the local newspapers and a memorial service was held at St. Mary's Church on 20th April. National newspapers continued for a time to write articles focussing on the heartbreak along with photographs of streets and schools, particularly in Northam, where many had lost relations.

Mayor Henry Bowyer of Southampton opened a relief fund 'for distressed dependants of the crew of the *Titanic*'. A national *Titanic* Relief Fund was also created and eventually collected over £413,000, the opening Lord Mayor of London being Sir Thomas Crosby. In

'Southampton's tribute to her dead heroes'. Men of the White Star Company on their way to St. Mary's Church.
20th April 1912.

Southampton City Heritage Collections

Above and below: White Star Company men entering St. Mary's Church. 20th April 1912.

Southampton City Heritage Collections

Southampton and District Pictorial

(WITH WHICH IS INCORPORATED "SOUTHAMPTON AMUSEMENTS.")

Vol. 1.—No. 4.]   WEDNESDAY, MAY 1st, 1912.   [Price One Penny.

Sunday's Memorial Service on the Marlands.

Above and below: Open air memorial service on Marlands.
28th April 1912.

Southampton Pictorial

THE PALACE

SOUTHAMPTON.

SPECIAL MATINEE

Wednesday, May 8th,

At 2.30, in Aid of the

MAYOR'S

"Titanic" —Fund

Under the Distinguished Patronage of His Worship the Mayor and Mayoress, Aldermen and Councillors, and other Influential Ladies and Gentlemen.

For Further Particulars See Small Bills.

Southampton Pictorial

1916 the fund was amalgamated to become the *Titanic, Empress of Ireland* and *Lusitania* Mansion House Relief Fund. The fund was available to dependants and relatives of crew and passengers lost in these disasters.

Money was raised in a plethora of ways including collecting by tin in the street, special charity concerts, fund raising sports events, memorium postcards and some of the earliest charity records including the dirge like 'Be British'. Many prominent individuals contributed.

HIPPODROME
SOUTHAMPTON.

Proprietors ... THE SOUTH OF ENGLAND HIPPODROMES, LTD.
Managing Director ... ... MR. WALTER DE FRECE
Resident Manager ... ... MR. H. YARDLEY

PRELIMINARY NOTICE.

A Special = Matinee

WILL BE GIVEN ON

WEDNESDAY, MAY 1st,

IN AID OF

THE MAYOR'S FUND

To relieve the sufferings of the Widows and Children caused through the terrible catastrophe which has overtaken the "Titanic."

:0:

The following Gentlemen have kindly consented to act as a Committee:— His Worship the Mayor; Sir Geo. A. E. Hussey; Col. Candy; Vascon. Sellors, Esq., Consul for Brazil; Dr. Russell Bencraft; Capt. Plunkett, Royal Mail; P. V. Bowyer, Esq., Chairman of Guardians; Mr. Alderman Sharp; Mr. Alderman W. Bagshaw; Mr. Alderman Ensor; Mr. Councillor Hair; F. E. Allen, Esq.; W. Bulpitt, Esq.; Archie Ede, Esq.; A. Foster, Esq.; Walter de Frèce, Esq.; George Gear, Esq.; A. G. Grainger, Esq.; W. Green, Esq.; F. A. K. Housell, Esq.; J. Laidman, Esq.; J. S. Medd, Esq.; A. E. Plumb, Esq.; W. Saunders, Esq.; W. Vincent, Esq.; H. Yardley, Esq.
From whom Tickets May be Obtained.

Notices for some of the many charity events and concerts which were staged to raise money for the Relief Fund.

Southampton Pictorial

Southampton alone collected £41,000 for the fund. Rea's (the coalers), among many others, contributed 100 guineas.

"There wasn't much in the way of assistance ... and I can quite clearly remember going to a concert ... which was in aid of the widows and orphans. These little concerts and charities ... were quite a feature of life."
Charles Morgan (City Heritage, Oral History)

'At a meeting of the A.O.K.'s on Thursday, a sum on £5 5s was voted to the Mayor's Titanic Disaster Fund. A sum of 8/- was also collected at the meeting and put into the Empire Theatre collecting box.'
(Southampton News 1912)

'A splendid programme has been arranged by the St. Mary's Ward Conservative Association (under the direction of Mr. Ben Living) for their concert in aid of the Titanic Fund on Tuesday next at the Deanery Schools. His Worship the Mayor and Mayoress are giving their patronage, and we sincerely hope they will have a bumper house.'
(Southampton News 1912)

'The local musicians belonging to the A.M.U. are arranging a promenade concert to be held at the Shirley Skating Rink on Sunday evening, June 16th. The proceeds to be devoted to the Titanic Disaster Musicians Hero's Fund.'
(Southampton News 1912)

SOUTHAMPTON AND DISTRICT LICENSED VICTUALLERS' ASSOCIATION.

TITANIC DISASTER.
RELIEF FUND

We are authorised by His Worship the Mayor to state that any member of the Trade who may desire to have Collection Boxes at their bars, may obtain same by applying to our Secretary, 4 Portland Terrace, Southampton.

W. INGRAM, Chairman.
W. E. WILTSHIRE, Secretary.

TITANIC DISASTER.

MR. HAROLD BINNING has great pleasure in announcing that

MADAME AMY SHERWIN

Has graciously offered to assist the Fund for the relief of the sufferers by giving a CONCERT at Southampton, at which the world-famous English Prima Donna,

STELLA CAROL, will sing.

Date and full particulars shortly.

Other smaller funds were also set up including one by the British Seafarers' Union who had lost nearly 300 members. They paid shipwreck and death benefits to surviving members and dependants, and in addition a Relief Fund was raised to give immediate help to sufferers.

The main relief fund was administered by the public trustees under the direction of the Mansion House council and executive committee in London with the help of local committees in Southampton, Liverpool and Exeter.

In Southampton the committee was made up of local dignitaries and administered by Woolley and Waldron of 8/10 Portland Place. One of its first tasks was to appoint a lady visitor.

May 28 1912

'A letter was read from the public trustee urging the advisability of the appointment of a lady visitor. Forthwith Mr Sevain addressed the meeting on behalf of the public trustee and emphasised the view that it should be desirable to appoint a lady professionally trained for such a post that she should be of good education and social standing and for choice someone not resident in Southampton.

A Miss Newman appointed at a salary of £100 per annum plus travelling expenses.'

Relief Fund Committee Minutes (Southampton City Records)

"Well, my mum lost her husband, her first husband, also her father-in-law. My name is May, the same as my mothers, but my father was a cousin to the first one that went down in the Titanic. We all went to Northam School and life to us younger children wasn't much affected by the Titanic because it didn't affect us personally. I can remember one or two little things, like a lady by the name of Miss Newman, who used to come from the Hawthorn Cottage in the centre of the Common. She used to ride her upright bicycle with her dalmation dog always in the front walking or running beside her and she used to come regularly once or twice a month, I think it was to see how my brother, who was you know a Titanic orphan, how he was getting on."

John Bartlett May (City Heritage Oral History)

The committees operated under a series of guidelines on eligibility and payout.

'The basis of calculation for the distribution of the fund is that the widows or other dependents of the sailors and officers who went down in the Titanic should receive a weekly grant approximately equivalent to half the victim's income.

No claimant may perceive from the fund larger financial assistance than was actually contributed by the deceased during his lifetime.

Dependants of the members of the ships band should be treated as passengers.

Allowances to widows, combined with their State pension, provided a minimum weekly income of £3 11s 6d. Widow dependants not eligible for a State pension, received a minimum weekly allowance of three guineas.

In addition special grants were usually made at Easter, in the summer and at Christmas, each equivalent to one month's allowance.'

(Daily Mail, October 5th 1912)

Collecting for The Telegraph Relief Fund. London 1912.

Southampton City Heritage Collections

Mayor Bowyer distributing relief to widows.

Southampton City Heritage Collections

There is no doubt that the money from the funds was desperately needed and gratefully received. Many children brought up on the fund gained a level of education and training they may not have been able to have had access to if their fathers had lived what with the vagaries of regular employment at sea.

But once again in the following extracts from the Relief Fund Committee Minutes we see reflections of the paternalistic nature of British Society at that time as the committee extended their remit to acceptable and non-acceptable social behaviour.

'That a grant of £25 be made to enable Mrs Bristow to take her children to the seaside.'

'That a grant of 5/- per week be made from compassionate funds for a period of three months in respect of paralysis caused through shock of disaster.'

'A request to be furnished with a list of the names and addresses of the dependants of members of the crew (other than the engineers) was submitted from the committee of the fund for a memorial to the stewards, sailors fireman etc and the sec was instructed to reply that the committee cannot see its way to grant this request to erect a memorial.'
(Sept 26 1913)

'Allowance discontinued as dependant is an inmate of the Southampton Workhouse.'
(Nov 27 1913)

'That the special grant of 5/- a week be discontinued as the surviving son is now earning on the *Olympic*.'
(Dec 22 1913)

'In connection with the grants for school fees, it was felt that some assistance from the fund might be extended to the cases of dependant daughters attending secondary or private schools at the time of the disaster.'
(Jan 29 1914)

'That Gladys Hamblyn (daughter aged 16) be apprenticed to Mrs Dora Hill, ladies outfitters, 130 Above Bar at a premium of £15 for 3 years.'

'That Melita Wallis (daughter nearly 15) be apprenticed to Mr Proust, hairdresser at a premium of £20 for a period of 3 years.'

'That Richard Edge (son aged 14) be apprenticed to Messrs Dixon Bros and Hutchinson (Marine Engineers Woolston) for a period of 5 years at a premium of £30.'
(April 23 1914)

'It was resolved that any member of the Committee attending meetings in London be entitled to charge first class fare and 10/- expenses.'
(May 28 1914)

'£10 for apprenticeship to French and Son Bootmakers and a sum not exceeding £7.7.0 for a bicycle if necessary - which is to remain the property of the committee.'
(May 31 1914)

'The Southampton Committee submitted certain correspondence which they had received from Messsr Francis White and Needham acting as solicitors for Mrs P., a widow dependent whose allowance has been stopped as the committee were dissatisfied with her mode of life.'
(Oct 16 1914)

'Acting upon information recived it was decided to suspend payment of allowance for the present to Mrs M. and her three children.'
(March 8 1918)

'It was reported that Mrs B. had again been before the magistrates on a charge of drunkeness and it was reluctantly decided to suspend her allowance for a period of 3 months.'
(March 8 1918)

'The committee do not see their way to place the widow on the fund as she had not been supported by her husband for two years before he was drowned. They however approved of a special allowance of 5/- a week for the maintenance of the child.'
(Dec 13 1918)

'To recommend Miss Newmans salary £150 per annum.'
(Feb 14 1919)

Relief Fund Committee Minutes (Southampton City Archives)

Edward Simmons aged one year. Son of Frederick Simmons, saloon steward who was lost. Edward was brought up on the disaster fund.

Southampton City Heritage Oral History

"I was born in York Road Freemantle in Nov 1911.... my father was a steward on board the Oceanic, then we moved to Millbrook Road ... and father was transferred to the Titanic and of course he went down when she sank."

"We had a lady visitor from the disaster fund, she used to come about once a month to see if I was being treated right... I was just five months old."

"I don't know what my mother had for her pension, but when she re-married she still drew a pension for me and I believe it was thirty shillings a month. She used to draw that at the London & Provincial bank which was on the corner by Holyrood. I know it eventually became the Titanic and Lusitania disaster fund because there used to be a little picture of the two ships on the top of the cheque that mother used to get."

"When I was growing up there were so many other orphans around about my age whose fathers had been killed in the war. When we were growing up there weren't a lot of young married men about, very few. There were elderly men and women, obviously women, but as far as young men were concerned, very very few. If there were they probably had something wrong with them probably consumption or something like that, there was a lot of that about"

"He was 23... and it didn't effect me, not with other kiddies, no sympathy and no jeering, I mean it was just natural for quite a lot of people not to have a father ...I just knew that he'd gone down on the Titanic and that he was drowned and that was about it. I just sort of accepted it."

"I went to Freemantle Church of England School when I was five .... it wasn't bad. I got on all right... I was seven when the war finished but there were still some lady teachers in the boy's school, Miss Wheeler, everybody was dead scared of her, she dressed rather mannishly wore a hard straw hat and a collar and tie and generally wore a blue cardigan. She used to shout and everybody was scared stiff of her."

"When I left school at 14 and mother didn't want me to go to sea obviously...any how Miss Newman the visitor from the disaster fund suggested I should be apprenticed to an upholsterer.... they paid my apprenticeship fees and bought my tools... £25.00 worth of tools, still got some of them now....5 years apprenticeship...Pascoe and Pascoe in Birmingham Street. I was 19 when I finished and then I went as an improver."

"This firm took people who were orphans. I met one who was just a bit older than me, Bert Akerman and later his younger brother joined. His father was drowned, an elder brother was also drowned, there were two Akerman's on the Titanic."

Edward Simmons (City Heritage Oral History)

"When I was a young girl at school in the infants, I went to school with a boy across the road and he had ringworm and I caught it and I was off school for six months, I had to have my hair all cut off and the Titanic people paid for me to go to a convalescent home at Worthing for a month because they thought I needed to get over it. And also when I was 14 they paid for me to go to a Commercial School to learn shorthand and typewriting, English".

Mrs Eames nee Geddes (City Heritage Oral History)

School logs throughout the town record the children affected by the disaster as here in Freemantle.

3-5-12 (Boys)

George Hawkesworth	Age 12
Arthur Hawkesworth	Age 8
Tom Nichols	Age 12
Charles Johnson	Age 12
Louis Hurst	Age 12
Reginald Biddlecombe	Age 12
Christopher Biddlecombe	Age 10
Jack Wormald	Age 9
Tom Stebbings	Age 9

All of whom lost a Father. I visited the home and reported on the cases to the Chairman of the Education Committee.

1912   449

Apr. 29th. Miss Newnam is absent today –

Apr. 30th. Miss Newnam is still away.

May 2nd. I regret to record several cases of infectious disease in the district – A child removed to day with scarlet fever was at school on Tuesday (Apr. 30)

May 3rd. Head Teacher is attending a Health Lecture this afternoon on the request of the Education Committee –

May 7th. I have distributed clothes to the children who were bereft through the "Titanic" Disaster –

Extracts from Northam School Logs. Note distribution of clothes to children who were bereft, and visit of Mayoress.

City Record Office

1912
May 21st. A child apparently recovering from scarlet fever was detected in school in a peeling state. I sent her home at once & reported to Dr Lander who has had the class rooms disinfected. All work & books belonging to the child have been destroyed –

May 23rd. The Mayoress visited this department this morning re the orphans of the "Titanic" victims.

May 24th. "Empire" Day: Lessons on the Empire &c are being given this morning – The children massed will sing their patriotic songs –

May 24th. School is closed for half-holiday in the afternoon.

A receipt was received from the Mayor for amounts subscribed to his fund on behalf of the sufferers from the loss of the S.S. *Titanic* by the children attending these schools:

Boy's Dept	£8. 15. 0.
Girls	£3. 5. 0.
Infants	£2. 6. 0

(Foundry Lane County Middle School Logs)

"TITANIC" RELIEF FUND.
SOUTHAMPTON AREA.

F. WOOLLEY, F.S.A.A.,
Secretary.

———

Telephone : 607.

5 *Portland Street,*

Southampton.

Please quote Name
and Number of
case. } *Stagg 613* .   14th January, 1913.

Dear Madam (or Sir),

I am directed by my Committee to inform you that your case has been considered with a view to relief from the permanent fund, and that the Mansion House Committee have authorised a payment to you at the rate of £ *15/6* per week (with a further sum of £ *3/-* per week in respect of your *one* children).

I, therefore, have pleasure in enclosing herewith a cheque for £ . in payment of the allowance for four weeks from the 1st instant. The cheque is payable over the counter at the Union of London & Smith's Bank, Holy Rood, Southampton, where you should call personally on Wednesday, 15th instant, between the hours of 1 and 3 o'clock. Should you be unable from any sufficient cause to attend at the Bank personally, please advise me, and other arrangements will be made for cashing your cheque. Your endorsement upon the cheque will be the only receipt required.

You are particularly requested to notify any change of address to me, and I am to inform you th the relief may be permanently or temporarily withdrawn by the Mansion House Committee at any time at their discretion.

The relief will be automatically terminated at death, or by the execution of any assignment, or the creation of any charge upon the allowance, also in the events undermentioned, viz. :

Widows--On re-marriage.
Children--Girls on attaining the age of 18.
      Boys on attaining the age of 16.
Other Dependents--Females, on marriage or on attain-
            ment of age 70, when Old Age
            Pension becomes payable.
      Males, age under 50, at the end of
            3 years.
      Age 50 and under 70, on attainment
            of age 70, when Old Age Pension
            becomes payable.

Mrs B Stagg

Yours truly,
F. WOOLLEY,
Secretary.

Letter to Beatrice Stagg, whose husband Jack was lost, informing her she would receive relief for her child.

Southampton City Heritage Collections

Titanic survivor Georgetta (Ettie) Dean with her daughter Millvina in goat cart in the garden of Ettie's parents at 'Bartley Farm', New Forest. Post disaster.

Private Collection

Below: An advert from the Southampton Pictorial.

Titanic survivor Bertram Dean in the garden of 'Bartley Farm', his grandparents home.

Private Collection

The White Star Line were about to begin a gradual decline in its fortunes. However, during 1912, despite *Titanic* and the problems on *Olympic*, and in 1913 the Line was still showing huge profits. The British Seafarer in characteristic fashion thundered against the injustice of this set against the conditions for the crew.

'We wish that every employee of the White Star Line could peruse the report of the directors... ...for the year ended December 31st (1913). The accounts show a profit on the years working of £1,082,227 2s. 8d. ... ...for 1913 the company pays 65% against 30% for 1912, the previous year marred by the Titanic disaster...

...But what of the men who work the ships? What is their share of all this wealth? Low wages and vile accommodation for the majority! 65%, and the stokers have to work their insides out! 65%, and full manning cannot be afforded! 65%, and stewards work for £4 5s per month! 65%, and men are herded together in rooms unfit for human beings. These men risk their lives while idle shareholders calmly draw their 65%! How long will the people stand this plundering?'

The British Seafarer (University of Warwick)

Inevitably as the years passed the number of people with a direct claim on the fund diminished.

'101 *Titanic* Fund dependants received £14,765 last year. It was revealed at the annual meeting of the Mansion House Council National Disasters Relief Fund in London that last year the sum of £14,765 was paid out to 101 dependants of the *Titanic* Relief Fund. Many of these dependants of the 1912 disaster live in the Southampton area.

Since 1912 the sum of £671,458 has been paid out in grants to dependants – more than one and a half times the amount originally subscribed by the public.

Last December, however, there was still the sum of £157,379 in the fund. The committee's report for 1952 showed that allowances and grants in the *Titanic* Fund were being maintained on the highest scale compatible with the financial position of the Fund as determined by periodical actuarial valuation.'

(*Titanic* Relief Fund, 27/7/53)

PAY RISE FOR *TITANIC* WIDOWS

An increase of 4s. a week to widows of men drowned in the *Titanic* sinking was announced at the annual meeting of the National Disasters Relief Fund yesterday. Other dependants are to receive another 2s. a week. These increases will date from October 1. There are 94 dependants many of them living in Southampton and district, benefiting from the *Titanic* Relief Fund which stands at $155,083.

(29/7/54 Echo)

During 1958/59 it was decided to wind up the fund converting it into annuities for the remaining dependants. The balance of the general fund was then transferred to the Shipwrecked Fisherman and Mariners Royal Benevolent Society. Today one person still receives money from the Relief Fund.

Titanic Fund Wound Up

Dependants of the *Titanic* disaster no longer receive direct grants from the *Titanic* Relief Fund established after the loss of the liner on her maiden voyage from Southampton in April 1912 it was revealed in London today.

During the last 18 Months annuities have been arranged for the dependants, as against the old method of grants which came out of the fund, administered by the Public Trustee under the direction of the Mansion House Council and Executive Committee.

It has always been the object of the Executive Committee that on the day that the last dependant dies, the fund shall be exhausted and also die. This has now been arranged by investing the remaining capital in the purchase of annuities for all dependants left.

An official at the Public Trustees office, in London told me: All the dependants have received a substantial increase as a result of this move. It was taken at a meeting of the Executive Committee and the Mansion House Council under the Chairmanship of the Lord Mayor of London.

This way not one penny of the funds capital will remain when the last dependant dies.

Under the old system the amount of assistance given varied with the conditions of the times and when the last dependant died an embarrassing large sum of money would have been left.

It is also more economical as the local committees at Southampton, London Liverpool and Exeter have been disbanded.

Mr R A Etheridge, ex-secretary of the Southampton committee of the *Titanic* Fund told me his committee disbanded early this year.

Nearly all of the 64 dependants still living live in and around Southampton. In 1912 there were about 1400 dependants who looked to the fund for help. They never looked in vain. Southampton alone collected £41,000 for the fund. In the heart of Southampton stands the Titanangel so that none shall forget.

(Echo October 16th 1959)

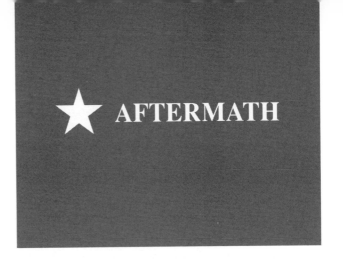

★ AFTERMATH

"Almost like murder wasn't it?"

Taken from the Isle of Wight in 1912.

Private Collection

The *Titanic* tragedy is a story of ifs, buts, might have beens, accidents, co-incidents, nearlys and, mostly, 'mistakes at the top'. But Charles Lightoller could also say with some justification, 'everything was against us'.

The Board of Trade's outdated lifeboat rules, so inadequate for the new giant ships, the captain's failure to appreciate the unusual ice conditions that year, the radio officer's failure to take a particularly crucial ice warning, the over confidence of Ismay, Pirrie and Captain Smith in *Titanic*'s 'unsinkability' and modern technology, the director's lack of imagination or financial cheese paring, Alexander Carlisle's failure to insist on providing *all* the lifeboats recommended by Axel Welin, the somewhat incomplete watertight compartmentalisation, the removal of the binoculars from the crow's nest, Murdoch's brave but misjudged decision to 'dodge' the berg rather than ram it, the inadequate boat drill, the failure of those responsible to adequately guide third class passengers to the boat deck...

As we have seen the effects on Southampton, town, docks and community, particularly the seafaring community, was devastating. Many people were barely able to speak of it for years. Pilot Bowyer studiously avoids mentioning the *Titanic* in his memoirs 'Lively Ahoy', apart from one reference to 'the late Captain E.J. Smith'. As soon as decently possible, the *Titanic* became a 'taboo' subject in the offices of the I.M.M. and the White Star Line, but the memory remained, the Relief Funds were regularly paid out to the bereaved, and the new memorials, simple or grand that were soon erected around the town, publicly perpetuated the names of some of the lost crew, and the great liner. Five *Titanic* orphans found a new home at the Seamen's Orphanage.

Combined with the grief and the bitterness there was justifiable moral pride in the known heroism and sacrifice for others of so many of the crew. On the other hand, in one instance, a crew survivor had a speedy fall from grace. Fireman James Thompson from Liverpool was sent to prison for one month in May 1912, for stealing a gold watch from a pub keeper in Southsea. After general laughter in the Southampton Borough Court as Alderman Hollis declared the watch of rolled gold, worth only 25 shillings instead of the owner's estimated £8, Mayor Bowyer asked
'On what ship did you last sail?'
Thompson: *'The Titanic.'*
The Mayor: *'Are you on the Inquiry?'*
Chief Inspector Allison: *'I understand he is getting 6/6d a day to remain in Southampton in case he should be called to give evidence.'*

Mayor Bowyer said that as Thompson had been saved from a disastrous shipwreck, Thompson ought now to have kept out of trouble.
(Hants Advertiser)

In June 1912 the Mayor of Southampton, accompanied by P.E. Curry and other local businessmen, paid an official visit to the Mayor of Le Havre where, en passant, commiserations were exchanged over the recent tragedy. Although human loss was irreplaceable, the loss of the ship was most definitely not the end of the mammoth luxury liner in the Southampton story. Puritans, harbour board officials, journalists or clergymen might thunder that the disaster was God's punishment for Edwardian materialists' love of luxury, but it was not the beautiful decoration or exotic facilities that caused the loss of life, as Lawrence Beesley appreciated. There was ample space on the boat deck for extra lifeboats to take all the *Titanic*'s complement. Extra boats were fitted to the *Olympic* in Southampton after the disaster with no practical difficulty, merely the expense. Shipping lines did not however take up the imaginative design of Harold J. Dartnall of Sholing Lodge, Itchen, *'a new safe method of boats launched down inclined slipways, by adopting a cruiser stern, with recesses down each side.'* **(Echo, 26 Feb 1913)**

In September 1912, White Star's David Blair won a 'Pictorial' prize for his photo from the *Majestic*'s crow's nest of her top deck swamped with newly lashed lifeboats. Perhaps the rush to get the ship out in service at a time of such intense international competition also consolidated the owners' and builders' tunnel vision before *Titanic*. But the lessons were learnt, the ships were improved and grew in size. *Olympic* was rebuilt in the winter of 1912-13, with a new inner skin, higher watertight compartments and full life saving equipment. Similar amendments were made to the longer, wider third sister ship, eventually named *Britannic*, which already incorporated many of *Titanic*'s improvements on *Olympic*. She was launched in February 1914, but her 48,000 tons had already been eclipsed by Hamburg America's *Imperator* which tendered off Southampton for the first time in 1913. The even bigger *Vaterland* followed in 1914. White Star's middle aged *Oceanic* was partially updated, with a modernised first class lounge, but was no competition for the mammoths.

Installing extra lifeboats aboard the *Olympic* in Southampton shortly after the disaster.

Southampton City Heritage Collections

Southampton AND DISTRICT Pictorial

(WITH WHICH IS INCORPORATED "SOUTHAMPTON AMUSEMENTS.")

Vol. II.—No. 106.]   WEDNESDAY, MARCH 4th, 1914.   [Registered at the G.P.O. as a Newspaper.   [Price One Penny

THE LAUNCH OF THE BRITANNIC.

Our pictures show the White Star leviathan Britannic shortly before and immediately after she left the stocks at Messrs. Harland and Wolff's shipbuilding yard at Belfast, on Thursday last. The launch, which was witnessed by some 30,000 persons, was a great success. The Britannic is the biggest British vessel yet built. She is a "50,000 tonner," and will take her place on the Southampton—New York service towards the end of the year.

The Southampton Pictorial of March 4th 1914 records the *Britannic* leaving the stocks at Belfast the week before.

Bert Moody Collection

A Gigantic Joke

Last week we ventured to call some of our contemporaries to book for applying the name *'Gigantic'* to the vessel which has recently been ordered by the White Star Line. This week we noticed that Mr. Bruce Ismay has been written to on the subject, and he has replied that the managers never had any intention of calling the new ship *Gigantic*. He added that she certainly would not be so named. How the name came to be accepted by the newspapers is difficult to say, but the first time we saw the name was in an American journal.

It was shortly after the maiden voyage of the *Olympic,* and an enterprising journalist in the States waylaid one of the stewards of the new ship. Some leg-pulling ensued, and the steward unfolded all the secret plans of the White Star Line to the unsuspecting pen man. 'Vessels of extraordinary size and length were being ordered, in comparison with which the *Olympic* was a mere flea bite, and the name of the largest of the new ships was given as the *Gigantic.*'
It was all a gigantic joke!
(Ship and Shore Maritime Notes and News. Southampton Times May 25th 1912)

But the prestige of White Star in Southampton, home of the *Olympic* and for the coming *Britannic* remained enormous. One quixotic instance of this is the memory of a very young housemaid, interviewed for a new job in about 1914-16 by the manager's wife, Mrs. P.E. Curry, in Bassett, not realising the Currys' close connection with the line.

"I wasn't being impudent. I said 'are you Curry's of the bicycle shop?' because there was a little bicycle shop at the Bargate when it was an archway, and you walked through it. Well that little shop, I suppose you couldn't sell a dozen bikes. I said 'Are you Curry's of the bicycle shop?' Oh crumbs, that did it. 'Bicycle shop, bicycle shop!!' She nearly spat at me. 'We're Curry's of the White Star Line!' All those big ships... Titanic an' all them big ones. That's the White Star Line, and 'course, I'm a bit flabbergasted so I came home, and I 'anded my card in... and had sixteen weeks on the dole."
Leah Mortimer (City Heritage Oral History)

The 'big ships' were here to stay, and Southampton would help to service and crew the Atlantic liners en masse until the late 1960s and even today with Cunard's *QE2*. The large hotel ship was the only realistic way to comfortably travel across the Atlantic before the advent of the jet plane in the late 1950s. After *Titanic*, *Britannic* was needed more urgently than ever to replace her, not supplement her as the third of the *Olympic* trio. The passenger market remained enthusiastic. Despite *Olympic*'s firemen's decision to have what Dr. Beaumont decried as *'a voyage off... the same thing did not occur to the public in America, for within a month we sailed to New York with over 700 in the first saloon alone.'*

White Star considered building a smaller ship at Belfast called *Germanic* (renamed *Homeric* after 1914) but abandoned the idea as war progressed. *Britannic* was completed as a hospital ship in 1915 and sunk in the Aegean in 1916. Her survivors included *Titanic* veterans Violet Jessop and Frank Priest.

After World War One, *Olympic*'s partners were the ex-German liners *Bismarck*, renamed *Majestic* and *Columbus*, renamed *Homeric* following war reparations. The *Imperator* became Cunard's *Berengaria*, joining the *Mauretania* and *Aquitania* in Southampton, following Cunard's move of its 'express' service to the port in 1919.

'Of course there was great rivalry between Cunard and White Star in Southampton, but it was all very friendly. It didn't stop my parents from mixing with White Star officers and personnel.'
(Maureen Howman, daughter of Captain Rostron)

White Star Dock was now renamed Ocean Dock, and was sometimes almost choked with three or four of Britain's 'Big Six' liners, or United States Line's *Leviathan*, ex-*Vaterland*. In later years, Cunard's *Queen Mary*, followed in time by the *Queen Elizabeth*, would usually tie up at the *Titanic*'s berth.

The White Star sheds, the last word in 1912, were replaced in 1950 by the magnificent Ocean Terminal, sadly demolished in 1983.

The numbing catastrophe of the *Titanic* could not destroy the progress of Southampton. But in the minds and hearts of the survivors, the bereaved, and those associated with her, the story lived on and is their own.

From left to right: *Berengaria*, *Leviathan* and the *Olympic* in Ocean Dock, 1920s.

Southampton City Heritage Collections

The Cornish Hotel, Orchard Place, near the docks. It catered to White Star's West Country and Cornish passengers and emigrants. This private temperance hotel, run by Fairburn, Martin and Fleet, is shown a few years after the *Titanic* disaster.

A.G.K. Leonard Collection

In 1982, Frank Prentice remarked to an ITV journalist *'It was almost like murder wasn't it?'* as he reflected on the lack of precaution and lifeboats. Many of the surviving crew continued to serve at sea for many years afterwards, some of them, like Sidney Daniels and Harold Phillimore, on the *Olympic*. Both were later appointed bedroom stewards to royalty, Sidney Daniels to the Prince of Wales on *Olympic* in the 1920s, and Phillimore in later days to the Duke of Windsor on the *Queen Mary*. He could also remember looking after Marie Lloyd on the old *Adriatic*. Rose 'Tish' Leahy, the widow of one of *Titanic*'s crew, whose daughter Audrey was born in 1912, later went to sea and became known as the Royal Stewardess, looking after various royals on the *Berengaria*. Frederick Fleet returned to sea, but later worked as a night watchman for Union Castle and at Harland and

Wolff's in Southampton before ending his career as an Echo newspaper vendor on a 'spot' in the town. *'I do it to while away the time'* he said. On one occasion in the 1960s, he met Mrs. Lightoller in the park and they reminisced. His favourite haunt was Freemantle Working Men's Club.

John Podesta left the sea in 1923 to work on shore. George Kemish, who disapproved for health reasons of the new oil fired engine rooms, remained at sea until the 1930s, wherever possible on those coal fired ships that remained in service. He considered having a tooth removed by a Russian lady dentist at Archangel during the Russian Revolution infinitely worse than being in the *Titanic* disaster.

Olympic had a busy 1920s career, when she was known as 'The Old Reliable'. She went to the breakers in 1935 following the Depression and enforced merger in 1934 of White Star with Cunard. Although White Star had carried the highest average of North Atlantic passengers in 1929, the company had suffered in the long run from its purchase from the I.M.M. by Lord Kylsant in 1926-7, and the stretching of its services in a new unwieldy group of shipping lines, including Kylsant's RMSP Co and later the Shaw Savill Line. He had also succeeded Lord Pirrie as chairman of Harland and Wolff. Plans to build a new 1000 footer at Belfast, the *Oceanic*, were aborted in 1930 as White Star went from profit into loss. In 1931 Lord Kylsant was arrested, tried and found guilty of falsely wording the 1928 RMSP Company share flotation prospectus, which was needed to pay back Treasury loans. White Star profits from 1927-9 were covering the needs of RMSP Co. Kylsant resigned and went to prison for one year. White Star remained ensnared in his venture in the Australian trade and the Aberdeen and Commonwealth Line, which was eventually sold off at a loss to the White Star Line of £1,487,807 in 1933. The world Depression hit the passenger trade harder, and many of the older White Star ships were sold off, although the new motor ship 'cabin' steamers *Britannic* (1930) and *Georgic* (1932), the last liners ever built for White Star, were proving a wonderful success.

Harold Sanderson had resigned in 1930, dying in Italy in 1932. In 1933 as things looked worse and worse for White Star, contact was even made with Bruce Ismay, and others, who proposed buying back the line from the trustees, and building more ships of the *Georgic* design. The plan was not feasible in the event and soon abandoned.

Cunard were in difficulties, over the Depression and had been obliged, in December 1931, to suspend construction of their own first 1000 foot giant (No. 534), eventually the *Queen Mary*, at Clydebank. The situation was resolved in late 1933 by the Chancellor of the Exchequer, Neville Chamberlain (following pressure from many sides) who announced the Government would lend the money to complete 534 and build a sister ship provided Cunard and White Star merged. The directors of both companies agreed. Cunard held a greater share in the new company. White Star proper was officially wound up in 1935. Cunard liners now flew the White Star flag below their own, and White Star flew the Cunard flag beneath theirs. Company colours were retained by the surviving fleet, although the old *Adriatic*, *Albertic* and *Calgaric* were sold for scrap by late 1934. *Olympic* and *Doric* followed in 1935, and the *Majestic* and *Homeric* in 1936. Many of the old White Star staff lost out, but others survived to serve in the new company.

For the first time in history four vessels in Southampton Docks today were flying the house flags of two companies.

It is the first outward and visible sign at the docks of the merging of the Atlantic interests of the White Star Line and the Cunard Line.

There happened to be three vessels concerned at the docks this morning – the White Star liner *Olympic*, which completed her voyage from New York yesterday, the Cunard liner *Aquitania*, which leaves this evening for America, and the Cunarder *Alaunia*, which called for passengers on her way from London to Canada.

Own Flags First

Orders were received this morning that the three ships should run up the house flags of both companies. The Cunard vessels had their own house flag at the main mast, with the White Star flag immediately underneath. The *Olympic*, on the other hand, had the White Star flag on top and the Cunard flag beneath.

The fourth vessel to fly the twin flags was the *Homeric*, of the White Star Line, which arrived at the docks after a successful cruise.

It will be remembered that the Cunard–White Star

A gangway at Ocean Terminal recalls the merger between Cunard and White Star.

Southampton City Heritage Collections

The withdrawn *Olympic* and *Mauretania* laid up in the Western Docks prior to scrapping in 1935. These new docks had been built on reclaimed land and completed in 1930. Taken by Frank Bealing.

Southampton City Heritage Collections

merger company was formed in accordance with an agreement made on December 30th last, between the Cunard Line, the Ocean Steam Navigation Company, and the Treasury, and it was registered with a capital of £10,000,000.
(Southern Daily Echo July 7th 1934)

'All the White Star officers had their promotion prospects relegated, behind those of the Cunard officers, so the wait was much longer, it was very hard.'
(Ethel Fitzgerald whose husband was Third Officer on the *Majestic*)

Another symbol of the old era, the famous time ball at South Western Hotel, was finally stopped and dismantled in early 1934. The new era *Queen Mary* numbered Joseph Chapman as well as Harold Phillimore in her crew. Arthur Lewis served on the *Mary* in her troopship years before ending his career with Red Funnel, which still numbered the veteran *Vulcan* in its fleet, well into the 1950s. Reginald Charles Burgess retired as head baker of the *Queen Elizabeth* in 1957. Stoker Ernest Allen, whose brother had been lost while Ernest swam to the upturned collapsible, ended his

career stoking the boiler of the Ordnance Survey building in Southampton.

George Rowe worked latterly at Thornycrofts, helping to fit stabilisers to the two *Queens* in the 1950s. Arthur Windebank spoke little of the *Titanic*, but helped Wilton Oldham on his book 'The Ismay Line'. Frank Evans refused to speak of it, it upset him too much.

Bealings continued to provide flowers for *Olympic* and the *Queens* until 1963. Rea's ceased coaling the Atlantic giants in the new oil era, but were still needed for Union Castle's *Arundel Castle* and *Windsor Castle* until the 1930s. Grey's victualled the *Queens*. One curious result of Cunard's move to Southampton in 1919 is that several of the crew of the old *Carpathia* (sunk in the war) also forsook Liverpool and became Sotonians, notably Captain Rostron and Second Officer James Bisset. Rostron commanded the crack *Mauretania* and *Berengaria*, and eventually wrote his memoirs. *'He was always terribly affected by the memory of the Titanic. He had also seen some of the bodies.'* **(Maureen Howman née Rostron)**

Rostron opened the new Odeon cinema in Southampton in 1936 and is buried in West End

The tug *Vulcan* (right) at *Titanic's* berth still hard at work. c.1947. *Queen Elizabeth* on left.

Real Photograph, Private Collection

cemetery. Bissett eventually commanded the *Queens*. William Collopy settled in Southampton, as did Francis E. Owen, assistant purser of the *Carpathia*.

None of the surviving officers of the *Titanic* ever became a Captain. Their association with the bridge of the *Titanic* was considered detrimental to any shipping line's image, despite their heroism, and Lightoller giving White Star a reasonable escape at the enquiries. Lightoller was moved to Liverpool after the war when he was not offered a post on the *Olympic*. Instead he served as chief officer on the old *Celtic* and left the White Star Line in despair and disgust in 1928.

P.E. Curry retired in 1931 and died suddenly in 1933. His extensive obituary in the Echo made no mention of the *Titanic*, although it referred to his work for the London and Southampton Committees of the National Disasters Relief Fund, and his chairmanship of the Committee of Southampton Seamen's Orphanage for Boys, and Southampton Sailors Home.

The paper observed of Curry

'A native of Liverpool, he came to Southampton at a time when the fortunes of the port were at a very low ebb, and when he passed from active service a vast transformation had taken place. Southampton had become the principal passenger port in the United Kingdom, and the part Mr. Curry had played in bringing the change was well known and appreciated by all. The moment he set foot in the town of his adoption he plunged with enthusiasm into the task of adding glory to its ancient traditions, and that he did to a very large measure succeed, there can be no doubt. If it was ever in his power to assist the underdog then assistance was readily forthcoming as a duty and a pleasure.'
(Southern Daily Echo, 1933)

C.A. Emanuel with his brother A.H. Emanuel, Southampton's Borough Coroner, who had represented *Olympic's* striking crew said *'I deplore his loss, because as I grow older my old friends and acquaintances seem to leave one by one.'*

One of Curry's sons became manager of White Star's office in Montreal. Today, the Currys' house, Thanet House at Bassett, like Captain Smith's, is long demolished, replaced by new housing, but the conservatory remains.

Although many of *Titanic's* surviving crew enjoyed brief fame and had their photos in national newspapers, they soon vanished from public view and were left to pick up the pieces of their life again. Charles Lightoller, back at Nikko Lodge on leave in 1913, had the unnerving experience of collapsing with shock in his cold bath after a hearty game of tennis. His wife found him staring in the air, caught once more in the drama of his struggle for life in the icy Atlantic.

Although some spoke or wrote of their involvement in the disaster, few can have guessed at the worldwide fascination with *Titanic* that would follow the publication of Walter Lord's book 'A Night To Remember', and the subsequent film. Several of the old crew, such as R.C. Burgess on the *Queen Elizabeth*, and George Kemish writing from Southampton, helped.

Others, like Sidney Daniels, F. Dent Ray and Joseph Boxhall advised in the film. More, including Violet Jessop, Sylvia Lightoller, Captain Smith's daughter Mrs. Cooke, and Marjorie Dutton née Collyer, attended the preview in London. At the Southampton opening night the audience included J. Whetten who had been on the *Olympic* on the fatal night:

'I have often wondered how many lives we could have saved had we both been on the same course... Nevertheless, everything that could be done was done that night. The whole crew was up and doing, stewards helping the deckhands to make

rope ladders, double banking in the stokehold, cooks getting hot food ready, bathroom stewards standing by... but, alas, we were too far away. Afterwards all the crew were silent, for they were too staggered to speak to one another. I often wonder how many survive of those who were on the Olympic.'

One name he remembered was Mr. Winter, the first class night watchman who woke him to break the news that shocked the world.

(Echo July 1958)

When the *Titanic* Enthusiasts of America set up in 1963, followed by their conventions from 1972, many of the remaining crew and passenger survivors and their families found themselves treated as celebrities, some of them flown in to the USA. *'It is good to know they are keeping the memory alive of Titanic in America'* reflected stoker Ernest Allan in 1964.

The Deans, Edith Haismann, Frank Prentice, Leo Hyland, Alfred Pugh, Arthur Lewis, John Podesta, George Rowe and others became 'Honor Members' invited to speak to packed audiences, and seeing themselves interviewed on screen.

Millvina, Ettie and Bertram Dean on the occasion of Ettie's 90th birthday. All *Titanic* survivors.

Southern Daily Echo

After Ettie Dean died aged 95, her son Bert and his wife Dorothy found a trunk:

'When we opened it we found some old clothes, including the childrens. I think they must have been the ones they had been wearing that night, but the moths had got at them and we had to throw them away.'

(Dorothy Dean, City Heritage Oral History)

Ettie had never travelled abroad again.

'She was never keen on boats afterwards. The furthest we would have gone sailing was the Isle of Wight.'

Millvina Dean (Echo 9th April 1992)

Bert Dean, a frequent visitor to City Heritage's offices in the 1980s, kept a close link with Woodlands, as Secretary for 25 years of the Anchor Darts Club at the Royal Oak pub in Woodlands.

'I don't remember anything of the actual event. But I have lived it over and over again as my mother told me, as I read books and magazines about the events.'

Bert Dean (Echo 16th February 1982)

While working at Husbands Shipyard, Bert met an older colleague and discovered he had not only been on the *Titanic* but in the same lifeboat, *"You must have been the little boy"*, he said. Bert died in April 1992.

Frederick Fleet committed suicide on 10th January 1965. One of his last letters from Southampton was to Edward Kamuda of the TEA.

'I don't know who my parents were. I have been an orphan all my life. My mother left when I was a baby, she went to a place called Springfield, Mass. I have been brought up in one of those homes, Dr. Barnardo's, till I was twelve, and then went to a training school till I was an Able Seaman. Been all kinds of companies ships, finished up with the sea in 1936. The Olympic was my last ship from the time I started deep sea 1903 I was no better off, pay in those days was very poor, I was always without money, always in debt.'

On 8th January 1965 he wrote Kamuda for the last time

'My dear friend. Just a few lines to let you know I am in deep trouble. I have lost my wife, also I am leaving my house, the place where I have been living. There is only my brother in law and myself, we cannot agree. From yours sincerely, Fred Fleet.'

(Courtesy Titanic Commutator, PO Box 51053, Indian Orchard, Mass. 01151/0053, USA)

For years Fred Fleet's grave was unmarked, but recently the *Titanic* Historical Society in the United States, with the help of Brian Ticehurst of the British

Frederick Fleet (right) lookout on the *Titanic*. In later life became a Echo paper seller in Southampton. 1961.

Southern Daily Echo

Above: *Titanic* steward Arthur Lewis and Mrs. Lewis celebrate their 70th wedding anniversary. Southampton 1972.
Below: *Titanic* fireman 'Wally' Hurst in later life.

Both Southern Daily Echo

Eva Hart, Millvina Dean & Edith Haisman open *Titanic* Voices Exhibition, Southampton Maritime Museum, 1992.

Southampton City Heritage Collections

Society, arranged for the erection of a gravestone on the site, with a suitable ceremony in honour of a famous citizen of Southampton.

The British *Titanic* Society has also hosted its own anniversary conventions at the Chilworth Hilton Hotel outside Southampton and arranged the faithful replication of the Musicians Memorial, lost when Southampton library was bombed, outside the new Mutual Assurance offices on the same site. The survivors and the descendants of survivors and victims maintain their link today as world interest in *Titanic* intensifies following the 1986 discovery of the wreck by Bob Ballard, the subsequent retrieval of 2,000 relics, and their exhibition in New York, Stockholm, Paris, and National Maritime Museum, Greenwich. The thriving international *Titanic* Souvenir and memento industry also finds a natural market in Southampton, for descendants, shipping enthusiasts and visiting tourists. The extensive collections relating to White Star and the *Titanic* of Southampton City Council are on display in Southampton Maritime Museum in an exhibition entitled 'Titanic Voices', which was opened in 1992 by *Titanic* survivors Edith Haisman, Eva Hart and Millvina Dean.

MEMORIALS AND MEMORIES

"April 15th. Very sad day"

In the many years that have passed since the *Titanic* disaster, Southampton has undergone a few more episodes in her long history.

For the first time since the 'French raid' in 1338 the town felt the full brunt of war once again in 1940 when the Luftwaffe dropped its deadly rain of bombs onto Southampton aiming to disable the docks and aircraft industries. Much of the town, especially the city centre, was destroyed with 250 people killed. However, by D-Day the town had recovered to be a major embarkation point for the allied liberation of Europe. As a recognition of the wartime role of the town and its people Southampton became a city in 1964.

The 'Gateway to the World' prospered in the 1950s and early '60s as its men and women continued to work on and service the ships sailing all over the globe.

The emergence of quick and affordable aircraft travel put the port and the city into a steady decline in the late 1960s and '70s. However, today once again, Southampton has emerged from a lean period as a major financial centre and with a port rejuvenated by the massive cargo tonnage of container ships and a continued interest in cruising with *QE2*, *Canberra* and *Sea Princess* based in the port.

Through all this time the memory of the *Titanic*, its passengers and crew, has remained strong in the city. Many memorials to the officers and crew have been erected throughout Southampton, some buildings with direct significance to the story still stand and many local people have been passed down stories of family involvement and connection with the disaster.

July 1912
74 Bullar Road
Bitterne, Southampton
Dear Sir
I have been inform by Mr F. Blake Superintendent Engineer of the White Star Line, Trafalgar Chambers on 10th that the body of my Beloved son Herbert Jupe which was Electrical Engineer no. 3 on the Ill Fatted Titanic has been recovered and Burried at sea by the Cable Steamer 'Mackay-Bennett' and that his silver watch and Handkerchief marked H.J. is in your possession. He bought him half of the same when he was at Belfast with the R.M.S. Olympic to have a new blade put on of Her Perpellors. We are extreemly obliged for all your kindness to my precious boy. He was not married and was the Love of our Hearts and he Loved his Home. But God gave and God has taken him. Blessed be the Name of the Lord. He has left an aceing Void in our home which cannot be filled. Please send along the Watche and the Handkerchief marked H.J.
Yours truly
C. Jupe
His mother is 72 last April 4th. His father is 68 last Feb 9th.
(Letter sent to Halifax, Canada from Southampton. Original spelling. Public Archives of Nova Scotia)

So many of the victims graves were on the sea bed. None of those few crew bodies that were retrieved were sent back to Southampton, but were buried instead at Fairview Cemetery, Halifax. In December 1912 the Echo published a photograph of the cemetery sent in by Mr. Dawes, a Freemantle resident, showing the temporary headstones including that of Luigi Gatti. A more symbolic sort of memorial was needed in Southampton. These memorials were indeed built, the grandest of which, to the *Titanic* engineers, was unveiled amid great ceremony on April 22nd 1914 by Sir Archibald Denny.

"Before the Titanic memorial was unveiled I and a Mr Grey, same age as me – 16 years, worked for a Mr Moore, a stationer on London Road ... he was supplied with photographs of the memorial before the cover went on ... Mr Moore gave me and Mr Grey from Chapel 2 or 3 dozen each ... and we sold postcards of that memorial at 4d a piece before it were unveiled to the crowds ..."
Len Harris (City Heritage Oral History)

"Every year when the date of the Titanic came he used to pop off on his bike and my mother used to say to me, 'You know where he's gone don't you?'. He never said anything, just used to go to the Titanic memorial and I suppose to pay his respects and to remember."
Joan Massey née Symons (City Heritage Oral History)

"We were having a lesson on the Titanic and I know I put my hand up and said that my father went down on the Titanic. (The teacher) said 'What did he do?' I said, 'He was a First Class Bedroom Steward.' 'Oh, we're not interested in that, it's only the engineers, they have a memorial'."
Marjorie Eames, née Geddes (City Heritage Oral History)

'A return of the deaths of seamen and fishermen reported to the Board of Trade in the year ended June, 1912, has been issued as a Blue Book. From this it appears there is a great increase as compared with 1911. Of the 236,418 seamen (excluding fishermen) employed in 1911, 165,159 were British, 43,127 were Lascars, and 28,132 were foreigners. Lascars include all Asiatics and East Africans (British and foreign) employed on vessels trading between India and this country, or entirely in Asiatic or Australian waters, and serving under agreements which terminate in Asia.

The total number of seamen whose deaths were reported in 1911-12 was 3,124, or one in every 76 compared with 2,204, or one in every 106 in 1910-11. The former figures, of course, include 673 seamen lost on the occasion of the *Titanic* disaster.
The British Seafarer, (University of Warwick)

Unveiling of *Titanic* Engineers Memorial, Andrews Park, Southampton. April 22nd 1914.

Southampton Pictorial

Spectators at the unveiling of *Titanic* Engineers Memorial. The public library is on the right. April 22nd 1914.

Peter Boyd Smith, Cobwebs

Slightly different view of above.

Corbishley Collection

Crowd facing the memorial.

Corbishley Collection

Procession of Boy Scout buglers, St. Mary's Church Choir and Clergy leaving the library.

Corbishley Collection

Speeches in front of the memorial.

Corbishley Collection

Titanic Crew Memorial on its original site. Southampton Common, 1915. (See page 282.)

A.G.K. Leonard Collection

Nearer, My God, to Thee.

There let my way appear,
      Steps unto heaven,
All that Thou sendest me
      In mercy given,
Angels to beckon me,
Nearer, my God, to Thee,
      Nearer to Thee.

Nearer, my God, to Thee, Nearer to Thee!
    E'en though it be a cross that raiseth me;
      Still all my song shall be,
    Nearer, my God, to Thee, Nearer to Thee!

Memorial souvenir postcards commemorating the lost *Titanic* issued by Bamforth and Co.

Southampton City Heritage Collections

Titanic crew memorial, Holyrood Church, 1994. This memorial was subscribed for by the people of Southampton and unveiled on 27th July 1915 by Mr Bullions Moody. The memorial originally stood on Southampton Common but was moved to its present site in 1972.

Southampton City Heritage Oral History

The recently renovated gravestones of *Titanic* crew members Frederick Fleet and Samuel E. Hemming in Hollybrook Cemetery, Southampton, 1994. Fleet's burial place was properly recognised when his friend Ed Kamuda and the *Titanic* Historical Society, Inc organised this new gravestone. They also paid for the cleaning up of Hemmings gravestone.

Brian Ticehurst/Southampton City Heritage Oral History

"Another memory is going with him (my father) to stand by the memorial to the men and women who lost their lives in the disaster. The engineers' memorial in the Andrews Park and the one which is now in Holyrood Church ruins, but which I remember as being on the Common, near what we call Cemetery Road... ...of course my father can't have known all the people but all number of names meant something to him and as a child I remember standing there and he'd say 'now so and so, he worked in such and such an office before he went to sea', or a lady's name 'she was the neighbour of your grandmother', things like that. It made such an impression on my parents."
Dora Caton (City Heritage Oral History)

"...and finally the ghastly noise of the people thrashing about and screaming and drowning, that finally ceased. I remember saying to my mother once, 'how dreadful that noise was' and I'll always remember her reply, 'yes but think back about the silence that followed it'... because all of a sudden the ship wasn't there, the lights weren't there and the cries weren't there.'
Eva Hart (City Heritage Oral History)

The musicians memorial was originally unveiled 19th April 1913 by the town's Sheriff Councillor W. Bagshaw in Southampton library. The library and memorial were destroyed during the Second World War. Through Brian Ticehurst, of the British *Titanic* Society, a replica memorial was unveiled (above) on the same site on 7th March 1990 by *Titanic* survivors, left to right: Edith Haisman, Millvina Dean, Bert Dean and Eva Hart.

Southern Daily Echo

"I have quite often heard my mother and father talk about the fact that every year when the anniversary came round they used to thank God... ...my father had been signed on as carpenter for the Titanic and was going away but two days beforehand he was working in the dock, he saw floating by a head with no body and hair about a yard long and it was such a shock to him that they had to call the doctor in and had to get him off the ship and on to the dockside and the doctor gave him some injection or other... ...that put him out long enough and he wasn't able to take his position on the Titanic so that's why my parents were thankful to God."
Iris Lee (City Heritage Oral History)

"My grandfather decorated the Titanic. A very sad affair that must have been, that day he lost a good customer. Yes, a great tragedy as far as Southampton was concerned to lose the queen of the ocean."
Raymond Bealing (City Heritage Oral History)

The grave of Sir Arthur Rostron, Captain of RMS *Carpathia*, West End Church, near Southampton.

Southampton City Heritage Oral History

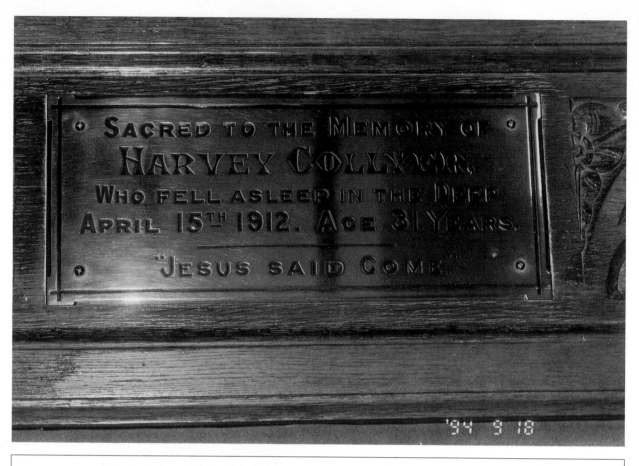

Above and below: Memorial to Harvey Collyer in St. Mary's Church, Bishopstoke, near Southampton, 1994.

Southampton City Heritage Oral History

Brooklyn, New York
Sun April 21st

My dear Mother and all,
I don't know how to write to you or what to say, I feel I shall go mad sometimes but dear as much as my heart aches it aches for you too for he is your son and the best that ever lived. I had not given up hope till today that he might be found but I'm told all boats are accounted for. Oh mother how can I live without him. I wish I'd gone with him if they had not wrenched Madge from me I should have stayed and gone with him. But they threw her into the boat and pulled me in too but he was so calm and I know he would rather I lived for her little sake otherwise she would have been an orphan. The agony of that night can never be told. Poor mite was frozen. I have been ill but have been taken care of by a rich New York doctor and feel better now. They are giving us every comfort and have collected quite a few pounds for us and loaded us with clothes and a gentleman on Monday is taking us to the White Star office and also to another office to get us some money from the funds that is being raised here. Oh mother there are some good kind hearts in New York, some want me to go back to England but I can't, I could never at least not yet go over the ground where my all is sleeping.

The small block of flats stand on the site of Captain Smith's house, Winn Road, Southampton. His house would have been similar to the one pictured on the left.

Brian Ticehurst/Southampton City Heritage Oral History

Sometimes I feel we lived too much for each other that is why I've lost him. But mother we shall meet him in heaven. When that band played 'Nearer My God To Thee' I know he thought of you and me for we both loved that hymn and I feel that if I go to Payette I'm doing what he would wish me to, so I hope to do this at the end of next week where I shall have friends and work and I will work for his darling as long as she needs me. Oh she is a comfort but she don't realise yet that her Daddy is in heaven. There are some dear children here who have loaded her with lovely toys but it's when I'm alone with her she will miss him. Oh mother I haven't a thing in the world that was his only his rings. Everything we had went down. Will you, dear mother, send me on a last photo of us, get it copied I will pay you later on. Mrs Hallets brother from Chicago is doing all he can for us in fact the night we landed in New York (in our nightgowns) he had engaged a room at a big hotel with food and every comfort waiting for us. He has been a father to us. I will send his address on a card (Mr Horder) perhaps you might like to write to him at some time.
God bless you dear mother and help and comfort you in this awful sorrow. Your loving child Lot.
Sent from Charlotte Collyer to her parents-in-law (Private Collection)

"My father was one of the last ones off and he was in the collapsible boat that was upside down in the water... ...he always said that, you know the captain of the ship, they say all sorts of things about what happened to him, well my father said somebody swam up to the boat and he couldn't get on because there were so many on there... ...he said 'good luck boys' and he went. My dad swore that was the captain that said that."
Rosina Broadbere née Hurst (City Heritage Oral History)

"Commander Boxhall told me he had worked with the makers of the film 'A Night to Remember' and had had all sorts of differences with the way they portrayed the story. He criticised the episode where the orchestra was playing to the end, saying that when one of the violinist's body was found his violin was strapped to his back. Undoubtedly there were heroes, but not everyone, he thought some of the male passengers would have cheerfully locked their wives in their cabins so that they could go first. When I first saw the film the story came over I suppose as glorified, you were proud to be British, that sort of thing. When I heard Boxhall's account I wasn't quite so proud."
Percy Toms

285

South Western Hotel, Southampton, 1994.

Southampton City Heritage Oral History

Malta, 3.12.1916
Dear Lamps
I am sorry I don't know your real name, I feel I must just thank you for looking after me, for putting me on the rope ladder (where) I didn't want to go, you were so splendid, one feels so proud of one's country where every man showed himself true British at such a time.
I thought about you the Sunday after and felt sure you were holding a little thanksgiving service for the crew. God bless you.
I hope we (shall) sail together again.
Yours truly E.A. (Matron)
Titanic Lookout George Symons (who was in the controversial lifeboat number 1) received this letter from the matron on board a hospital ship whose life he helped to save when the ship was torpedoed during World War One (Private Collection)

"It was terrible, lots of shouting and people crying as she went down, people were so upset, never heard anything like it, you could hear the screams of all the people that was left on deck, it was really terrible."
Edith Haisman née Brown (City Heritage Oral History)

Looking down Canute Road, Southampton, 1994.

Southampton City Heritage Oral History

Children in the playground of Northam School, 1992.

Southampton City Heritage Oral History

The Grapes public house, Oxford Street, Southampton, 1994. Many of the crew used this pub before embarking *Titanic*.

Southampton City Heritage Oral History

Southampton Docks, 1994. From the area *Titanic* berthed looking over towards South Western Hotel.

Southampton City Heritage Oral History

"Later I became a friend of Ismay Drage who was the nephew of Mr Bruce Ismay, and I used to stay with them in London and then once they took me to lunch on Hill Street with the Ismays and of course Mrs Drage, naturally she knew I'd been on the Titanic, said (well of course I wouldn't have) 'don't say anything about the Titanic', because she said 'it ruined my brother's life!'.

Eileen Schefer née Lenox-Conyngham (City Heritage Oral History)

"I just stopped at home. After a couple of days I went down with quinsy, a reaction had set in apparently. I was on the dole then for about six months and I went back on the Olympic and stopped right there. I did roughly two hundred voyages on the Olympic, backwards and forwards to New York each time."

Sidney Daniels (City Heritage Oral History)

"But what could I do? In the water it was everyone for themselves."

Ernest Allen, still haunted by the memory of a girl struggling in the water. (Echo 1964)

"He never spoke about it very much. I remember once when we were children, I don't know how old I was but he did come one day and say that the Daily Sketch, or one of those, were running a series on the Titanic, and he said to me you may read something that is a bit detrimental but don't believe all you hear. And I think he would have spoke about it then but being a youngster I never really bothered. He was my dad and I loved him. When the Mary, when she was first there, we cycled down to Millbrook Point and we went up on the bridge and he stood there looking at it and looked very sad and he said, 'That's where the Titanic broke in half, out there'."

Joan Massey née Symons (City Heritage Oral History)

Acknowledgements and Bibliography

Acknowledgements

Andrew Acquier

Gill Arnott

Mrs M. Anscombe

Rod Baker

Mr F. Banfield

Mr J. Beckett

Nancy Bealing

Mr Bell

Peter Boyd-Smith

Patrick Bogue

Viscount & Viscountess Bridgeman

Mrs J. Bromage

Harold Campbell

Dan Chadwick

Mr & Mrs D. Connor

Lawrence Cooper

Alan Corbishley

Amy Cozens

Stephen Croad

Dr Ronald C. Denney

Mrs Betty Denny

Mrs Diane Edwards

Ethel Fitzgerald

Mrs Joan A. Ford

Lindsay Ford

Mr Jack Fry

Richard Garrett

Miss Jane Gale

Mr & Mrs F. Giles

Julian Gollogly

Aubrey Grey

Ivor Guest

David Harries

Mrs J. Hartnett

Mr F.C.R. Hocking

Mrs M. Howman, née Rostron

Bryan I. Hunt

Mrs D.C. Hyslop

David Hutchings

D. Isitt

Vera Jones

Ed Kamuda (Titanic Historical Society)

Mr B. Kemish

Richard de Kerbrech

Anne de Lasta (Rio Tinto Zinc)

Alan Leonard

Ian Leith

Ken Marschall

Mr & Mrs Richard May

Peter McGaw

Bert Moody

Ray Mursell

Fred and Claire Murley

Mrs Oakley

Mrs F.E. Owen

Mrs Degna Marconi Paresce

Miss Catherine Pearson

Mr Bob and the late Mrs Jean Peck

Mr Mike Petty

Mr Garton Playdon

Peter Prior

Lee Raymond

Peter Reid

Steven Rigby

G.W. Robinson

John Seaman

Cynthia Skipwith

Mary South, née Simmons

Brian Ticehurst

Peter Turrall

Edwina Vardey

Kay Welham

John Whitaker

Rodney Norman Wilkinson

George Williams

Nancy Young

While every effort has been made to trace and acknowledge all copyright holders, we would like to apologise should there have been any errors or omissions.

THE LARGEST VESSEL & THE LARGEST FLOATING CRANE IN THE WORLD, THE WHITE STAR LINER "TITANIC."
LENGTH 882 FT 9 INS. EXTREME BREADTH 92 FT 6 INS. HEIGHT 104 FT. GROSS TONNAGE 46,380 LEFT BELFAST FOR SOUTHAMPTON ON APRIL 2ND AND
SAILED FROM SOUTHAMPTON FOR NEW YORK ON HER ILL-FATED MAIDEN VOYAGE ON APRIL 10TH SANK AFTER COLLISION WITH AN ICEBERG OFF
THE COAST OF NEWFOUNDLAND ON MONDAY APRIL 15TH AND OF THE PASSENGERS AND CREW TOTALLING 2,358 ONLY 705 WERE RESCUED

Titanic at Harland and Wolff Shipbuilders, Belfast, 1912. From an original postcard.

Southampton City Heritage Collections

Willsteed postcard shows *Titanic* decked in flags on Good Friday, 1912. Coaling is in progress.

Southampton City Heritage Collections

Interviewees and Correspondents

Molly Adams, née Stewart
Tom Atkinson
Raymond Bealing
Ben Benham
Rosina Broadbere, née Hurst
Dora Caton
Dorothy Cross
Sidney Daniels
Rose Dawson, née Major
Millvina Dean
Dorothy Dean, née Sinclair
Roy Diaper
Marjorie Eames, née Geddes
Mrs J. Fagin
Alfred Fanstone
Martha Gale
Arthur Gibbs
Edith Haisman, née Brown
Leonard Harris

Eva Hart
Lois Jacobs née Brown
Tom James
Iris Lee, née Jeans
Bert Lester
Joan Massey, née Symons
John Bartlett May
Charles Morgan
Leah Mortimer
Frank Scammell
Eileen Schefer, née Lenox-Conyngham
Clare Seagrave, née Hendricks
Edward Simmons
Cynthia Skipwith
Roland Southwell
Ernest (Jack) Smith
Percy Toms
Elsie Whitfield
John Wright

Oral History Interviewers

Sheila Jemima
Donald Hyslop
Dan Chadwick
Christine Tanner
Carl Major

Tim Caves
Chris Howard-Bailey
Paul Ferguson
Sharon Taaffe

Addresses and Contacts

Any correspondence relating to this publication should be sent to:

The Editors
'Titanic Voices'
City Heritage
Civic Centre
Southampton
SO14 7LP
United Kingdom

Where photographs or articles are credited to the following organisations, they can be contacted direct to:

Southampton Archives Service
Southampton City Council
Civic Centre
Southampton
SO14 7LY
United Kingdom

Southern Daily Echo Library
Southern Newspapers PLC
45 Above Bar
Southampton
SO14 7AA
United Kingdom

Local History Librarian
Reference Library
Civic Centre
Southampton
SO14 7LW
United Kingdom

SPECIAL THANKS
Also thanks to Nigel Overton, Simone Joyce, Jill Neale, Janet Hall-Patch and all our City Heritage colleagues past and present.

View from Cowes, Isle of Wight, as *Titanic* departs on her journey.

Peter Pearce Collection

Ingenieur Minard tendering *Queen Mary* at Cherbourg in the 1950s. Built in 1911 by Harland and Wolff as White Star tender *Nomadic,* she and her sister, the *Traffic,* tendered *Titanic* at Cherbourg. Since 1977 she has been a floating restaurant on the River Seine in Paris under her original name. The last White Star ship afloat.

Southampton City Heritage Collection

Titanic Societies

Those with a continuing interest in Titanic may like to join one of the following organisations:

The British Titanic Society
PO Box 401
Hope Carr Way
Leigh, Lancs. WN7 3WW
Journal: *The Atlantic Daily Bulletin*

The Titanic Historical Society, Inc
PO Box 51053 Indian Orchard
Massachusetts 01151-0053
United States of America
Journal: *The Titanic Commutator*

Titanic International Inc.
Post Office Box 7007
Freehold, New Jersey 07728-7007
United States of America
Journal: *Voyage*

Titanic Society of South Africa
PO Box 256, Crown Mines 2025
Johannesburg, South Africa
Journal: *The Titanic Chronicler*

The Auckland Titanic Club
c/o The President
13 Watling Street
Mt. Eden, Auckland 4
New Zealand
Journal: *The Liner*

The Switzerland Titanic Society
c/o Lindi Erni
Postfach 123
CH-8613
Uster 3
Switzerland
Journal: *Titanic Post* (in German)

Also specialising in Titanic and other ocean liner memorabillia:

Peter Boyd-Smith
Cobwebs Ocean Liner Memorabillia
78 Northam Road
Southampton
United Kingdom

Institutions

Adrian Osler (Science Museum, Newcastle)
Mike Stammers, Alan Scarth, David Williams (Merseyside Maritime Museum)
Mike McCaughan, Kenneth Anderson (Ulster Folk & Transport Museum)
Michael Cook, Adrian Allan, Andrea Owens (University of Liverpool Archives)
Michael Moss (University Archives Glasgow)
Mary Shepherd, Rita Bryan, David Hodge (National Maritime Museum, Greenwich)
British Sailors Society
British Titanic Society
Titanic Historical Society, Inc
Society of Gonzaga, Dublin
Sue Woolgar, Andrew George and staff (Southampton Archives Service)
Richard Preston and staff (Southampton Reference Library, Hants County Library)
University of Southampton Record Series
Department of Transport, Marine Accident Investigation Branch
J. Farrugia (GPO Archives)
The Modern Records Centre, University of Warwick
The Rail, Maritime and Transport Union
Kathleen Chapman (Shipwrecked Mariners Society)
Sarah Woodcock (Theatre Museum, London)
The Friends of Southampton City Museums and Art Gallery
Hibbert Beer photograph reproduced by kind permission of S.B. Publications

Bibliography

Books

R.B. Adams, *Red Funnel and Before*, Kingfisher, 1986.

R. Anderson, *White Star*, Stephenson, 1964.

J.H. Beaumont, *Ships and People*, G. Bles, 1920s.

L. Beesley, *The Loss of the Titanic*, Heinemann, 1912.

Sir J. Bisset, *Tramps and Ladies*, Angus & Robertson, 1959.

Board of Trade, *Investigation into the Loss of SS Titanic*, London, 1912.

G.W. Bowyer, *Lively Ahoy*, Broadbere (Southampton), 1930.

M. Bown & J. Simmons, *Titanic in Old Postcards*, Braintree, 1988.

P. Boyd-Smith, *Titanic From Rare Historical Reports*, Brooks Books, 1992.

S. Bullock, *Thomas Andrews, Shipbuilder*, Maunsel, 1912.

M. Davie, *The Titanic, the Full Story of the Tragedy*, Bodley Head, 1986.

C.F. Dendy Marshall, *History of the Southern Railway*, Ian Allan.

R.C. Denney & E. Hart, *Shadow of the Titanic, A Survivors Story*, Greenwich University Press, 1994.

Lady Duff Gordon, *Discretions and Indiscretions*, Jarrold, 1932.

J.P. Eaton, C. Haas, *Titanic, Triumph and Tragedy*, PSL, 1986.

J.P. Eaton, C. Haas, *Falling Star*, PSL, 1990.

J.N. Faulkner & R.A. Williams, *The LSWR in the 20th Century*, David & Charles, 1988.

A. Gracie, *The Truth About the Titanic*, 7 Cs Press, USA, 1973.

I. Guest, *Adeline Genée, Her Years of Dancing in Six Reigns*, 1958.

Sir B. Hayes, *Hull Down*, Cassell, 1920s.

M. Harding O'Hara, *Hands Off the Titanic*, Countrywise, 1989.

D. Hutchings, *RMS Titanic*, Kingfisher, 1987.

S. Jemima, *Chapel and Northam, An Oral History of Southampton Docklands*, S.C.C., 1992.

R. de Kerbrech & D. Williams, *Cunard White Star Liners*, Conway, 1990.

A.G.K. Leonard, *Southampton in Old Postcards*, European Library, 1992.

A.G.K. Leonard & R. Baker, *A Maritime History of Southampton in Picture Postcards*, Ensign, 1989.

C. Lightoller, *Titanic & Other Ships*, Ivor Nicholson & Watson, 1935.

W. Lord, *A Night to Remember*, Allen Unwin, 1976.

W. Lord, *The Night Lives On*, Viking, 1986.

LSWR: *Inspection of the New Deep Water Dock*, Southampton, June 8, 1911.

D. Marconi, *My Father Marconi*, F. Muller, 1962.

G. Marcus, *The Maiden Voyage*, Allen Unwin, 1969.

K. Marschall & D. Lynch, *Titanic An Illustrated History*, Madison Press, 1992.

J. Maxtone-Graham, *The Only Way to Cross*, Macmillan, 1972.

J. Montlucon/N. Lacoudre, *Les Objets du Titanic La Memoire des Abimes*, Fondation Electricite de France, 1989.

B. Moody, *One Hundred & Fifty Years of Southampton Docks*, Kingfisher, 1988.

B. Moody, *Southampton's Railways*, Waterfront Publications, 1992.

M. McCaughan, *Steel Ships & Iron Men*, FBP, 1989.

M. McCaughan, *Titanic*, Ulster Folk & Transport Museum, 1982.

M. Moss & J.A. Hume, *Shipbuilders to the World, 150 Years of Harland & Wolff*, Blackstaff Press, Belfast, 1986.

P. Padfield, *The Titanic and the Californian*, Hodder & Stoughton, 1965.

C. Pellegrino, *Her Name Titanic*, Hale, 1988.

L. Reade (Edited by E.P. De Groot), *The Ship That Stood Still*, Patrick Stephens Ltd., 1993.

Sir A. Rostron, *Home from the Sea*, Cassell, 1931.

The Shipbuilder, *Olympic & Titanic*, Souvenir Number, 1912.

Southampton Harbour Board, Minutes.

A. Temple Patterson, *Southampton – A Biography*, Volume 3, Macmillan/Southampton University Press, 1970.

B. Ticehurst, *The Titanic, Southampton's Memorials*, Kingfisher, 1987.

A. & B. Watson, *Roster of Valor*, *The Titanic – Halifax Legacy*, 7 Cs Press, USA, 1984.

D.L. Williams, *Docks and Ports*, Southampton, Ian Allan, 1986.

J. Wincour (Ed), *The Story of the Titanic As Told By Its Survivors*, Dover Publications, New York, 1970.

US Enquiry, *Investigation into the Loss of SS Titanic*, Washington, 1912.

Articles

Journal of British Titanic Society, Atlantic Bulletin, Spring 1991.

Black Jack (Journal of Southampton Branch of World Ship Society), Winter, 1990 (article by B. Moody, 'Construction of the Ocean Dock').

Chart and Compass (article by Miss E.N. Blair).

Hampshire Advertiser, 20 May 1927 (article on J. Rea & Co).

Hampshire Magazine, October 1985 (article by Eric Gadd: 'Modest artist, Walter Dane Bryer').

Hampshire Magazine, August 1985 (article by Mary L. South: 'The Short, Busy Life of Fred Simmons').

Ireland of the Welcomes, September-October 1992 (article by Father Eddie O'Donnell, S.J. 'One Ship That Did Not Make It Across the Atlantic… The Story of Father Browne').

Oral History, Spring 1991, 'The Sea', Hyslop & Jemima (The Titanic and Southampton).

'Stamp News', 19 September – 2 October 1985 (article by J. Seaman), 'Posting from the Titanic'.

The Pier Review, No. 8, March 1932 (Southend Corporation) … Article by J. Scarrott, 'The Loss of the Titanic', Part I, The Sailing of the Titanic.

Titanic Commutator Articles (Journal of Titanic Historical Society, Inc)

December 1964, J. Podesta, 'I Survived the Titanic Disaster'.

Vol 22, April 1969, S. Rogers Cook, 'The Last Voyage of RMS Titanic'.

December 1968, 'Mercy Mission', by W. Collopy.

June 1965, E. Allen, 'He Tried to Save His Brother and Missed the Boat'.

April 1966, Arthur Lewis, 'A Shattered Star Foretells Disaster'.

No. 29, December 1970, R.D. Burgess, 'The Titanic Was His First Voyage'.

No. 29, December 1970, C.L. Doughtrey, 'The Right Ship at the Right Time'.

No. 29, September 1972, 'Never Doubt Your Mother'.

Fall 1978, 'Account of Edith Russell'.

Sales Catalogues

Christie's, South Kensington, Titanic Sale, April 1992 & Maritime Pictures, May 1994.

Onslow's, Titanic Sales, April 1986 – April 1994.

Sotheby's, Manuscripts, July 1991.

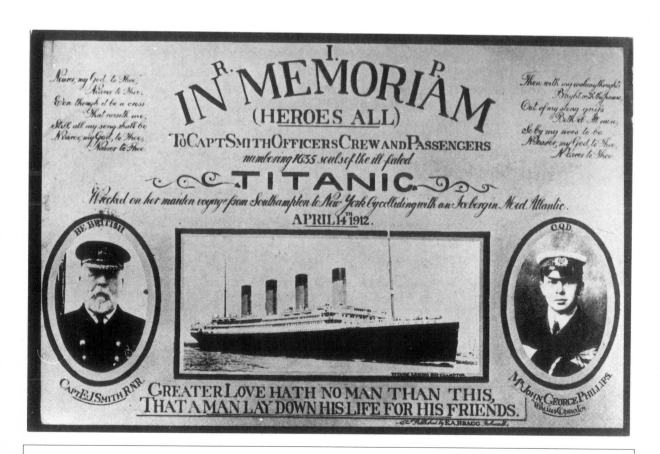

One of many memorial cards issued after the disaster.

Southampton City Heritage Collections